THE TUBE HAS SPOKEN

FILM & HISTORY

The Film & History series is devoted to creative scholarly works that focus on how feature films, documentaries, and other forms of media represent and interpret history. Books in the series explore the significant impact of motion pictures on our society and analyze films and television programs from a historical perspective. One goal of the series is to demonstrate how historical inquiry has been reinvigorated by the increased scholarly interest in the intersection of film and history. The Film & History series includes both established and emerging scholars and covers a diverse array of films.

Series Editors
Peter C. Rollins and John E. O'Connor

THE TUBE HAS SPOKEN

Reality TV & History

Edited by Julie Anne Taddeo
and Ken Dvorak

THE UNIVERSITY PRESS OF KENTUCKY

Scholarly publisher for the Commonwealth,
serving Bellarmine University, Berea College, Centre
College of Kentucky, Eastern Kentucky University,
The Filson Historical Society, Georgetown College,
Kentucky Historical Society, Kentucky State University,
Morehead State University, Murray State University,
Northern Kentucky University, Transylvania University,
University of Kentucky, University of Louisville,
and Western Kentucky University.
All rights reserved.

Editorial and Sales Offices: The University Press of Kentucky
663 South Limestone Street, Lexington, Kentucky 40508-4008
www.kentuckypress.com

Library of Congress Cataloging-in-Publication Data

The tube has spoken : reality TV and history / edited by Julie Anne
Taddeo and Ken Dvorak.
    p.   cm. — (Film & history)
  Includes bibliographical references and index.
  ISBN 978-0-8131-2553-4 (hardcover : alk. paper)
  1. Reality television—History and criticism. 2. Reality television
programs—Social aspects. I. Taddeo, Julie Anne. II. Dvorak, Ken, 1950–
  PN1992.8.R43T83 2009
  791.45'6—dc22
                                          2009027966
ISBN 978-0-8131-3388-1 (pbk. : alk. paper)

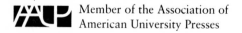

Contents

Foreword   vii
    DEBORAH A. CARMICHAEL

Acknowledgments   ix

Introduction   1
    JULIE ANNE TADDEO AND KEN DVORAK

Part I: Reality TV as Social Experiment

Citizen Funt: Surveillance as Cold War Entertainment   11
    FRED NADIS

From Social Experiment to Postmodern Joke: *Big Brother* and   27
    the Progressive Construction of Celebrity
    LEE BARRON

From the Kitchen to 10 Downing Street: *Jamie's School Dinners*   47
    and the Politics of Reality Cooking
    JAMES LEGGOTT AND TOBIAS HOCHSCHERF

The Patriotic American Is a Thin American: Fatness and   65
    National Identity in *The Biggest Loser*
    CASSANDRA L. JONES

Part II: Class, Gender, and Reimaging of Family Life

Disillusionment, Divorce, and the Destruction of the American   83
    Dream: *An American Family* and the Rise of Reality TV
    LAURIE RUPERT AND SAYANTI GANGULY PUCKETT

"The television audience cannot be expected to bear too much   98
    reality": *The Family* and Reality TV
    SU HOLMES

Reality TV and the American Family   123
    LEIGH H. EDWARDS

Shopping, Makeovers, and Nationhood: Reality TV and   145
    Women's Programming in Canada
    SARAH A. MATHESON

Babes in BonanzaLand: *Kid Nation,* Commodification, and   171
    the Death of Play
    DEBBIE CLARE OLSON

Part III: Reality TV and the Living History Experiment

"A Storybook Every Day": Fiction and History in the   197
    Channel 4/PBS House Series
    JULIE ANNE TADDEO AND KEN DVORAK

"What about giving us a real version of Australian history?":   217
    Identity, Ethics, and Historical Understanding in Reality
    History TV
    MICHELLE ARROW

Living History in Documentary Practice: The Making of   236
    The Colony
    AURORA SCHEELINGS

Contributors   257

Index   261

Foreword

Reality TV continues to grow in popularity as television programming that offers "real," albeit edited and scripted, experiences before the handheld camera and proliferates to include children (*Kid Nation*) and animals (*Pet Psychic*). With roots in documentary film, originally used for education or persuasion, and television news, including heart-wrenching human-interest stories, reality TV has both expanded and blurred definitions of broadcast content and, some would argue, standards of acceptable conduct. Although television is an influential visual medium, much of the attraction of reality TV relies on backstory. The narratives often attract sympathy or create empathy. Room makeovers on shows like *Deserving Design, Trading Spaces,* and *Designed to Sell* include stories of personal self-sacrifice, feuding siblings, and expectant couples. *A Baby Story* takes the viewer into the delivery room. These narratives connect with shared realities, as if they were *Life* and *Look* magazine photos put into motion to tell the touching tales in every detail.

Other shows rely less on heartwarming narratives and more on voyeurism and vicarious experiences. Although *Survivor* and *The Amazing Race* take armchair travelers around the globe, backstories and backstabbing provide the entertainment. Julie Chen, the steamy host of *Big Brother,* "welcomes another gaggle of exhibitionistic houseguests to the . . . compound, where their sleazy psychodramas are sure to remedy any self-esteem issues you may be having" after watching the tenth season.* Sleaze and sex sell, human conflict entertains, and the possibility of winning a million dollars is always attractive, especially if more than fifteen minutes of fame comes with the cash. Consumers can share their own realities on QVC or HSN,

---

*From the *Big Brother* Web site, http://television.aol.com/show/big-brother-10/10230987/main?flv=1&icid=templatized_tv_shows.M.

calling in not only to buy products, but also to explain the joy of shopping. Nancy Grace on CNN uses caller commentary to explicate current events, usually a news story of a sensational kidnapping or murder.

Daytime programming appears to target women, whereas prime-time offerings aim for mixed audiences, yet the many online sites announcing auditions for reality TV seek far more young women than men. Some of those casting calls include:

> Are you a beautiful, young woman in her 20's who knows what she wants? A rich, older man who can give you all the things you deserve . . . clothes, cars, money, jewelry, trips. . . . Do you stop at nothing to find your Sugar Daddy? We want to meet you!
> Major cable network now casting attractive, fun, outgoing recently divorced women.
> Looking for attractive female MMA fighters between the ages of 18 and 28 to interview for a TV pilot pitch.*

Surely if these shows make it to the airwaves, there will be some enticing backstories to examine.

Reality TV asks questions of gender, race, ethnicity, and socioeconomic status as played out on the smaller screen, and it offers historians and those in film or cultural studies some complex areas of study. This volume tackles many of the complexities of reality TV, setting high standards for future exploration. By looking to early network shows like *Candid Camera,* as well as PBS productions such as *An American Family,* scholarship can begin to examine the metamorphosis of television from its own backstory to current programming. We can begin to understand the tales being told about cultural perceptions and historical dynamics through the study of reality TV in all its manifestations, from baby stories to babes, from man against nature to man versus woman, from home improvement to improving life at home. And, finally, what might the future be for reality TV? How will television programming intersect with YouTube or MySpace? And what will the coming changes reveal about how we tell our stories or how we are told about our history and culture? Thankfully, there are scholars equal to the challenge of searching for answers to these important questions.

DEBORAH A. CARMICHAEL
MICHIGAN STATE UNIVERSITY

---

*Found at www.realitytvcastingcalls.com, one of many such Web sites.

Acknowledgments

Life often takes you in directions you least expect, and this is true of my relationship with my coeditor, Julie Anne Taddeo, with whom I first discussed this project during a telephone call in 2002. She inquired about my call for papers distributed on H-Net for a proposed anthology on the PBS historical Homes series. Julie, a British historian steeped in Victorian texts, gravitated toward "classy" productions such as *1940s House* and *Manor House,* whereas I, a fan of the western and cowboy boots, wanted to compare such tame British fare to PBS's *Frontier House* and *Texas Ranch House.* Working together as coauthors and coeditors, we discovered that such programs were not simply a guilty pleasure for us as viewers, but another valuable resource for understanding the complex relationship among history, myth, and current social and political concerns.

Since that phone call, Julie and I have guest-edited two issues of *Film & History* devoted to scholarship on reality TV and history. Throughout this process we have been encouraged and supported by Peter C. Rollins and John E. O'Connor, who pushed us to look at all angles of this genre: as a tool for teaching and learning about history, as an experiment in documentary and film, and as a way to measure the pulse of contemporary society in the United States and other Western nations. We are honored with their friendship; they are true mentors for so many of us fascinated with the study of film and television and its cultural influence on our global society.

The University Press of Kentucky, notably Stephen Wrinn and Anne Dean Watkins, has been incredibly supportive of this collection, even before we sent our proposal. This collection is, of course, the sum of its parts, and our contributors have been gracious and patient, often given deadlines with only two weeks' notice. They also forced us to look beyond our own intellectual interests as historians and to envision the interdisciplinary connections that a study of reality TV promised. Finally, both Julie and I would like to thank our families for putting up with us as we sometimes used as an excuse (however legitimate) from household chores the necessity of watching more TV!

JULIE ANNE TADDEO AND KEN DVORAK

Introduction

As the title of this anthology suggests, reality TV is both a historical and a programming phenomenon. From Allen Funt's *Candid Camera* of the 1950s to 2007's *Kid Nation,* reality TV owes much of its format and techniques to the documentary genre, in particular the camera's focus on "ordinary" citizens and the drama and humor of their day-to-day lives evoked by the fly-on-the-wall approach. Reality TV has certainly come a long way since the hidden cameras of *Candid Camera,* and the breadth and variety of programming reflects the larger historical context driving content and ratings. PBS's *An American Family,* for example, showed a family in crisis, the feminist and sexual revolutions of the 1970s serving as its backdrop. Three decades later reality TV shows about supernannies and wife swapping take place in a postfeminist society in which families farm out parenting and domestic duties but nevertheless still cling to traditional notions of motherhood. Critics may write off reality TV as trash or fluff, but the essays in this collection demonstrate how social and cultural trends inevitably shape the productions and audience reactions.

Although many of the following articles look at American TV shows, we also include Australian, British, and Canadian programming, which reflects not only the transnational appeal of reality TV, but also culturally specific concerns about individual and national identity. Programs like *Outback House* and *Big Brother* are just a couple of the programs analyzed in this collection, which explore the tensions between individual and community, the enduring legacy of racial, class, and gender inequality, the transformative power of technology in our daily lives, the creation of celebrity, and the breakdown of public and private spheres. Our authors also discuss the historical evolution and the potential and limits of the genre of reality TV as a whole. Representing various points of view—those of scholars of history, literature, and communications, and even a filmmaker whose work on the making of *The Colony* was suppressed because of her insistence on her project's honesty—this collection showcases how pivotal reality TV is to any study of popular culture's past, present, and future.

The idea for this collection first emerged when we guest-edited a special issue on reality TV for *Film & History: An Interdisciplinary Journal of Film and Television*. The overwhelming response we had to our call for papers suggested that scholars were aware not only that reality TV was not a passing trend but also that its relationship to history demanded attention. That latter realization is what even the most recent scholarship on reality TV still ignores. The media scholars Anita Biressi and Heather Nunn (*Reality TV: Realism and Revelation,* 2005), for example, focus on the hybridization of genres, exploring reality TV's roots in the documentary format, and Jonathan Bignell's *Big Brother: Reality TV in the Twenty-first Century* (2005) looks at the direction television culture is taking in the new century and how reality TV breaks with previous conventions. Annette Hill's *Reality TV: Factual Entertainment and Television Audiences* (2005) examines reality TV as a catch-all that tells stories about "real people"; *Understanding Reality TV* (2005) by Su Holmes (one of our own contributors) discusses how reality TV has constructed celebrity, fandom, surveillance, and the politics of representation for its audiences. Mark Andrejevic's *Reality TV: The Work of Being Watched* (2003) traces how surveillance-type programs like *Big Brother* have altered our attitudes about voyeurism and the increasingly important economic role played by the work of being watched, whereas *Shooting People: Adventures in Reality TV* by Sam Brenton and Reuben Cohen (2003) offers a harsh critique of the psychological ramifications of shows like *Survivor* and how viewers' attitudes about larger issues (such as war) have been influenced by reality TV.

Such studies of reality TV, while contributing to our own understanding of voyeurism and the authenticity of performance, have been done primarily by communications scholars and media critics. As historians, the editors of this collection have prompted their contributors to approach the topic of reality TV with specific questions in mind: for example, how has the genre evolved and what larger social, political, and cultural forces have affected reality TV programming? What do these programs say about their specific historical moment? How do reality TV programs treat and redefine history? We are especially interested in what Roy Rosenzweig describes as the role of the media as national educator. His 2000 national survey concluded that Americans felt a strong relationship to the past but that much of this feeling was based not on history books or classes taught by professional historians; instead, many connected to the past through family histories, the collection of memorabilia, museum excursions, and, tellingly for our purposes, reality TV. Rosenzweig concluded his findings with a warning to fellow scholars that we can no longer ignore that television has become a primary component of "national memory." Our contributors have certainly heeded Rosenzweig's command, and the essays that follow confirm how reality TV both reflects and defines national memory, as well as individual and collective identity in America and abroad.

Our analysis begins by discussing reality TV as a social experiment. Producers, subjects of the camera's gaze, and viewers of reality TV all take part in these televised experiments, which both challenge and reaffirm certain social mores and practices. In "Citizen Funt: Surveillance as Cold War Entertainment," Fred Nadis returns us to the early days, before reality TV even had a name, when *Candid Camera* turned our cold war paranoia about surveillance into a laugh-inducing gimmick. Allen Funt's "experiments in human nature" gently poked fun at his subject (or victim, depending on one's perspective) but also, according to Nadis, conveyed a serious message about conformity and blind obedience to authority that stood in stark contrast to the show's peppy theme song, "Smile, You're on *Candid Camera*." The subjects of Funt's seemingly playful look at mass psychology, however, were not in on the joke. How different such an approach to self-revelation seems from the more recent crop of reality TV programs, in which spouses freely discuss sources of marital conflict and parents complain about their children's bad behavior before millions of viewers. Though critics bashed Funt as a hypocrite and unscrupulous torturer, he proudly accepted his status as voyeur and made it acceptable for TV audiences to play that role as well.

Funt's turning of the camera on "regular Joes" has become a basic ingredient of reality TV, and as Lee Barron explains in "From Social Experiment to Postmodern Jokes: *Big Brother* and the Progressive Construction of Celebrity," ordinary men and women now apply to appear on such programs, hoping to achieve instant celebrity status for doing very mundane things. Using the U.K. version of *Big Brother* and its offshoot, *Celebrity Big Brother,* Barron contemplates the scripted nature of reality TV and the role of the producer in manipulating the "celebritizing" process. Lost in the process has been the original intention of the program to be a social and psychological experiment and exercise in surveillance and coping strategies. Barron captures the carnivalesque spectacle of the *Big Brother* household and the media frenzy surrounding its residents.

Whereas *Big Brother* transforms the ordinary citizen into a household name, another recent trend in reality TV is the program spearheaded by an established celebrity whose purported mission is to educate as well as to entertain audiences. In "From the Kitchen to 10 Downing Street: *Jamie's School Dinners* and the Politics of Reality Cooking" James Leggott and Tobias Hochscherf discuss how the celebrity chef Jamie Oliver's effort to improve the quality of food served to children in British state schools triggered a national debate about the paternalistic role of the welfare state. As Prime Minister Tony Blair (1997–2007) promoted a vision of a classless society, Oliver's tours of school cafeterias in largely working-class areas of England exposed (not always intentionally) stark divisions of class and gender. In addition to the serious social, political, and health issues Oliver's show highlighted, Leggott and Hochscherf trace Oliver's own evolution as a reality TV star as he juggles his masculinity with the feminized environment of the kitchen.

Oliver nobly tries to improve the diet and health of Britain's youth (while promoting his cookbooks and boyish good looks), but *The Biggest Loser* aims to reshape the American adult body. Cassandra Jones, in her essay "The Patriotic American Is a Thin American: Fatness and National Identity in *The Biggest Loser*," looks at one of the most popular staples of reality TV, the individual in need of transformation at the hands of "experts." Jones describes the *Survivor*-like challenges the overweight contestants endure to "cure" themselves of fatness. The third season of *The Biggest Loser*, however, goes even further, equating bodily transformation with patriotism, positing the ideal American body as a thin body. Isolating the contestants on a Western ranch, the program upholds the myth of the self-made man (and woman) and reveals how the frontier informs our notions of fatness and weight loss.

The setting for reality TV programs need not be isolated ranches or exotic locales. As the essays in part 2, Class, Gender, and Reimaging of Family Life, indicate, when the camera is turned on the home and a family's most private moments, plenty of drama unfolds. In "Disillusionment, Divorce, and the Destruction of the American Dream: *An American Family* and the Rise of Reality TV," Laurie Rupert and Sayanti Ganguly Puckett examine Craig Gilbert's groundbreaking documentary that chronicled the day-to-day experiences of the William C. Loud family of Santa Barbara, California. With the parents on the brink of divorce, a wife discovering feminism, and a confused son expressing his homosexuality, the Louds were a dream come true for a director intent on exposing the myths behind the American dream and the bourgeois ideal of Home, Sweet Home. Rupert and Puckett not only provide a detailed analysis of the twelve-part series and its roots in documentary practice, but also show how Gilbert's use of editing and video confessional influenced future reality TV programs.

A year after PBS aired *An American Family*, British TV responded with its own version, *The Family*, focusing instead on a working-class household. Su Holmes's essay, " 'The television audience cannot be expected to bear too much reality': *The Family* and Reality TV," describes the class and gender politics surrounding the media debate over the program and the questions *The Family* provoked about privacy and television's role in reshaping the boundary between public and private. Like Gilbert, the director of *The Family* responded to charges of sensationalism by describing the program as a documentary, rooted in its specific social and political context. Looking at the American and British versions side by side, Holmes shows just how important such context is; the language and behavior of the upper-middle-class Louds are shaped by the therapy culture and "let it all hang out" ethos so prevalent in 1970s America, whereas the working-class Wilkinses, living in council (i.e., publicly subsidized) housing, frequenting the pub, and uttering profanities, worried middle-class critics about the image of postcolonial Britain the program would project overseas.

Three decades later, reality TV programs about the family may no longer aim for the seriousness of the documentary format, but as Leigh Edwards argues in her essay, "Reality TV and the American Family," shows like *Who Wants to Marry My Dad?* and *Trading Spouses* continue to put cultural anxieties about the family on display. Edwards explores the rhetoric of the family in crisis that permeates much of reality TV programming and how various programs contribute to the long-running "family values" debate. Tracing recurring narrative tropes in reality programs about the family, Edwards understands the source of the appeal of the "family circus" that "portrays real people struggling with long-running cultural problems that have no easy answers." Viewers have the voyeuristic opportunity to peer into other people's households (from celebrity families to ordinary parents seeking help from British nannies) and witness the reality of diverse family practices. Noting that the current definition of the family is up for grabs, Edwards leaves us with the intriguing possibility that viewers might one day have nostalgia for the Osbournes as a model of the postmodern American family.

Edwards looks at families in need of a makeover, and part of the makeover process involves the reinforcement of certain beauty ideals and consumer practices. American reality makeover programs from *The Biggest Loser* to *The Swan* have their international counterparts, but as Sarah Matheson argues in "Shopping, Makeovers, and Nationhood: Reality TV and Women's Programming in Canada," Canadian cable channels aimed at female viewers sometimes put their own unique spin on this format. Matheson situates her discussion within a larger history of debates about women's television programming in Canada that accompanied the rise and decline of second-wave feminism. But critics of reality TV, who already lament its role in dumbing down popular culture, need not fear that current "lifestyle programming" oppresses women or reinforces sex-role stereotypes. Using the consumer advice program *The Shopping Bags* and the makeover series about plastic surgery *Plastic Makes Perfect*, Matheson describes how such programs complicate or disrupt discourses surrounding gender, nation, and television.

An altogether new type of nation is created in the reality TV program *Kid Nation*, which, according to Debbie Clare Olson in her essay "Babes in BonanzaLand: *Kid Nation*, Commodification, and the Death of Play," deliberately bombards children with threats to their innocence. In *Kid Nation* forty children, aged eight to fifteen, are charged with creating their own "brave new world" in Bonanza City, without any help or interference from adults. A show that stirred up controversy before it even aired, *Kid Nation* challenges its young participants to act like adults, dangling $20,000 gold stars as the price for their childhood. Olson reads the program as a paradoxical comment on a youth-obsessed society that nevertheless denies children the pleasures of play, teaching them to embrace consumer capitalism and class and gender prejudices to survive in a social Darwinian nightmare. That this experiment was not the ratings failure some critics predicted suggests the voyeuristic pleasure evoked by the dismantling of the fiction of childhood innocence.

Reality shows like *Kid Nation* and *The Shopping Bags* continuously prompt critics to lament the decline of quality television programming. The final part of this collection, Reality TV and the Living History Experiment, looks at a subgenre of reality TV known as "living history" or "hands-on history," described by its producers as "TV with a purpose." Britain's Channel 4 initiated the format with *The 1900 House,* and its ratings success has since led to similar programs in the United States and Australia. But, as the following articles suggest, these programs raise troubling questions about historical authenticity and reveal the pervasiveness of national myths. In 2002 London's Institute of Historical Research hosted a conference on the theme History and the Media to explore the benefits and pitfalls of historical reality TV programming. Though many scholars regarded any involvement with the media as selling out, others argued that programs like *1900 House* could in fact "convey the immediacy of history." As the historian David Cannadine pointed out, in Britain alone historical reality TV has led to a surge in interest in history among the general public; coined "the new sex" by the media, historical programming continues to feed into nostalgia for the past but also reveals how the media have taken over "as the prime educator about the past" for a majority of viewers.

Julie Anne Taddeo and Ken Dvorak use the Anglo-American productions *Regency House Party* and *Texas Ranch House* to explore just how difficult it is to make "real" history. The producers and time-traveling volunteers are guided not by historians but by their own assumptions about the past, most of which derive from fictional representations (TV, novels, and movies). As the guests visit at the Regency-style manor, they try to reenact their favorite Jane Austen novels; the cowboys in *Texas Ranch House* live out their John Wayne fantasies, proving, as the producers put it, their "true grit." The volunteers also experience the clash of their twenty-first-century sensibilities with their nineteenth-century re-created environments and value systems, which prompts them to rewrite their own fictions of the past, to reject gender and racial inequality and defy any authority that stands in the way of their individual happiness.

This need of both the producers and volunteers to write a more "ethical" version of the past also shapes the Australian living-history programs *The Colony* and *Outback House.* In her essay " 'What about giving us a real version of Australian history?': Identity, Ethics, and Historical Understanding in Reality History TV," Michelle Arrow critiques the refusal of these productions to tackle the violence of colonialism in Australia's past. Arrow is particularly interested in how Australian viewers have responded to the issues raised in these programs. Is it even possible to present a heroic pioneer experience while omitting the convict origins of Australia or white

Australians' dispossession of indigenous peoples? These concerns sparked an ongoing debate among not just academics but also politicians and the media about the very nature and responsibility of history.

Aurora Scheelings, armed with the dual credentials of academic and documentarian, further explores the limits of living history programs that aim not only to re-create the past but to record "the experiences of those who relive it." In her essay "Living History in Documentary Practice: The Making of *The Colony*," Scheelings describes the confrontation that ensued with *The Colony*'s producers and director over the making of the documentary she had been commissioned to film. Though she, like Arrow, notes some of the problems involved in the program's content (in particular the treatment of relations between aboriginals and white settlers), her main focus is the issue of the production process. Her involvement in *The Colony* offers rare insight into what she sees as the "ever-hybridizing world of documentary and factual program making" and how this hybridization negatively affects the presentation of historical "truth."

Reality TV continues to generate scholarly analysis, including the development of university courses examining this global phenomenon and the cultural significance of its programming. These shows, whether they aim to beautify and slim their contestants, teach children how to be adultlike consumers, instruct adults how to dance a nineteenth-century waltz, or simply document the day-to-day experiences of an English family in a re-created wartime suburb, continue to attract television audiences eager to empathize with their plights or even relish their failures. The importance of reality TV and the paradigm shift it has caused in television viewing and audience participation points to a more pervasive shift in cultural attitudes about self-exposure and the relationship between the individual and an increasingly global community. Will Internet social networking sites such as YouTube and Facebook replace reality TV productions? Or will electronically created avatars serve the individual cravings of people constantly seeking adventure, romance, and celebrity? These current and future trends in popular culture will no doubt be tackled by other scholars, and we hope that this collection contributes to a lively debate.

PART I

Reality TV as Social Experiment

FRED NADIS

Citizen Funt

Surveillance as Cold War Entertainment

A New York City bus station phone operator receives a series of phone calls from an annoying customer. In the first call he asks the operator for the scheduled departures and the length of the trip. In the second call he asks if he will get a seat and if the bus drivers are good. The third call brings further questions: Do the buses ever get lost? Is Spring Valley a nice town? How many stops along the way? Can the driver make a special stop to pick him up at 114th and Broadway? When he calls the fourth time, he asks to speak to another operator. The exasperated operator responds, "I've told you all about the buses; do you want to know how often they clean them maybe?" The customer asks again the departure times. Then he asks if the buses have reclining seats.

Throughout the call we hear only the phone operator's voice, with its New York working-class accent; we sense her general good humor and the caller's difficulty flustering her, then her rising aggravation balanced by her fellow feeling for the caller, about whom between calls she wonders out loud to a coworker, "Where was he when they passed out the brains?" The caller was the thirty-three-year-old Allen Funt, and the recording was made in 1947 for his radio series *The Candid Microphone*. In this radio show he explored ways to provoke unrehearsed behavior that would eventually crystallize in the *Candid Camera* sequences he filmed off and on from the late 1940s until his death in 1999.

In provoking these unrehearsed responses, Funt thought of himself as a researcher, conducting experiments in human nature; in his sketches he dared his victims to act badly and dared his audiences to consider what "acting badly" meant. In the bus station operator sequence, we as listeners come to admire the phone operator. She is polite but nobody's patsy. By the sequence's finish, when he asks if he'll get lost in Spring Valley, she sings

Allen Funt in his role as television "researcher" on *Candid Camera*. Courtesy of PhotoFest.

out, "Take a chance!" Along the way Funt has tested her character—or, to use a more old-fashioned coinage, her "virtue"—and, with her, the virtues of the working public in cold war America.

Frequently, Funt's surveillance "victim" would not fare as well as the bus station phone operator. For example, in one sequence for *Candid Camera* in 1963, Funt filmed a young man in a suit and fedora boarding an elevator crowded with Funt operatives. Before the elevator doors close, the Funt extras turn to the back of the car. The young victim notices this, then casually turns backward. Next the extras slowly turn forward; again the young man, baffled, does the same. They continue to put him through his paces, for example removing and then replacing their hats. The victim mirrors them. While Funt's voiceover commentary stresses the humorous nature of the young man's plight, he serves him up as a "treat" and a warning about conformity.

Concerns about privacy, conformity, decency, and American charac-ter were rampant in the late 1940s and early 1950s, when Funt's shows emerged on radio and television. This was the age of loyalty oaths, fears of un-American activities, Communist infiltration, organized crime, and public panics over comic books and juvenile delinquency. In 1947, just one year before *Candid Microphone,* the Truman administration had established the national security state apparatus, which included the formation of the National Security Council and the CIA, as well as an expanded FBI with authority to run background checks on federal employees. Funt's use of surveillance for entertainment addressed the public's concerns about threats to privacy in a time of rampant paranoia. And though Funt's entertainments quietly probed 1950s Americans for their "good citizenship" qualities, creating a comic inversion of the HUAC hearings, his critics inevitably questioned what sort of citizen these shows' creator was as well.

The Apprenticeship of Citizen Funt

Funt was born in Brooklyn in 1914 to immigrant German-Jewish parents. He graduated from high school at age fifteen and went on to study fine arts at the Pratt Institute and Cornell University. No introverted artist, he was feisty and streetwise. To gain respect in his Brooklyn neighborhood, during his childhood he began boxing, and he continued as a member of the Cornell Boxing Club; his scrappy appearance and manner later aided him when he asked outrageous favors and questions of people on camera. After graduating from Cornell in 1934 with a degree in fine arts, and recognizing that he was "no Matisse," Funt landed an entry-level job in advertising in Manhattan and soon found a niche as an "idea man" for radio shows.

Drafted during World War II, Funt continued his show business apprenticeship in the U.S. Army Signal Corps, where he produced radio shows and fund-raising events for war bonds. In *Behind the Dog Tag: The Show That Makes GI Wishes Come True,* Funt would field GIs' bizarre wishes, for example, "to go swimming in beer," and find a way to grant them. He also created a radio show that fielded GI complaints called *The Gripe Booth.* According to Funt, GIs tended to become tongue-tied when the red light flashed on for recording, so he began to record them earlier, in secret, while casually bantering, to get better and more candid communication from his subjects. This was a breakthrough for him. According to his 1994 memoir, "As soon as I was discharged from the army and returned to New York, I tried to create a radio show using hidden microphones. . . . I wanted to create a program that would simply record the beauty of everyday conversation . . . pure eavesdropping" (Funt with Reed 26).

The results, made with a wire recorder in diners and other public venues, frequently consisted of weak banter and background noise that tended to be unfit for his radio show *Candid Microphone*. Occasionally the hidden microphone would pick up gems, such as when two handicapped veterans in a veteran's hospital talked about how difficult it was to deal with the public's inquiries about their disabilities. Too often, though, there was not enough drama in these secret recordings. Funt claims that he finally hit on the proper formula while hiding a microphone in a dentist's office. A customer interrupted him, and in a fit of inspiration, Funt began to examine her mouth, then told her that she didn't have any wisdom teeth at all, which led to a heated exchange on tape. With this improvisation, Funt left behind the role of silent eavesdropper and took on the role of dramatic provocateur.

His further exploration of his gimmick gained for *Candid Microphone* popular acclaim and a following that included numerous New York intellectuals. The sociologist David Riesman, for example, in *The Lonely Crowd* (1950) cited a *Candid Microphone* sequence as evidence that consumerism had led to the emergence of an "other-directed" personality anxious to smile and please (121). In addition to being reviewed in the New York dailies, Funt and his innovative shows were the subject of articles in *Life,* the *New Yorker,* and the *Saturday Evening Post;* he also became the model for the roguish television producer Golk, who revels in shouting, "You're on camera!" to his media con-game dupes in Richard Stern's energetic novel *Golk* (1960).

Braced by this early appreciation, Funt continued his experiments, pranks, and improvisations and helped define himself as a new sort of "auteur." A publicity photo from the late 1940s shows Funt in his office, tie loose, arms crossed, and one leg up on a chair as he gazes bleary-eyed past three workers with earphones who are splicing wire recordings. Like a jazz album photograph showing musicians and producers in a relaxed studio, this portrait suggested a certain insouciance and world-weariness in Funt and his young staff. His wised-up, technically capable portrayal announced a new sort of artist at work: a practical joker, sociologist, and confidence man. Like the swindler Rinehart in Ralph Ellison's 1952 novel *Invisible Man,* who prowls the streets of Harlem impersonating a preacher and a pimp, Funt—who also published his first memoir in 1952—could "be" anybody—dentist, grocer, butcher, hotdog vendor, driving instructor, wrestler, annoying presence on a street corner, even HUAC investigator. And he was able to evoke melodic inspirations from his "instrument"—the anonymous people he referred to, alternately, as "subjects" and "victims." He was no Matisse, but a new kind of artist primed for the age of radio and television.

A year after his radio debut, Funt took his format to television. The show pleased audiences even though it did not fit preexisting genres or broadcasters' notions of television's strengths as a medium. In 1948, when *Candid Camera* first aired, television was in its infancy; many believed that the small screen with its poor image quality was best for live events, which offered a feeling of immediacy and connection. Hollywood-made telefilms such as detective series were suspect. One critic argued that such artificial shows "break the link between human and human. The viewer loses his sense of being a partner and instead becomes a spectator" (Boddy 81). Much of the early television programming was live, whether talk shows, quiz shows, variety shows, or live dramas and staged spectaculars that drew from the New York City theater talent pool.

Funt blended curiously into this mix of live programming. He began on a local ABC broadcast with Ken Roberts as his cohost, Philip Morris as the show's sponsor, and plenty of shots of Roberts and Funt puffing on their sponsor's cigarettes. To meet television's demands for immediacy, Funt gave off-the-cuff introductions to his films and ongoing commentary or banter with his cohost during the live broadcast. In so doing he solved the problem of maintaining immediacy and a sense of intimacy with live audiences. In the 1960s, when *Candid Camera* became a national success on CBS, Funt relied on the same format, working with a string of urbane partners that included the acidic, witty talk show host Arthur Godfrey, and later the more self-effacing Durward Kirby and Bess Myerson, a former Miss America.

Selling his show to local networks, while also working on industrial films and producing phonograph recordings of his radio material, Funt soon became a wealthy man. In 1951 he purchased a large estate on the Hudson River that he and his wife Evelyn dubbed White Gates. There they took to living in high style with their three children, as the original ten-acre purchase spread out into a hundred acres. Funt struck a jaunty style, commuting to work in a phone-equipped white Thunderbird, relying on a tape recorder to capture his inspirations, pleased to get comments on his show from a toll collector every Monday morning.

Candid Methods

When Funt gained prominence in the 1950s and 1960s, he offered inter-viewers a standard account of *Candid Camera*'s five basic categories: (1) pure observation of the ordinary; (2) wish fulfillment; (3) human frailties; (4) the small crisis; (5) the exposé of tricks of the trade (Martin 93–94). Funt insisted that he could spend hours admiring the different ways in which people smoked, ate spaghetti, or descended staircases. The "pure observation" that he had attempted in early *Candid Microphone* segments by recording in diners and veterans' hospitals had by the 1960s become compendiums of simple events set to music, whether a montage of numer-ous bowlers bowling, babies' crying set to opera music, or stylish traffic cops at work directing the flow of traffic in time with a jazz score.

The category of "wish fulfillment" involved the viewer's identifying with Funt, the provocateur, as he played out a transgressive or risqué fantasy, attempting, for example, to pick up girls in Central Park, or to order a set lunch special at a diner and repeatedly ask the irritated waiter to make substitutions ("Vegetable soup, I don't like vegetable soup. Can I change the soup for some fruit salad?"). In another wish fulfillment fantasy he would nonchalantly hand a cab driver a fifty- or hundred-dollar bill and wait for the cabbie to complain he couldn't change it.

"Human frailties," in his formula, meant exposing an individual's vanity, greed, or weakness in the face of social pressure. His camera would catch people primping in front of a mirror, for example, or getting increasingly aggravated as he asked for favor after favor. He would use difficult words in an improper context and prompt absurd responses from subjects who didn't know the word's meaning but wouldn't admit it, as when he asked, "Did you know that elevator is retroactive?" or, "Who do you think is the most superfluous actress acting today?"

His exposés of tricks of the trade, which aligned his shows with cru-sading journalism, included candid tapes he made of trickery in the loan industry and on used car sales lots. In one such sequence he talked with a professional wrestler about how he could fix a fight and was assured that 99 percent of all fights were fixed, and those that weren't were "no good" because they bored audiences. Such exposés could also benefit businesses, as when he created sales training films that highlighted bad salesmanship.

The heart of his show, however, was in the small crisis. His creation of these small crises anticipated the work that the social psychologist Leon Festinger in the late 1950s termed cognitive dissonance. Much of this research could be traced to postwar funding related to understanding shifts in public opinion and concerns about conformity and totalitarianism. Such communications research examined how subjects handled the unexpected—if what is going on is baffling, or contradicts a person's received wisdom, ethics, or common sense, how does she or he resolve the situation? How do people manage to reduce the dissonance and related anxiety? The majority of Funt's sequences fit this category, which in his hands involved people handling the minicrisis of the practical joke. How do people in telephone booths respond, for example, when an elephant comes and blocks their exit?

For this category of research, Funt, like a silent comedy director, often highlighted people's reactions to machines that went haywire. In linking comedy and automation, Funt was following a long tradition. Writing in an era of increased industrial regimentation, the early twentieth-century French philosopher Henri Bergson argued that "the attitudes, gestures and movements of the human body are laughable in exact proportion as that body reminds us of a mere machine" (75). Bergson called laughter the corrective for such rigidity. Funt produced his work in a new era of social regimentation, and his audience's laughter "corrected" revealed behavior patterns.

In one *Candid Camera* sequence, we see an office worker at first amused, and then fluttering around in dismay as a mimeograph machine begins to fling out sheet after sheet of paper. In a more elaborate setup, a new cook in a bakery is positioned at a conveyor belt to put whipped cream on cakes. The cakes come at much too fast a pace. The worker is a morose little fellow who responds in much the same way as a Harry Langdon or Charlie Chaplin might. He finally can only scoop the cakes up and place them higher up the conveyor line, knowing they soon will return. Further exploring the grammar of slapstick, Funt hired Buster Keaton to imitate an accident-prone customer at a diner and recorded the results.

In another sequence, Funt set up a trampoline store and focused his camera on hired secretaries as a client would come in, begin testing a trampoline, bounce higher and higher, then crash through the ceiling and disappear. One nonchalant secretary, who has seen it all, simply sits there puffing on her cigarette, refusing to offer a response.

Other crisis sequences offered sharp social commentary. A classic example involves Funt summoning a locksmith to his office to open the locks holding his secretary chained to her desk so she can take a short lunch break. Although outraged and concerned for her well-being, the locksmith ultimately only urges Funt at least to rubber-coat the chains. When Funt asks, "Is there a rubber-coated chain they use for this purpose?" the locksmith weakly replies, "No one uses it for this purpose here. . . . Out West maybe" (McEvoy 116).

His networks wanted broad humor, but Funt stressed in interviews his concerns about conformity and weakness in the face of authority. Here he was in step with the sociologists and intellectuals of the era then dissecting the psychology of mass culture and dynamics of totalitarianism. Funt's concern was quite overt in the sequence from 1963 in which the young man in the fedora boards an elevator crowded with Funt operatives. Funt brought out the same message with a lighter tone when he placed a sign saying "Please step only on the black squares" in a shoe repair store with a checkerboard tiled floor. We then see victims of all ages politely hopping and skipping across the square tiles, eager to please.

In addition to its basic formula of manufacturing an absurd yet often telling crisis and documenting the shifting reactions of the subjects, *Candid Camera* relied on the dramatic epiphany of what Funt dubbed "the reveal"—that is, the moment when the crisis has peaked and the subject is informed he or she is being filmed. In the reveal all the building tension of the scene is resolved and dissonance evaporates. Men and women might hide their faces while overcome with emotion, burst out laughing, hug Funt, or, in one woman's case, pull him down onto a bed and roll around with him. The reveal ultimately became the show's trademark, as exemplified by the show's peppy theme song, which ended with "Smile, You're on *Candid Camera*."

Hidden Microphones and Documentary Ethics

Funt's show appealed to broadcasters because it was inexpensive; it appealed to audiences because it was amusing; and it appealed to intellectuals because it was a curious hybrid—taking up the documentary cause that had been supremely important in the 1930s and 1940s, while also paralleling the work of postwar sociologists, psychologists, and documentarians. Yet his shows were also open to charges that he was exploiting his humble subjects for the amusement of a middle-class audience.

Similar complaints had plagued earlier efforts at "artful surveillance" with hidden cameras; for example, in the late nineteenth century, the portable "detective" camera was introduced, making new, quick, candid photographs possible. Some of these cameras were built into bowler hats, cravats, walking sticks, and picnic baskets.[1] Middle-class subjects spluttered over the photographs taken of them without consent. Members of the working class or "exotic" groups have traditionally been more appropriate subjects—or victims—of documentary studies. The crusading journalist Jacob Riis used his camera to invade slum life and depict sordid scenes in sweatshops, tenement alleys, police lodging quarters, and cheap saloons to build support for his reform agenda. Likewise, documentary classics such as Robert Flaherty's *Nanook of the North* (1922) reinvented the lives of the Inuit as exotic, premodern others.

Funt confirmed his preference for humble subjects in a 1960 interview in the *New Yorker,* stating, "The lower the class, the more comfortable I am." His interviewer stressed that Funt, with his Brooklyn accent and Stanley Kowalski persona, was able to make "humbler subjects feel right at home, and thus softens them up for lines of questioning that in the mouths of less earthily gifted interrogators might cause suspicion, resentment, or, worst of all, silence" (Flagler 73). Funt also admitted to cruelty at times, noting that it was intrinsic to humor. In an early interview he commented, "If you want to know what holds the man together . . . you apply a real jolt and see where the cracks appear" (Flagler 74).

Funt, however, also believed his shows had "uplift." His first LP record anthology from the *Candid Microphone* series included Funt's introduction in which he made a case for his democratic realism, or "candid portraits in sound," casting himself as a latter-day Walt Whitman, eager to celebrate democracy. He noted: "These are the plain everyday kind of people you never see in the headlines or in the movies or on the stage; authors create copies of them; history counts them and sorts them and finally lumps them all together. They have no single name except as Americans and their voice is not remembered except as a chorus. They make themselves heard here as individuals . . . unposed, unrehearsed, and completely off-guard."

In his writings Funt argued that he was after something bigger than just cheap laughs or cruel fun. What he did was a combination of art and science. Funt, like any artist working in a realist mode, wanted to capture real life. One of his goals was to make "a photograph of the way a man spends his entire working day—every public minute of it. This may not be great entertainment, but it certainly should have a place in the time capsule of this civilization" (Funt 205). He added that his crews had already photographed one man traveling from "place to place" using seven different hidden cameras and seven crews. Trying to break completely free of the *Candid Camera* gimmick, in 1963 he developed the short-lived television show *Pictures of People.* He and his staff used three mobile television studios that traveled the country, inviting people to present themselves as they liked, completely aware that they were being recorded. The program did not last the year.

Like the highbrow cinema verité filmmakers who followed, Funt reveled in the poetics of everyday life captured on film. Yet his idea of realism was more directly drawn from the terms of the 1950s debate about television's strengths. Trying to achieve the more immediate, direct sense of the real that suited television, Funt's sketches often deflated classic Hollywood moments. He would, for instance, hop into a taxi and order the driver to "follow that cab," and he inevitably was turned down; one cabbie remarked, "How do I know where he's going?" Another driver said, "I don't do nothing like that, Mister. I just take you to places, not after other cabs." In 1962 Funt hired William Saroyan to script the ways that a customer in a carpeting store would react when told that an anonymous client had made all his payments for him. Funt noted that in his actual takes, no customer nobly refused being let off the hook.

The Case against Citizen Funt

A provocateur onscreen and off, instead of trying to shake the label of "voyeur," Funt proudly titled his early autobiography *Eavesdropper at Large* (1952). He also explored what it might mean to be a public voyeur, one who rejects the legitimate boundaries of the private sphere during the cold war. Announcements of the end of privacy were endemic in the 1950s and 1960s.[2] Books such as Vance Packard's *The Hidden Persuaders* (1957) reported on how the advertising industry manipulated an audience's emotions. Packard followed this book with *The Naked Society* (1964), which detailed various invasions of privacy, whereas the U.S. Supreme Court decision in *Griswold v. Connecticut* (1965) underscored the right to privacy when a couple sued for the right to receive birth control material through the mail.

Funt intentionally gave his footage the feeling of a wiretap or surveillance film. He insisted on a stripped-down aesthetic for his show, as apparently only one camera recorded a scene to give the audience a surveillance-camera perspective. Sequences were concluded and connected with lap dissolves that showed Venetian blinds closing on a scene, blacking it out and opening to the next. The audience, like the host, was a Peeping Tom, engaged in fun that paralleled government surveillance and censorship. When people swore on the radio or screen, Funt's people would dub in a woman's voice sweetly saying, "Censored."

Continuing to explore the realms of realism and secrecy, Funt took his *Candid Camera* to various European countries and then to the Soviet Union in 1960 and managed to smuggle candid films made in Moscow— which Soviet authorities had apparently "fogged"—out from behind the Iron Curtain, including tried-and-true-bits in which Funt or an operative reads a newspaper over someone's shoulder or a pretty young woman asks passersby to help carry a suitcase filled with concrete. They also filmed observational footage of, for example, Russian families posing for snapshots in front of a cannon. Funt insisted that he was on a "subversive mission—I wanted to show that the Soviets were actually human beings" (Funt with Reed 134). The promptings for Funt's U.S.S.R. mission were similar to the simple humanism of Edward Steichen's 1955 touring show, The Family of Man, a compilation of photographs from artists worldwide that showed daily life around the globe and stressed universal, shared values and the necessity of institutions such as the United Nations to undercut cold war tensions.

In line with this humanistic Family of Man approach, the mainstream press frequently portrayed Funt as a connoisseur of the "little guy" whose show, if at times "impudent," was ultimately harmless, often hilarious, and even instructive. Yet, perhaps because of his canny abilities, Funt became the target of some very literate critics, housed largely at the *New Yorker,* who saw themselves as the true defenders of the "little guy" whom Funt exploited.

The *New Yorker*'s Philip Hamburger, one of Funt's most savage critics, writing in 1957, made "hypocrisy" Funt's prime sin. Hamburger began by arguing that Funt had "succeeded, I think, in reducing the art, the purpose and the ethics of the 'documentary' idea to the level of the obscene." Comparing Funt's efforts to the earlier work of the documentary filmmaker Robert Flaherty, which he insisted showed respect for the dignity of his subjects, Hamburger berated Funt for being a tempter who was "sadistic, poisonous, anti-human, and sneaky" (73).

Two and a half years later another *New Yorker* writer, John Lardner, joined the attack. Far from being the "benevolent student" of his species that Funt passed himself off as, the producer was actually a "torturer" who had fewer scruples than a government wiretapper. In his lengthy diatribe, Lardner painted a diabolic portrait of Funt along the lines of Melville's sinister Confidence Man. He described one sketch in which Funt placed a twenty-dollar bill in a revolving door and another in which Funt put twenty-dollar bills in the pockets of suits in a tailor shop, then commented that these twenty-dollar deposits were "the standard wages of temptation on 'The *Candid Camera*.'" Lardner concluded his critique by voicing the wish that Funt leave alone the "man on the street" and instead apply "his great gift for aggressiveness to men in public life, beginning at the top" (60).

Golking Funt

The novelist Richard Stern explored such a possibility in his short novel *Golk* (1960). Stern, a fan of Funt's programs, recalled "laughing so hard at one [showing] that I fell into the aisle of an Iowa City theater" (*One Person* 392). In his rise and fall narrative, Stern homed in on Funt's ambitious, streetwise characteristics while shaping his Funt character, Golk, into a mythic trickster and father figure. Stern's depiction oscillates between Golk as a jaded, manipulative monster and Golk as a tough populist genius. The book extols a Golk who skewers highbrows with his street tactics, who taps the natural artistry of his subjects, and who projects a democratic presence, so that his becomes "the world's own voice."

At the novel's pivot, Golk, sated with fame and useless power, decides to leave entertainment behind and to expose the corrupt and powerful. Golk announces, "We're going to be the education of the audience. Not the blackboard-and-seats kind, but demonstrators, dramatizers, the portrayers of corruption, connivance, of the tone and temper of the world they live in and don't understand" (101). Although Golk knows he cannot hope to last with such strategies, he prefers a "noble stint, a clean job." Then follow three "golks" of Washington insiders and lobbyists. Soon after, the network forces Golk off the show, after which his underlings take over and quickly run the program into oblivion. Golk, with his chameleon knack, heads out West and then fades behind the scenes to become a stagehand in Hollywood.

In his own life Funt made some dramatic changes but avoided Golk's flameout. In 1964 Funt divorced his first wife and married his secretary from *Candid Camera,* Marilyn Ina Laron. Funt left behind the town-and-country style and became a zany urbanite in a ten-room apartment that one breathless journalist insisted had a "nuttiness in every room." The kitchen, for example, included two ovens, two stoves, two refrigerators (one just for his wife's "No-Cal"), and two freezers as insurance against the time when "things break down."

The second marriage survived a plane hijacking to Cuba in February 1969 (many of Funt's fellow passengers thought it was only a *Candid Camera* trick in bad taste) but only briefly survived a second disaster, Funt's discovery in 1972 that his accountant had embezzled more than $1 million since 1961. Several years later Funt divorced his second wife, who later wrote two books on the problems a wife faced in a celebrity marriage, the first, from 1979, titled *Are You Anybody?*

After his business and personal upsets, Funt, like Golk before him, finally moved West. He claimed Los Angeles was not a city for him—though he had made a career of turning ordinary people into media beings, he disliked the lack of authenticity of Los Angeles. It was, he said, a place "where everyone looks and acts like a movie extra. They dress in costumes, speak in no particular accent, and seem to be starring in a movie that is running in their heads" (Funt with Reed 176). He settled instead on a 1,200-acre parcel of real estate in Big Sur and began turning it into a working ranch that included a small outbuilding for Native American art.

What Do You Say to a Naked Formula?

To avoid Golk's fadeout, Funt had nowhere to go creatively but to introduce his formulas into different media. One such realm was business consulting: from the 1950s he created many industrial films and filmstrips relying on *Candid Camera* formulas. A second realm was academia: Funt made several film compilations and produced textbooks for introductory psychology courses based on *Candid Camera* sequences and even taught psychology in Carmel. He also entered a third realm, that of risqué entertainment, with the X-rated film *What Do You Say to a Naked Lady?* (1970). Distributors paired it with the X-rated *Last Tango in Paris* and, at the height of the sexual revolution, it became a financial success.

Turning to sex as a topic was a reasonable extension of *Candid Camera*'s mixture of practical jokes, Peeping Tom tactics, and boundary exploring. In addition to candid interviews with people about their ideas regarding sex, sexual experiences, and beliefs, *What Do You Say* largely involved surveillance footage of male subjects' encounters with naked female models who held, as fig leaves, purses containing hidden microphones. In the footage we see these men ogle pretty nude women, try to ignore them, gallantly offer to cover them, pursue them with wolfish stares, or break out in laughter after the naked lady has left the scene. The film's peppy title song, now pure kitsch, kept the proceedings light. As an example of the new sexual permissiveness of the 1960s, the film has not aged well. It distorted the usual *Candid Camera* formula, since the wrong people were being "stripped"—not Funt's ordinary people, but fetching operatives. Nevertheless, Funt later produced nearly forty half-hour shows for the Playboy Channel that "poked fun at the way people react to nudity and sex."

Funt went on to make the feature film *Money Talks* (1972), an uneasy mix of gags and social commentary about money, livelihood, and poverty. A third feature, *Smile When You Say I Do* (1973), centered on the theme of marriage and was prompted by his own difficulties in his second marriage. Overall, the restraints of television network sponsorship—and the social restraints of pre-1960s culture—tended to evoke better work than the relative freedom of his finally realized film experiments.

Though Funt produced only *Candid Camera* specials after the 1967 cancellation of the regular series, in 1998 his oldest son, Peter Funt, long involved in *Candid Camera*, began producing the program again for CBS. But the never-ending show, continuously in reruns somewhere in the world, had inevitably suffered aesthetically. Even Funt, before his death in 1999, said his show looked "quaint" by modern television standards.

The latest incarnation of *Candid Camera*, of course, is surrounded by its progeny: the many reality television shows that borrow Funt's strategies of low-cost production, constant surveillance, voiceover, and editing to tweak real life into entertainment. "Meet Joe Schmo" (2003), for example, featured a young man who auditioned to be on a *Survivor*-style reality show but was not told that he would be the only "genuine" cast member. Everyone else was working from a script to set him up. In this show, then, the several-minute surveillance observation of *Candid Camera* was stretched into a season-long experiment in dissonance. The series ended, inevitably, with the filmed reveal.

Such tweaking no longer raises the same outcry it once did—even serious documentary filmmakers, who long ago distanced themselves from *Candid Camera* and its secret-camera tactics, often admit that their works are, in the filmmaker Frederick Wiseman's words, "reality fictions." At his best, Funt, with his tricks and reveals, circled the problem of making his show both real and entertaining, but he found it insoluble. *Candid Camera*'s success remained, perhaps, in its uneasy blend. Turning surveillance to artistic ends evoked moral ambiguities as well as fascination. Was Funt's camera eye cruel or humane? Were Funt's subjects exploited or ennobled? Were they caving in to authority, being good sports, or both? Was his empathy an illusion, or was Funt, like the fictional Golk, despite his crudities, a genuine artist with a social vision?

A product of the quiet liberalism of the 1950s, *Candid Camera* was made at a time when boundary-probing entertainment still was expected to have uplift. If the many loyalty committees of the era wished to be arbiters of good citizenship, the moderate left also wished to have its say. In their documentary work, folklorists, sociologists, and cinema verité filmmakers sought to expose both the nobility and the folly in the lives of their subjects. Like the era's psychologists, documentarians also explored the social pressures that people faced. *Candid Camera,* with a theme song that noted that "When You Least Expect It, You're Elected," consistently surveyed the American scene, while probing ideas of good citizenship and threatened democracy.

Acknowledgment

This article is republished courtesy of the editors of *Film & History: An Interdisciplinary Journal of Film and Television Studies.*

Notes

1. See Gunning for a discussion of the rise of the hidden camera at the turn of the twentieth century.

2. Nelson, for example, argues that during the cold war, confessional poetry emerged at the same time as concerns about invasion of privacy.

Works Cited

Bergson, Henri. "Laughter." *Comedy*. Ed. Wylie Sypher. Garden City, NY: Doubleday, 1956. 74–79.

Boddy, William. *Fifties Television: The Industry and Its Critics*. Urbana: University of Illinois Press, 1990.

Festinger, Leon. *A Theory of Cognitive Dissonance*. Stanford: Stanford University Press, 1962 [1957].

Flagler, J. M. "Profiles: Student of the Spontaneous." *New Yorker,* December 10, 1960.

Funt, Allen. *Eavesdropper at Large: Adventures in Human Nature*. New York: Vanguard Press, 1952.

Funt, Allen, with Philip Reed. *Candidly, Allen Funt: A Million Smiles Later.* New York: Barricade Books, 1994.

Gunning, Tom. "Embarrassing Evidence: The Detective Camera and the Documentary Impulse." *Collecting Visible Evidence*. Ed. Jane M. Gaines and Michael Renov. Minneapolis: University of Minnesota Press, 1999. 46–64.

Hamburger, Philip. "Peeping Funt." *New Yorker,* January 7, 1957.

Lardner, John. "Harsh Voice from the Past." *New Yorker,* July 4, 1959.

Martin, Peter. "I Call on the *Candid Camera* Man." *Saturday Evening Post,* May 27, 1961.

McEvoy, J. P. "Eavesdropper without Inhibitions." *Reader's Digest,* August 1948.

Nelson, Deborah. *Pursuing Privacy in Cold War America*. New York: Columbia University Press, 2002.

Riesman, David. *The Lonely Crowd*. New Haven: Yale University Press, 1963 [1950].

Stern, Richard. *Golk*. Chicago: University of Chicago Press, 1987.

———. *One Person and Another: On Writers and Writing*. Dallas: Baskerville Publishers, 1993.

LEE BARRON

From Social Experiment to Postmodern Joke

Big Brother *and the Progressive Construction of Celebrity*

> Television it is, reality it's not. (Baggot 24)

> The invention of Chantelle was a superb piece of casting. (Peter York, quoted in Aspinall 2006, 154)

According to Su Holmes, one of the significant factors to emerge from the growth of reality TV is that it "has made it impossible to escape the fact that we have seen an appreciable rise in the number of 'ordinary' people appearing on television" ("All you've got" 111). It is this process that this essay will explore, examining the reality TV program *Big Brother* and especially its counterpart, *Celebrity Big Brother,* within the context of its transmission in the United Kingdom. Following a discussion concerning the development, nature, and critical reaction to *Big Brother,* I will focus on the palpable congruence between *Big Brother* and celebrity discourse and the increasingly discernible "celebritization" effect *Big Brother* perennially bestows on many of its contestants, particularly in recent years. Indeed, when examined retrospectively, many of the prominent or infamous moments of *Big Brother* are explicitly connected to this increasing reality TV–celebrity connection. Although the study of media stars has a significant history within film studies and sociology (Dyer; Alberoni; Monaco; DeCordova; Gledhill), recent years have seen the emergence of a solid and progressive body of research dedicated to mapping out the culture and status of contemporary celebrity (Rojek; Turner; Evans and Hesmondhalgh; Cashmore, *Beckham* and *Celebrity/Culture;* Marshall; Holmes and Redmond; Redmond and Holmes), much of which pays acute attention to the rise of "fabricated celebrities" created through appearances on reality TV shows. When viewed in retrospect, *Big Brother* represents a steady convergence between a "people show" narrative and the establishment of a particular mode of celebrity, a celebrity type constructed by the *Big Brother* audience, but more crucially by the show's producers. Drawing on the approach of Erving Goffman, I will discuss the increasing prevalence of individuals reflexively recognizing the potential of *Big Brother,* a process that serves to undercut the "reality principle" of the format through the adoption of strategic fronts designed to appeal to voting viewers and fellow housemates in order to postpone eviction from the house, with all its risks of anonymity.

Though I will discuss the means by which successive ordinary people can and have become celebrity figures through sustained television exposure on *Big Brother,* I will also examine a singular case study in the show's history, an event that occurred in the United Kingdom: *Celebrity Big Brother* 2006 and its winner, Chantelle Houghton. The significance of this case stems from the fact that Chantelle entered *Celebrity Big Brother* as a non-celebrity, a "fake celebrity" furnished with a script and a specific assignment: to convince her celebrity housemates that she was indeed famous. Not only did she achieve this objective, but she subsequently became the winner of the show and the most mediated figure to take part in the program: a true star. After *Big Brother,* Chantelle embarked on a celebrity fairy-tale life, complete with her own television show. This deliberately engineered television experiment served to illuminate the manner in which reality TV can direct cultural interest to the various individuals who appear within it, to demonstrate the ways in which the producers of *Big Brother* strive to reflexively manipulate, or at least foster, the celebritizing process, and to illustrate the degree to which reality TV and celebrity have become steadily intertwined. This symbiosis therefore is the culmination of *Big Brother*'s significant trajectory since its first broadcast in 2000 in the United Kingdom.

I will discuss how, since its first transmission, the U.K. version of *Big Brother* has progressively and decisively developed away from the trappings of psychological and social experimentation, a game show but one with a socially aware veneer, into an entertainment spectacle, a Boorstinian pseudo-event in which the celebritization process not only is left to external media (newspapers, celebrity magazines) but is increasingly engineered by *Big Brother*'s producers. The sum effect is that, as some commentators state, the radical nature of *Big Brother* has given way to a battery of gimmicks and the conscious and active creation of celebrity contestants while they are still contestants. If *Big Brother* has a discernible trajectory from 2000 to 2007, this, arguably, is it.

Reality Television, Big Brother, *and "Ordinary" Celebrities*

Surveying the history of media and, in particular, television in relation to the subject of celebrity, Tunstall notes: "Personal celebrity pre-dates the modern media, but in recent years general and media celebrity have moved closer and closer and are now virtually identical. . . . The television age took further something which radio had begun—the manufacturing of fame largely through appearances on the electronic media" (1). Certainly this trend is manifest in relation to the inexorable rise of the television genre commonly dubbed reality TV, particularly the reality game-show formats such as *Survivor* and especially *Big Brother.* The cultural responses to reality TV initially bore a distinctly Frankfurt School–flavored pessimism and critical cynicism. Contrary to any social experimental "mission state-ments," reality TV, for many commentators, was argued to offer no social-psychological insights at all but instead merely to represent "a mixture of banality and emotional pornography" (Barnfield in Cummings et al. 47). For others it was an emergent genre explicitly predicated on turning its "characters' vices into virtues" (Cashmore, *Celebrity/Culture* 189), and in its predictability and set format, it is arguably a mode of television texts that limits and preestablishes "the attitudinal pattern of the spectator" (Adorno 169), based as it is on mass audience participation. Such nega-tive approaches were corroborated in the case of the reactions to *Loft Story,* the French version of *Big Brother.* Although a significant ratings success, *Loft Story* was also subjected to various demonstrations by the protest group Activists against Trash TV, which called for the program to be removed from air, and whose protests included demonstrators outside the television studio brandishing placards that read, "With trash TV the people turn into idiots" (Hill 4).

Conversely, other commentators perceived the development of reality TV as an unprecedented advance in television, seeing it as a medium by which the audience is actually empowered and rendered active. In this analysis, reality TV has represented a dynamic development whereby the masses have actually been granted the ability to actively direct the narra-tive rather than simply receive transmissions in a docile, passive manner

(Andrejevic; Tincknell and Raghuram 2002). Furthermore, in relation to the example of *Big Brother* and its broadcast in Denmark, some politically minded critics viewed it as an incisive and instructive social experiment because of the ways in which the format is fundamentally based on "human relations, intimacy and security" (Biltereyst 100).

The history of reality TV stretches back to at least the 1960s in "people shows" such as *Candid Camera* and through the 1990s within docudramas and docusoaps, including *The Family, An American Family,* and *Airline.* Other notable examples include the do-it-yourself (DIY) Webcam experiments in the 1990s (Turner), broadcasts such as that of the American student Jennifer Ringley, who created videos of her everyday life in her apartment, revealing domestic and personal events ranging from brushing her teeth and studying for college, to having sex with her boyfriend, all broadcast on the Web as "Jennicam" to millions of viewers (Bazalgette). Reality TV's prime exemplar in terms of influence, significance, and popularity, however, is undoubtedly *Big Brother.*

 Big Brother was originally developed by Endemol Entertainment in the Netherlands in 1999 and would be subsequently syndicated in numerous countries, including France, Germany, Italy, Poland, South Africa, Australia, and America. Seamlessly combining television and Internet surveillance (Griffin-Foley), *Big Brother* was launched in the United Kingdom on Channel 4 in the summer of 2000, becoming "the definitive example of a whole range of programmes which have deployed combinations of the syntactical elements of forced confinement, competitive individualism and emotional conflict as entertainment [such as] *Castaway 2000, Survivor, Pop Idol, Fame Academy* [and] *The Salon*" (Tincknell and Raghuram 2006, 255). *Big Brother* is essentially an "interactive reality TV game show" (Thornborrow and Morris 246), culturally designated by the iconic symbol of an all-seeing eye that knowingly and explicitly referenced George Orwell's dystopian novel *1984* (the major difference being that the contestants *welcomed* the all-pervasive gaze of the camera). Its set consists of a specially constructed Big Brother House, which is fitted extensively with cameras that serve to monitor the housemates twenty-four hours a day. Furthermore, "The contestants are given tasks to perform in return for extra food and other treats, and to encourage them to interact in various ways and get to know one another. Every week, they each nominate their least favorite housemate, the two contestants with the most nominations are announced and the public are invited to vote one of them out of the house. In this way the contestants are gradually whittled away, and whoever is left in the house at the end of the series is the winner and gets a cash prize" (Cummings et al. xii). Throughout the *Big Brother* experience, contestants conventionally have no contact with life outside the house, and their social interactants are restricted to their housemates until they are evicted. Their only moments of privacy are attainable within the "diary room," where they speak to "the imaginary figure of 'Big Brother'" (Tincknell and Raghuram 2002, 202). Hence, the process is akin to that of the inmate world articulated by Goffman, by which individuals enter institutions, bringing with them values from a "home world"—ways of life and activities taken for granted—that, on the point of admission to the institution, are subject to curtailment (*Asylums* 23). The enforcement of mortification is also evident: within the Big Brother house, the contestants are referred to only by their Christian names; shower and toilet areas are communal; they are permitted to bring with them into the house only a limited number of personal items (which are routinely removed if contestants break the house rules); and they must endure periodic humiliation in the form of participation in tasks set by the omnipotent Big Brother to secure rewards and luxuries. Abstention results in group penalization and frequently the failure to complete the task.

Given the ubiquity of cameras, the dominant motif of *Big Brother* is surveillance; watching is at the heart of the narrative. Consequently, personal space is at best restricted, if not entirely removed: "*Big Brother*'s title connotes entrapment, restriction and control, and *Big Brother* was marketed at first as an experiment about how human society works, with the contestants like rats trapped in a laboratory maze. As if in a psychology test, the selfishness of desiring the first series prize of £70,000 conflicted with the contestants' need to gain loyalty from their housemates" (Bignell 118–119). Such control evokes Foucault's conception of the idealized "disciplined society" (and its primary institutions—the military, factories, hospitals, and prisons): "the gaze is alert everywhere" (195). *Big Brother* is Foucault's (or, rather, Bentham's) "panopticon" in idealized form (with shades of Zimbardo's 1971 Stanford prison experiment), constructed and utilized for purely entertainment purposes, but reflecting the primary effect of the panopticon: "to induce in the inmate a state of conscious and permanent visibility" (Foucault 201). *Big Brother,* however, arguably represents a three-step panopticon: the contestants are subject to the gaze of the media and related professionals—from the producers, presenters, and psychologists to the newspapers and magazines that constantly discuss, dissect, and speculate on the various housemates; the contestants are subject to the scrutiny of the viewing public, and they must subsequently strive to project favorable and entertaining impressions of themselves if they are to forestall premature eviction; and finally (and most directly), the housemates constantly observe each other, forming alliances, trying to second-guess other contestants, analyzing, and developing appraisals on which they will ultimately base their decisions to nominate or not nominate others for eviction. Such internal surveillance is the staple of diary room discussions with Big Brother. And it is this combinatory panoptic process that confers a peculiar glamour, an aura conducive to an emergent celebrity status.

For many commentators, the intrinsic appeal and distinctiveness of *Big Brother* is that it specifically involves real people, individuals who have been "plucked from obscurity and turned into stars, not because of any special talent, but just because they seem personable" (Cummings et al. xii). Thus, reality TV is a genre predicated on the erosion of discrete borders, actively blurring "the conventional boundaries between fact and fiction, drama and documentary and between the audience and the text" (Roscoe 474). It is a televisual experience "located in border territories, between information and entertainment, documentary and drama" (Hill 2). As Barnfield states, "Our collective willingness to watch such material indicates an erosion of the distinction between public and private, an end to intimacy" (Cummings et al. 63); *Big Brother* is an environment in which the contestants freely make "themselves into a spectacle" (Scannell 276) and as such become, to lesser and greater degrees, celebrity figures.

For Holmes the development of reality TV, and *Big Brother* in particular, has resulted in a palpable rise in the number of "ordinary" people who now are able to appear on television and who, by being on the program, are inevitably granted the status of "celebrity in process" ("All you've got" 119). Yet it is a very novel form of celebrity because "celebrity in *Big Brother* is lacking some of the fundamental discourses of the success myth, largely the emphasis on work and traditional conceptions of talent" ("All you've got" 119), although it may be argued to accord to some extent with the "discovery narrative" (Turner), in which an anonymous individual suddenly finds fame and media attention. In *Big Brother,* however, there is rarely any sense of "achieved celebrity"; it is, rather, an "attributed

celebrity" (Rojek) status because for those who participate, celebrity is ostensibly achieved through leisure, by frequently doing nothing. Ultimately,
Big Brother deliberately places "ordinary people in an extraordinary situation . . . a world in which anyone can feel the glow of celebrity" (Holmes,
"All you've got" 131–132). Moreover, like most categories of celebrity, it
requires constructing agents. As Rojek states, although it may not always
be apparent, celebrities are by and large "constructed": "Their impact on
the public may appear to be intimate and spontaneous. In fact, celebrities
are carefully mediated through what might be termed chains of attraction.
No celebrity now acquires public recognition without the assistance of
cultural intermediaries who operate to stage-manage celebrity presence
in the eyes of the public. 'Cultural intermediaries' is the collective term
for agents, publicists, marketing personnel, promoters, photographers"
(10). Although agents and related media (newspapers, magazines, and
television) are significant players in the celebrity-construction process,
in *Big Brother* the television audience becomes a key agent in ensuring
the continuing visibility of the contestants because it is the viewers who
control the fate of the housemates. Although primarily a television event
(Kilborn; Scannell) on both terrestrial and satellite channels, *Big Brother*
is also streamed across the Internet, a factor that grants the audience a
distinctive "*idea* of agency" (Tincknell and Raghuram 2002, 2006), and
as the motto of Big Brother consistently proclaims regarding the fate of
nominated contestants: "*You decide.*" Such apparent viewer freedom, however, is not always so clear-cut. *Big Brother,* with its apparent trappings of
psychological experimentation, is broadcast on commercial television, and
thus entertainment is a crucial factor. Viewed retrospectively, *Big Brother*
has steadily become a larger spectacle, and the original "reality" concept
has increasingly been eclipsed by the game-show dimension. In this sense,
reality TV and *Big Brother* arguably fall within Pierre Bourdieu's analysis
of popular television, a field significantly influenced by the dual forces of
commercial and economic constraints. As Bourdieu argues: "On the whole
the management of television is determined by the channel owners, by the
agencies which pay vast amounts of money to have their commercial clips
screened or by the state which raises public money to fund it" (quoted in
Marlière 200). The recent history of *Big Brother* in the United Kingdom
supports this contention and displays the way in which the *Big Brother*
format has changed and has been periodically embroiled in media and
social debates. For example, the influence of advertising that Bourdieu

identifies was graphically demonstrated by the withdrawal of *Celebrity Big Brother*'s commercial sponsor, Carphone Warehouse, in the wake of the racist bullying controversy involving Jade Goody (and to a lesser extent the model Danielle Lloyd and former S Club 7 pop singer Jo O'Meara) and the Bollywood actress Shilpa Shetty. The contretemps dominated its 2007 broadcast and generated some 44,500 viewer complaints (Tryhorn), marking this edition of *Celebrity Big Brother* as the most problematic in the show's history. This transmission would see the Goody-Shetty storm reach a national and international level of media coverage and even involve the British police. Thus, *Celebrity Big Brother* became not merely a media event but the grounds for an international incident between the British and Indian governments. Yet, for all of the uproar, the controversy was a primary contributor to the success of the show; indeed, 23 percent of the available TV audience tuned to Channel 4 to see the housemates nominate for eviction Jade Goody and Shilpa Shetty, the two people at the center of the storm (Brook), and 7.4 million viewers watched Goody's post-eviction interview (Tryhorn). A controversial broadcast thus resulted in a massive upsurge in viewing figures.

For Bourdieu, contemporary television has been marked by an increasing emphasis on ratings and the steady replacement of potentially politically divisive and problematic programs with more universally appealing entertainment formats, particularly soap operas. Although Marlière points out that Bourdieu's position is rather sweeping and polemical, *Big Brother* nevertheless conforms to his cultural assessment of television formats; consequently, although a democratic ethos seemingly informs *Big Brother* through audience participation, this is supported by acute production control. But the direction and codes of *Big Brother* are, like other forms of media, the subject of negotiation. As Golding states: "The term *mass* media and *mass* communication should not obscure the variations within the audience and the vastly different ways in which people use the media. Even television, the mass medium par excellence, has by no means a homogeneous reception" (9). Yet, though Golding refers to television per se and is referring to different age groups, classes, and genders, this assessment is equally valid when applied to the varying receptions of *Big Brother* as expressed in Internet discussion forums. The integration of *Big Brother* with its Web site constitutes a primary and potent example of media convergence within popular television and the media industry (Bignell), and *Big Brother* is thus argued to be a key exemplar of "a new symbiotic relationship between television and the Web" (Deery 171). This convergence includes Webcasts that, unlike the edited television program, is a live, unedited version in which fans can engage with the *Big Brother* text, and an important aspect of this mode of consumption is the way in which it generates debates about the "reality" of reality TV. As Jones's ethnographic fan study of *Big Brother* revealed, "Undoubtedly the role of technology will offer a window onto a totally new world of fact-based television, but, audiences may well continue to ask themselves, the fundamental questions, 'Is it fact?,' 'is it fiction?,' 'is it real?' or 'is it faked?'" (419).

This sense of ontological uncertainty is a central aspect of *Big Brother* for the contestants also. As Holmes states: "The concept of who is 'being themselves' or who appears to be performing for the camera is a crucial criterion in how the housemates judge and perceive one another, and equally in viewer discussion of the programme—Adele Roberts in series three persistently nominated fireman Jonny Regan for eviction because 'he isn't being true to himself—he's putting up a mask, being a joker. I don't think I've met the real Jonny yet'" ("All you've got" 128). The perception by the viewer that a participant is putting on a front is more likely because of the degree of visibility the housemates have, via television transmission and Internet live streams. Hence, the presentation of self is an intrinsic aspect of forum debate and illustrates a further connection of Erving Goffman's articulation of social interaction to *Big Brother*. A prominent component of Goffman's analysis is the idea that social actors can be interpreted as being manipulative performers always engaged in creating a front in their relations with other social actors. In the process of social interaction, individuals are continuously communicating (giving and giving off) self-impressions in all they do. Goffman explicates such social process by use of the metaphor of theatrical performance. Onstage, actors have the task of presenting themselves to the audience as particular characters in a play, and they must make it manifest exactly which role is being played, an effort assisted through the use of costume, props, scenery, and movement, as well as dialogue. They are also aided by other actors on the stage and those behind the scenes. When individuals enter a setting or occasion, they are faced with the task of communicating to others who and what they are. The only way others can judge what type of person another individual is comes initially through that person's conduct and appearance. Consequently, social actors use the resources at their disposal to communicate an impression to a given social "audience" to effectively put on a show "for the benefit of other people" (Goffman, *Presentation* 28). Moreover, much like theaters, social settings can be divided into front and back regions. The front region is where the performance is given, whereas the backstage area is conventionally cut off from public view, usually physically, so that the audience is unable to witness what is occurring there. *Big Brother* potently, deliberately, and *visually* lifts this dramaturgical curtain to provide near-total spectator access to the housemates' lives in the various zones of the Big Brother house: "The private space of the *Big Brother* house becomes public" (Bignell 157). This arguably is the show's primary source of fascination. Therefore, the audience, spread across various media outlets, *sees* the various dramatic displays: the confrontations, interactions, and donning and discarding of fronts as the various contestants interact and express their "true feelings" in the solitary sanctuary of the diary room. Consequently, as part of the process of becoming a successful housemate the contestants confront a paradox: because they are the subjects of such pervasive inspection, they must strive to put on a show in order to survive. If they do nothing of note to endear themselves to the viewers and their housemates, eviction is a risk; however, too much of a performance risks denunciation—on the grounds of being a fake—by spectators and contestants alike.

This process rapidly became evident following the success of the first U.K. broadcast in 2000 and has become a clearly visible trend: reflexive constants are fully aware of the rewards that can be obtained as a result of participating. In essence, since 2000 *Big Brother* has retreated from reality, or real people being themselves, in favor of a parade of larger-than-life characters steadfastly engaged in the maintenance of an entertaining front. As Holmes states, in the wake of such unprecedented exposure and the possible rewards of appearing on *Big Brother* (the original winner, Craig Philips, released a pop single and is still something of a U.K. television personality, appearing on a number of DIY shows), the contestants on the second and third seasons of *Big Brother* began to exhibit a self-conscious awareness of the conventions of the format. As the *Big Brother 3* winner, Kate Lawler, stated, "It's amazing to think the whole nation is watching *us*" (Holmes, "All you've got" 118). One of the key examples of this phenomenon was another instance of celebrity reflexivity in which the process of becoming a celebrity though exposure in the Big Brother house was a subject of conscious producer-led experimentation in 2006. In this instance, fakery became a virtue and the key to both *Big Brother* success and the achievement of celebrity status. It illustrated the ways in which the *Big Brother* format was undergoing transformation.

Celebrity Big Brother *2006: Twisting the Format to Construct a Star*

On leaving the Big Brother house, numerous contestants have forged careers in the media industry, whether working as a model (Orlaith McAllister), radio DJ (Richard Newman), or television presenter (Brian Dowling). In some cases, most notably that of Jade Goody, a contestant in the 2002 *Big Brother,* celebrity status stemmed from effectively just being oneself in public and in media spheres; for others the glare of celebrity rapidly faded with the end of the *Big Brother* narrative. But regardless of duration, the equation is invariably *Big Brother* = celebrity status, however temporally limited this status may be. In the United Kingdom, however, Channel 4 transmitted the first edition of *Celebrity Big Brother* in 2001 as a means of turning this process on its head: well-known faces would elect to live in the Big Brother house and subject themselves to the viewers' gaze. This represented not merely a significant moment in *Big Brother*'s history and development, but also a distinctly novel one, by which the dramaturgical curtain was visually raised to expose celebrities' lives and their private behavior. As Hill states, unlike the conventional *Big Brother,* which deals with people drawn from the general public, *Celebrity Big Brother* "takes celebrities and turns them into 'ordinary people,' before releasing them back into the world of the media" (38).

Although the meta-narrative of the *Celebrity Big Brother* format is more or less the same as that of *Big Brother* (though the running time is much shorter, usually three weeks), the major divergence is that in the world of *Celebrity Big Brother,* the viewer (ideally) "knows" the contestants who enter the house. But, unlike earlier versions, *Celebrity Big Brother* 2006 would take the form of an unprecedented media experiment, an experiment designed to act as a cultural barometer charting who could constitute and, crucially, be accepted as a celebrity within contemporary British society. The setup for this incarnation of *Celebrity Big Brother* was as follows: joining the likes of the pop performers Pete Burns, Preston, and Maggot; the actors and entertainers Traci Bingham, Rula Lenska, and Michael Barrymore; the model Jodie Marsh; the former Football Association secretary

Faria Alam (famous for a relationship with Sven Göran Eriksson, at the time the England National Football Team manager); the basketball star Dennis Rodman; the controversial Respect politician George Galloway; and the "pop singer" Chantelle Houghton. There was a twist, however. A failed applicant for *Big Brother 6*, Chantelle Houghton was actually a non-celebrity. She had been selected by the show's producers and set a special task on entering the Big Brother house: to maintain a front in order to convince the rest of her housemates that she too was a celebrity, a pop singer with a girl band who had had one minor U.K. hit single. If she failed in this project, she would be instantly evicted from the house. But her tenure in the house was sealed when she survived a *Big Brother* task that compelled the housemates to organize themselves in a line in order of their famousness. Out of the lineup of eleven, Chantelle came ninth, and her position in the house was thus secured. Moreover, as Paul Flynn notes: "She pulled off the deception with casual aplomb, warming to her fake ID as a pop star in the imaginary five-strong girl group Kandy Floss ('With a K!')"; and it was Chantelle who would survive the voting process and who would become the eventual *Celebrity Big Brother* winner in a finale that attained a record 7.5 million viewers (Plunkett).

Evaluating this outcome, Peter Bazalgette, chairman of Endemol, which produced this *Celebrity Big Brother*, concluded: "It was a very clever joke by the production team. . . . Nobody thought for a moment she'd end up winning. It's hilarious. It's very Channel 4—that's where you'd expect to find this kind of slightly postmodern convoluted joke" (Aspinall 147). Hence, Chantelle would be dubbed "the celebrity who became a celebrity by pretending to be a celebrity" (Aspinall 49–50). Chantelle's numerous appearances after *Celebrity Big Brother* in mainstream U.K. celebrity and lifestyle magazines, from *Heat* and *Star* to *OK!* and *Hello,* represented a form of media-driven "Chantelle-mania" that focused on numerous aspects of her life, such as her fashion tastes, her shopping trips that exhibited her conspicuous consumption in the wake of her newfound fame, and her changing hairstyles and hair color, a process Rojek refers to as the media "frenzy of reportage and cod punditry" (150).

Furthermore, *Celebrity Big Brother* 2006 emphasized the way in which gimmicks and twists beyond the surveillance brief were now a staple of the format. Although claims are made about the unedited and real nature of *Big Brother,* the Chantelle edition served to highlight the degree of producer-led orchestration that dominates reality TV. Especially in regard to the Chantelle joke, reality TV exemplifies Daniel Boorstin's concept of the pseudo-event. Boorstin (a theorist whose analyses are especially cogent in the era of reality TV) argues that pseudo-events represent a "synthetic novelty," the prefix pseudo having derived from the Greek meaning "false, or intended to deceive" (9). Pseudo-events are purposefully produced by the media to fulfill a constant demand for ever more spectacular diversions from reality. They are not spontaneous events but occur because someone has deliberately planned them. Moreover, they are planned and staged "for the immediate purpose of being reported or reproduced" and arranged "for the convenience of the reporting media" (Boorstin 40). Ultimately, a pseudo-event is planned to achieve the maximum publicity, drama, and public interest (Merrin 54–55). The concept of the pseudo-event is therefore particularly applicable to reality TV and specifically to *Celebrity Big Brother*. The invention of Chantelle was a deliberate marketing tool to differentiate *Celebrity Big Brother* from its non-celebrity counterpart, to maximize public interest with the fake celebrity twist. Moreover, as Boorstin argues, celebrities themselves represent "human pseudo-events." So, with regard to Chantelle, Boorstin's analysis manifests itself at two levels: she was a pseudo-event created within a pseudo-event. The event was the transformation of Chantelle from ordinary and everyday into a star, a process transmitted as a live event. On leaving the Big Brother house, Chantelle Houghton had effectively become "Chantelle," going on to live a life that would exemplify and epitomize Boorstin's now classic definition of celebrities, those individuals who are "well-known for their well-knownness" (57). Moreover, although it is by now a well-worn definition of celebrity, it is especially apt in relation to reality TV because, for many other *Big Brother* participants, "well-knownness" by way of television is invariably the primary qualification. As Turner contends, the various *Big Brother* housemates who have achieved some degree of media renown are the very "epitome of the fabricated celebrity" (60).

Big Brother, *Celebrity, and Staving Off Format Fatigue*

In defining contemporary celebrity, Rojek points out that "although God-like qualities are often attributed to celebrities, the modern meaning of the term celebrity actually derives from the fall of the gods, and the rise of democratic governments" (9). This is appropriate because, as Andrejevic claims, a major consequence of the development and popularity of reality

TV is the "democratization of celebrity" that it has apparently produced. In the era of reality TV, Andrejevic argues, it is no longer presidents, prime ministers, and pop, rock, or movie stars whose lives are open to public debate: "Now it will be the private life of the person on the street—of anyone who trains the webcam on him—or herself—or anyone who makes the final casting call for 'The Real World' " (268). But what exactly is being celebrated? In trying to answer this question, Holmes, using the example of the eviction moment on *Big Brother,* argues that it is the "staging of the physical encounter between the televisual/screen self and the media. Until this point the contestants have surrendered all power over their image, allowing *Big Brother* and the media to make of them what they would. It is at this stage that the participants can exercise an element of discursive control over their image. They comment on their representation in the programme and their experiences in the house, and describe events in the first person" ("All you've got" 131). But in the face of a potentially celebratory active relationship between reality TV and audiences, the blurring of distinctions between the celebrity and the non-celebrity, Bourdieu's cultural pessimism remains. Gray cynically concurs: "Mass consumption is maintained by breaking up consumers into a multitude of shifting niche markets, each catering to a carefully crafted and continually refined illusion of individuality. This strategy is most highly developed in interactive television programmes such as *Big Brother,* which instil the illusion that celebrity is a universal entitlement that everyone can enjoy if they are lucky enough to be selected by everyone else" (207–208).

On *Celebrity Big Brother* 2006, Chantelle was the lucky person. Her success was not implicitly linked to any inherent charisma, nor would one assume that the public was necessarily projecting any charismatic attributes on her. Instead, it was her very non-celebrity status that was the primary attraction and key marketing aspect and that marked her out from a very early stage as the likely winner of the event *because* of her novelty factor. Because Chantelle was selected by the producers and given her script, the setup was carefully engineered, and she subsequently received the majority of the media publicity surrounding the show. Thus, like many *Big Brother* contestants, she was effectively a celebrity from the first day of transmission. And this is the fundamental aspect of *Big Brother*—it is a narrative. In terms of the official rationale of the show, with its apparent "liveness" and reliance on the authorial and dynamically active audience, Tincknell and Raghuram cite Ruth Wrigley, executive producer of the U.K. version, stating that the *Big Brother* team does not seek "to impose their own perspective on the show—they [want] it to be as truthful as possible . . . [reporting] facts without editorial comment" (2006, 257).

Yet, as Tincknell and Raghuram point out, reality TV is as dependent on narrative as any other form of media; the key difference is that a sense of narrative structure is imposed *after* the footage has been recorded. Thus, a story is constructed through editing and the pervasive use of voiceover, all of which help produce a "preferred version" of events (2006, 257). Hence, *Celebrity Big Brother* 2006 was dominated by the Chantelle narrative, and her success was the logical conclusion to the series. This was the *point* of the exercise, "postmodern joke" or not, and she helped ensure that this edition would serve as an appealing and entertaining quirk in the conventional format. Other than being personable and forging a chaste and furtive romance with a housemate, Chantelle exhibited no latent star quality of any discernable kind. And this was enough, as she did become the *star* of the experience, despite not being a "genuine" celebrity.

Nonetheless, this is, for some commentators, the key problem in the history of *Big Brother* and its progressively dynamic interface with the discourses of celebrity, and it is the prime mover in the progressive degeneration of the format. From 2000 to 2007 *Big Brother* changed radically; Chantelle-type gimmicks and radical changes to the format increasingly came to the fore.[1] As Ramchandani argues, alternative reality TV shows in the wake of *Big Brother,* such as the talent-singing contest *X Factor,* encourage people to make the most of their abilities, to become famous and achieve celebrity status through the showcasing of a genuine singing talent that is endorsed by the voting public. But for Ramchandani, *Big Brother* has steadily but decisively retreated from the process of rewarding virtues:

> When it first came to our screens in the summer of 2000, *Big Brother* was a thrilling high-concept idea: a live human zoo, a Milgram or Zimbardo-style social experiment brought to national television, a real-time version of *Lord Of The Flies*. Seven years after lovable Craig beat Anna and donated all his prize money to fund his mate's heart and lung transplant, the programme has lost its charm, having been twisted and twisted again by Endemol and Channel 4 in a desperate attempt to combat inevitable format fatigue. *Big Brother* has become a manipulative piece of broadcasting that takes advantage of the worst side of everybody.

In 2000 "ordinary" was acceptable and unique as a televisual experience, as it enabled viewers to immerse themselves in the minute-by-minute
lives of people just like themselves, but as the format has developed dramatically and decisively since 2000, the ordinariness of contestants has
progressively developed into something else. The ways in which *Big Brother*
has developed and has represented its various contestants is radical. The
first U.K. transmission of *Big Brother* was characterized by its avowedly
low-key, minimalist Big Brother house and comparatively inconspicuous
presentation of contestants. Although it would become *the* media spectacle
of that summer, initially *Big Brother* was implicitly focused on the group
dynamic of the ten housemates and on how they dealt with the social isolation of the experience: the emotional crises, tensions, conflicts, and sexual
attractions that emerged in the course of the project. Moreover, the social-
psychological aspects of the experiment were in the central foreground.
Big Brother was always intended to be a game show, but it was arguably
more than this; it was an extraordinary televisual exercise in surveillance
and psychological coping strategies of those living under such prolonged
scrutiny. Celebrity status for the contestants was a potential and eventual
by-product. It came *after* appearances on *Big Brother*.

As the format has continued on a yearly (sometimes biyearly) basis,
however, subsequent editions of *Big Brother* (in the United Kingdom at
least) have progressively and strenuously emphasized the spectacle of the
program. This is evident in the scale of more recent editions, now lasting
some three months rather than the original ten weeks, and the star factor.
This is a component that is accentuated by the producers and is palpable
in the mode by which contestants now enter the house. Rather than the
original en masse entry, the various contestants now go into the Big Brother
house in a manner that deliberately serves to perpetuate the entrance segment and that self-consciously mimics the red-carpet aesthetic of the movie
premiere. In recent editions of *Big Brother*, the "ordinary" contestants
enter the house before a carnivalesque multitude of raucous spectators
and a host of media personnel (television cameras and photographers),
accompanied by the animated officiating of the host, Davina McCall. This
process serves not merely to introduce the various contestants to the audience by providing a basic biography (which it does), but more explicitly
to initiate the process that will watch these anonymous individuals become characters in the media landscape and media discourses. Moreover,

contestants now frequently amplify this, stressing celebrity connections or a celebrity "aura" upon entering the house—whether it is personal or family relationships with celebrities or, in the case of *Big Brother 8*'s Chanelle Hayes, a self-professed physical likeness to a celebrity, Victoria "Posh Spice" Beckham, coupled with a determined aspiration to be "just like" Beckham and to live a similar "celebrity life." In the space of some eight years it is this aspect that constitutes the fundamental transformation that has occurred on *Big Brother*. Now, for many of the contestants, the experience of *Big Brother* is secondary to the celebrity status they will obtain by participating.

Therefore, if, as Boorstin maintains, the development of "the Graphic Revolution gave us the means for fabricating well-knownness" (47), then reality TV and its epitomizing example, *Big Brother,* have arguably perfected the process, constituting as it does a perennial media spectacle complete with a new generation (or cast) of "everyday" but carefully selected embryonic celebrities who will (the producers hope) provide a good story, romance, controversy, and, above all, entertainment.

Yet, as Ramchandani intimates, this ever more palpable quest for entertainment and increasingly marketable (and self-reflexive) contestants, controversies, and scandals, aligned with the twists and convoluted tinkering with the program's structure to enhance its spectacle, possibly indicates that *Big Brother* may soon be nearing its end as a viable, attractive, and popular format. Consequently, where it once made television history as a revolutionary and daring televisual form at the forefront of an entirely new television genre, *Big Brother* may soon be consigned to history.

Note

1. The U.K. 2008 version of *Celebrity Big Brother* saw yet another format twist. Billed as *Big Brother: Celebrity Hijack* and broadcast exclusively on the cable/satellite channel E4, this show saw a collection of non-celebrity housemates live under the surveillance and direction of a number of celebrity figures, such as Matt Lucas, Kelly Osbourne, Roseanne Barr, Alan Cumming, and Joan Rivers, who variously adopted the mantle of Big Brother and set a number of tasks for the contestants to complete.

Works Cited

Adorno, Theodor. *The Culture Industry.* New York: Routledge, 2001.

Alberoni, Francesco. "The Powerless 'Elite': Theory and Sociological Research on the Phenomenon of the Stars." *Sociology of Mass Communications.* Ed. Denis McQuail. Middlesex: Penguin Books, 1972. 75–91.

Andrejevic, M. "The Kinder, Gentler Gaze of Big Brother Reality TV in the Era of Digital Capitalism." *New Media and Society* 4.2 (2002): 251–270.

Aspinall, Julie. *Oh My God! The Biography of Chantelle.* London: John Blake, 2006.

Baggot, Jim. *A Beginner's Guide to Reality.* London: Penguin, 2005.

Bazelgette, Peter. "Why We're Right about Celeb BB." *Observer,* February 25, 2007.

Bignell, Jonathan. Big Brother: *Reality TV in the Twenty-first Century.* Basingstoke: Palgrave Macmillan, 2005.

Biltereyst, Daniel. "Reality TV, Troublesome Pictures and Panics: Reappraising the Public Controversy around Reality TV in Europe." *Understanding Reality Television.* Ed. Su Holmes and Deborah Jermyn. New York: Routledge, 2004. 91–111.

Boorstin, Daniel. J. *The Image: A Guide to Pseudo-Events in America.* New York: Vintage Books, 1992.

Brook, Stephen. "Big Brother Ratings Hit 5.7m." *MediaGuardian,* January 19, 2007.

Cashmore, Ellis. *Beckham.* Cambridge: Polity, 2002.

———. *Celebrity/Culture.* New York: Routledge, 2006.

Cummings, Dolan, Bernard Clark, Victoria Mapplebeck, Christopher Dunkley, and Graham Barnfield. *Reality TV: How Real Is Real?* London: Hodder & Stoughton, 2002.

DeCordova, R. *Picture Personalities: The Emergence of the Star System in America.* Urbana: University of Illinois Press, 1990.

Deery, June. "TV.com: Participatory Viewing on the Web." *Journal of Popular Culture* 37.2 (2003): 161–184.

Dyer, Richard. *Stars.* London: BFI, 1982.

Evans, Jessica, and David Hesmondhalgh, eds. *Understanding Media: Inside Celebrity.* Maidenhead: Open University Press, 2005.

Flynn, Paul. "A Star for Our Times Is Born in Elstree." *Guardian,* January 28, 2006.

Foucault, Michel. *Discipline and Punish: The Birth of the Prison.* Trans. Alan Sheridan. New York: Pantheon, 1977.

Gledhill, Christine, ed. *Stardom: Industry of Desire.* London: Routledge, 1991.

Goffman, Erving. *Asylums.* London: Penguin Books, 1991 [1961].

———. *The Presentation of Self in Everyday Life.* Middlesex: Penguin Books, 1959 [1956].

Golding, Peter. *The Mass Media.* New York: Longman, 1974.

Gray, John. *Heresies: Against Progress and Other Illusions.* London: Granta Books, 2004.

Griffen-Foley, Bridget. "From *Tit-Bits* to *Big Brother*: A Century of Audience Participation in the Media." *Media, Culture & Society* 26.4 (2004): 533–548.

Hill, Annette. *Reality TV: Factual Entertainment and Television Audiences.* New York: Routledge, 2005.

Holmes, Su. " 'All you've got to worry about is the task, having a cup of tea, and doing a bit of sunbathing': Approaching Celebrity in *Big Brother*." *Understanding Reality Television.* Ed. Su Holmes and Deborah Jermyn. New York: Routledge, 2004. 111–136.

———. "It's a Jungle Out There! Playing the Game of Fame in Celebrity Reality TV." *Framing Celebrity.* Ed. Su Holmes and Sean Redmond. New York: Routledge, 2006. 45–65.

Holmes, Su, and Sean Redmond, eds. *Framing Celebrity.* New York: Routledge, 2006.

Jones, Janet Megan. "Show Your Real Face: A Fan Study of the UK *Big Brother* Transmissions (2000, 2001, 2002)." *New Media & Society* 5.3 (2003): 400–421.

Kilborn, Richard. *Staging the Real: Factual TV Programming in the Age of Big Brother.* Manchester: Manchester University Press, 2003.

Marlière, Philippe. "The Impact of Market Journalism: Pierre Bourdieu on the Media." *Reading Bourdieu on Society and Culture.* Ed. Bridget Fowler. Oxford: Blackwell, 2000. 199–212.

Marshall, P. David. *Celebrity and Power: Fame in Contemporary Culture.* Minneapolis and London: University of Minneapolis Press, 1997.

Merrin, William. *Baudrillard and the Media: A Critical Introduction.* Cambridge: Polity Press, 2005.

Monaco, James, ed. *Celebrity: The Media as Image Makers.* New York: Delta, 1978.

Plunkett, John. "A Summer of Reality." *Guardian,* May 12, 2006.

Ramchandani, Naresh. "Why Big Brother Doesn't Have the X Factor." *Guardian,* June 25, 2007.

Redmond, Sean, and Su Holmes, eds. *Stardom and Celebrity: A Reader.* London: Sage, 2007.

Rojek, Chris. *Celebrity.* London: Reaktion Books, 2001.

Roscoe, Jane. "*Big Brother* Australia: Performing the 'Real' Twenty-four-Seven." *International Journal of Cultural Studies* 4.4 (2001): 473–488.

Scannell, Paddy. "Big Brother as a Television Event." *Television & New Media* 3.3 (2002): 271–282.

Thornborrow, Joanna, and Deborah Morris. "Gossip as Strategy: The Management of Talk about Others on Reality TV Show 'Big Brother.' " *Journal of Sociolinguistics* 8.2 (2004): 246–271.

Tincknell, Estella, and Parvati Raghuram. "Big Brother: Reconfiguring the 'Active' Audience of Cultural Studies?" *European Journal of Cultural Studies* 5.2 (2002): 199–216.

———. "Big Brother: Reconfiguring the 'Active' Audience of Cultural Studies?" *Understanding Reality Television.* Ed. Su Holmes and Deborah Jermyn. New York: Routledge, 2006. 252–269.

Tryhorn, Chris. "Celebrity Big Brother Racism Row Timeline." *MediaGuardian,* May 24, 2007.

Tunstall, Jeremy. *The Media in Britain.* London: Constable, 1983.

Turner, Graeme. *Understanding Celebrity.* London: Sage, 2004.

JAMES LEGGOTT AND TOBIAS HOCHSCHERF

From the Kitchen to 10 Downing Street

Jamie's School Dinners *and the Politics of Reality Cooking*

In an average week in September 2007, viewers of British television would have had difficulty avoiding programs with some kind of cooking element. On terrestrial television there were at least a dozen weekly or daily shows of this sort, including the magazine show *Saturday Kitchen* (BBC1, 2006–), the celebrity cookery show *Ready Steady Cook* (BBC2, 1994–), competitive reality formats like *Britain's Best Dish* (ITV, 2007), *The Restaurant* (BBC2, 2007), and *Hell's Kitchen* (ITV, 2004–), documentary cookery shows such as *The Wild Gourmets* (Channel 4, 2007), and the most recent series by the cookery superstars Nigella Lawson, Ray Mears, and Jamie Oliver. Viewers with access to digital, cable, or satellite television were able to watch countless other examples of this broad-ranging genre of programming, including an entire channel (UKTV Food) devoted to the subject. For a nation not renowned for its culinary prowess, this seemed remarkable. Had the United Kingdom suddenly changed into a nation of gourmets *au fait* conversant with terms such as sauté, tapas, and al dente, or was this cluster of programming more the result of format evolution?

As part of a wider trend toward lifestyle programming in both daytime and prime-time television,[1] the upsurge of cookery shows is certainly not unique to British television culture, as a quick glance at television guides across America and continental Europe would confirm. Though such programs are undoubtedly part of a global programming trend toward a diversified and demand-led broadcasting culture, however, cookery shows in other countries have hardly ever become part of political discourse, as they have recently in the United Kingdom.

In particular, the four-part series *Jamie's School Dinners*, first broadcast on Channel 4 in 2005, and a one-off sequel shown the following year, generated considerable debate about governmental versus parental

The Galloping Gourmet, Graham Kerr, started his cooking career in England. *The Galloping Gourmet* ran from 1968 to 1971. Courtesy of CBC/PhotoFest.

responsibility not only among academics from various disciplines but also in the UK media in general (Spence). The program charted the attempts by the celebrity chef Jamie Oliver to improve the quality of food served to children in British state schools as well as to raise awareness of nutritional issues. It showed Oliver taking charge of the provision of food in two schools that were struggling to produce fresh meals on a limited budget; one in Greenwich, a suburb of London, and another "up north" in County Durham.

Jamie's School Dinners was part of Oliver's cross-media "Feed Me Better" campaign to draw attention to the links between the serving of junk food and Britain's rising levels of child obesity, heart disease, and other dangerous conditions. The show, and the campaign behind it, generated mostly sympathetic coverage and demands for the government to intervene to arrest the health "time bomb" predicted by Oliver and others. Audiences were able to follow as the celebrity cook and new political activist presented a petition of 300,000 signatures to Prime Minister Tony Blair, who committed a budget of £280 million to better ingredients and training. The campaign also met with a degree of hostility, however, as it was denounced by some as a wearying new strain of Oliver's ubiquitous self-promotion, and by others as a prime example of the paternalistic tendencies of both the state and the cultural-culinary establishment.

Most significantly, though, the program and the controversy around it exposed stark divisions of gender and class that may not have been expected in twenty-first-century Britain under Blair's New Labour government. At the same time, *Jamie's School Dinners* has value as an indicator of how British television culture has evolved in recent years. Part celebrity soap opera, part makeover and swap show, Oliver's program exemplifies the trend (in the United Kingdom and elsewhere) toward increasingly hybrid reality formats, as well as the contemporary media's tendency for self-referentiality, interactivity, and convergence.

Public Service Broadcasting (PSB) and Tele-Intervention

With its impulse to entertain but also to educate, and ultimately to bring about social and political change, *Jamie's School Dinners* can be seen as British public service broadcasting rebooted for the twenty-first century's multichannel, digital landscape. The twenty-fifth anniversary of Channel 4 television in 2007 produced some academic and journalistic reflection on its achievements since 1982, and on whether its goal of producing minority-targeted programs and films of the kind not being broadcast elsewhere was being fulfilled. For many, the channel's shift in the 1990s toward more youth-centered, commercially minded programming had diluted its radicalism and relevance.[2] When first broadcast by the channel in 2000, the U.K. version of the Orwellian game show *Big Brother* was not only the first of its kind, but arguably defensible as a social experiment (Bignell, Frau-Meigs, Andrejevic). More than five years later, it was widely felt that successive seasons of the show, like other reality formats broadcast by the channel, were indistinguishable from those produced by other broadcasters such as the BBC (itself the source of ongoing scrutiny of its direction and purpose) (Collins).

Significantly, in a four-page *Sight and Sound* interview with key members of the channel's creative personnel, *Jamie's School Dinners* was cited twice. Jeremy Isaacs, the founding chief executive of Channel 4 who left in 1987, lamented that its "balance [had] got out of hand" in recent years, but he acknowledged that "there are still wonderful programs like *Longford* [Channel 4, 2006—a drama-documentary about the Earl of Longford's relationship with the Moors Murderers] and *Jamie's School Dinners*" (Jivani 29). No doubt on the defensive, Kevin Lygo, the channel's director of television since 2003, argued that the way forward was to "find a subject that's entertaining and exciting and tells human stories but also has a social purpose—like *Jamie's School Dinners*" (Jivani 31).

Jamie's School Dinners quickly became a pawn in debates around Channel 4 and the fulfillment and adaptation of PSB directives (Born 777–779), and in 2007 the regulator and competition authority for the U.K. communications industries, Ofcom, challenged Channel 4 to clarify its intentions before decisions were made about financial support. Stung by widespread condemnation of sensationalist programs like *Celebrity Big Brother* and a documentary featuring images of a dying Princess Diana (*Diana: The Witness in the Tunnel*, June 6, 2007), the chief executive Andy Duncan argued that programs such as *Supernanny* (Channel 4, 2004–) and *Jamie's School Dinners* "do serve a public purpose" (Osborne). In his New Statesman Media Lecture, Duncan again drew attention to the program as an example, alongside *Wife Swap* (2003–), *Green Wing* (2004–2007), and *Unreported World* (2001–, all Channel 4), of "high-risk projects that challenge current orthodoxies and offer new insights" (Great Britain). In a Parliament Select Committee session relating to the BBC's charter review, Duncan placed the show together with the channel's seasons of themed programs on torture, immigration, and sex trafficking, arguing that these were the "sorts of things that certainly no one else is going to do if you are chasing a profit, but equally the BBC will not do either" (Great Britain). At the same committee session, Luke Johnson, the channel's chairman, described *Jamie's School Dinners* as "probably one of the finest examples of public service broadcasting in terms of impact for many, many years" (Great Britain).

But it was not just a self-congratulatory Channel 4 that trumpeted the significance of *Jamie's School Dinners* as a work of educational television that was also entertaining, celebrity-driven, and unashamedly populist.

Writing in the *Guardian*, David Liddiment praised it as "one of the best examples of a public service program so far this century," and he went on to say: "What is wonderful about *Jamie's School Dinners* is that it defies just about all the green paper rules about what makes a public service programme. It is reality TV and not even an entirely original format. . . . Here is an example of that much vilified genre, reality TV, that is informing the public with shocking truths, mobilising public opinion and prompting grass-roots action for change." As Liddiment notes, this example of "tele-intervention" was not entirely novel, following as it did earlier examples of socially orientated documentaries that struck a popular chord, such as the notorious 1984 edition of *World in Action,* in which a young Tory M.P. (Matthew Parris)—who had criticized the jobless as "work-shy"—was challenged to spend a week living entirely on unemployment benefits. That program played a role in challenging widespread attitudes of the time, and it was arguably a forerunner to the swap formats that would grip viewers twenty years later.

Hybrid Television

Although not without precedent, *Jamie's School Dinners* is clearly a program of its time. Its hybridity of form is exemplary of more general trends in British television, which has arguably changed over the past ten years as much as British society has done under Blair's and Brown's New Labour governments. The United Kingdom has experienced a period of economic growth and stability unrivalled in its twentieth-century history, and British television has witnessed dramatic changes, such as the introduction of vertically integrated global media corporations, the rise of digital broadcasting systems, and the outsourcing of production by both public and private channels. Furthermore, an increasingly competitive broadcasting market has prompted a radical realignment of programs, schedules, and formats.

Many of these trends are demonstrated by *Jamie's School Dinners,* which fuses dramatic and documentary modes and in characteristically postmodern fashion resists categorization as either a prime-time or daytime format. This pull toward hybridization in contemporary television (and culture) has been well documented (Thornham and Purvis 154–164), but *Jamie's School Dinners* is still remarkable for its multiplicity of generic influences.

As such, *Jamie's School Dinners* combines not only aspects from the two formats that had dominated British culinary-related programs until the late 1990s (the studio- or kitchen-set instructional program, and the travelogue in which a roving chef samples exotic food and drink from around the world) but also other lifestyle formats. In fact, in addition to drawing elements from traditional cookery and lifestyle formats (Oliver shows local chefs how to prepare inexpensive and healthy meals), *Jamie's School Dinners* incorporates stylistic and structural elements from make-over formats like *Changing Rooms* (BBC1 and BBC2, 1997–2004) and *What Not to Wear* (BBC1, 2002–), the ultimate aim here being to change school meals and fight obesity. Also influential are documentaries like *Panorama* (BBC1, 1953–), as can be seen in Oliver's attempts to expose political and social problems, and celebrity docusoaps like *The Osbournes* (MTV, 2002–2005), as the show is arguably as much about the chef as about the campaign. *Jamie's School Dinners,* moreover, consciously uses characteristics of swap formats—a true staple of Channel 4's reality of-ferings—such as *Faking It* (2001), *Wife Swap, Supersize vs Superskinny* (2008), and *30 Days* (2005–) as the millionaire chef changes places with a school dinner lady.

Furthermore, *Jamie's School Dinners,* from its name to its visual and editing styles, bears many of the hallmarks of Oliver's auteurist stamp. An authoritative voiceover commentary (from the actor Timothy Spall) pro-vides objective narrative linking, but Oliver's voice and opinions dominate, whether in the form of direct, companionable addresses to the camera or in conversation with others. Moreover, the show self-consciously shies away from the stylized editing and camera work that characterize many a make-over television program in favor of more spontaneous, amateurish visuals. The jagged, unpolished look of the program happens to be the customary aesthetic of the cheaply made docusoap, but it is also a defining feature of Oliver's television work, from *The Naked Chef* (BBC2, 1998–1999) to *Jamie at Home* (Channel 4, 2007–), which usually strives to match a breezy, unfussy style to the chef's youthful, down-to-earth persona. Like *The Naked Chef* and Oliver's major advertising campaign for the super-market chain Sainsbury's, *Jamie's School Dinners* makes prominent use of a driving British pop soundtrack, particularly in sequences where Oliver is traveling cross-country in his car. The program, which won the award for "most popular factual programme" at the 2005 National Television Awards, thus works directly and indirectly to promote the Jamie Oliver "brand," which encompasses restaurants, books, live shows, musical downloads, podcasts, and cookware. Although few would challenge Oliver's sincerity of purpose, a sequence in which he encourages school-children to sing a ditty entitled "Try Something New" cannot help putting U.K. viewers in mind of his role as the public face of Sainsbury's, which uses a very similar slogan ("Try something new today"). It would seem that a conflict of interest over his commercial endorsements had led the BBC—which had "discovered" Oliver in *The Naked Chef*—to terminate his contract before his arrival at Channel 4.

Jamie's School Dinners also conforms to other film and broadcasting trends, not least the campaigning documentaries of U.S. filmmakers such as Michael Moore and, in particular, Morgan Spurlock, whose McDonald's-baiting *Supersize Me* (2004) used a similar challenge-based narrative to make its propagandist message about nutrition more palatable. In the United Kingdom Oliver's program builds on and expands an existing fad, as it was not the first—or the last—to incorporate concerns about obesity in a reality format. Though ITV's *Fat Club/Celebrity Fit Club* (2002–)—in which overweight members of the public, then celebrities, compete to lose weight—and BBC3's therapy–reality TV show *Freaky Eaters* (2003–) have dubious educational merits, Channel 4's *Ian Wright's Unfit Kids* (2006)—on which a famous ex–soccer player was given six months to reduce the level of body fat in a group of children—and *You Are What You Eat* (Channel 4, 2004–) were clearly modeled on Oliver's template. In all these cases, the narrative hook was the question of whether the individuals or celebrities would succeed in their tasks. Unusually, for a competitive reality show, *Jamie's School Dinners* was unable to provide such a satisfying climax, instead projecting its message into the wider political and cultural arena. The follow-up program, *Return to Jamie's School Dinners*, offered a delayed resolution, setting out the advances that had been made as a result of the campaign, but it was important to stress that the task was far from complete.

Oliver's support for young school children is far from being completely altruistic, given his personal financial profit; nevertheless, his seemingly genuine commitment to tackling poverty relates *Jamie's School Dinners* to another contemporary trend in reality TV, one that focuses on the benevolence of the very wealthy. In addition to business-oriented shows such as the U.K. version of *Dragon's Den* (BBC2, 2004–)—in which inventors pitch their business ideas to a panel of wealthy experts—or *The Apprentice*

(BBC2, 2005–), *Jamie's School Dinners* has much in common with *The Secret Millionaire* (Channel 4, 2006). In this show, a millionaire (usually self-made) goes undercover in a troubled urban community to decide who is most deserving of his or her charity. Oliver's 2002 program for Channel 4, *Jamie's Kitchen,* was in the vanguard of this trend for the philanthropic makeover format, bringing together a group of disadvantaged teenagers to prepare food in his restaurant Fifteen. By forcing their participants to compete, however, these shows would seem to imply that socialism is a spent force and that the deserving poor must perform to survive—a message shared by Blair-era feature films such as *The Full Monty* (Peter Catteneo, 1997) and *Billy Elliot* (Stephen Daldry, 2000).

The Celebrity Chef and Prime-Time Television

Jamie's School Dinners now takes its place within an eclectic range of prime-time cookery programs like *Hell's Kitchen* and *The Restaurant* that combine the appeal of a celebrity involvement with the satisfaction of a challenge or competitive story line. An intriguing aspect of the show is the insight the audience gets into Oliver's personal and public lives, and the effects of the overlaps between the two, which make the subject as exposed as—in fact, more than—the participants of celebrity shows like *Celebrity Big Brother* (Channel 4, 2001–) and reality sitcoms like *The Osbournes* (Gillan). There is an uncomfortably invasive moment when Oliver's wife, Jools (the former model Juliette Norton), who has been seen making flippant complaints about her husband's work-life balance, is distressed by allegations in the U.K. press about Oliver's infidelities and has to be comforted by him offscreen.

Although domestic intimacy—albeit mostly of an ersatz kind—is important to many cooking programs, the manner in which *Jamie's School Dinners* conflates Jamie Oliver the businessman, celebrity cook, private individual, father, husband, and political activist into one "crossover" television product is remarkable. Though this can be understood as typical of the blurring of the private and the public spheres in reality TV, the show is also readable as a coming-of-age story and as a strategy to modify Oliver's star persona. Paradoxically, this involves the projection of his work into the public arena of politics through an acceptance of the camera in his private home life.

After a brief television appearance as an apprentice at the renowned London restaurant The River Café, Oliver's international fame was kick-started by his funky 1998 series, *The Naked Chef,* a program designed as an antidote to old-school British screen chefs such as Delia Smith. Oliver's boyish charm and informal cockney dialect seemed groundbreakingly maverick and certainly a change from someone like Smith, whose reliable, mumsy delivery and recipes have led to her reputation as a person who "will never let you down" (Fort)—despite her rather out-of-character fame in the United Kingdom for a seemingly inebriated outburst on the terraces of a soccer club for which she is a shareholder. While promoting the preparation of food as a leisure and lifestyle activity rather than a dull domestic chore, Oliver reconciles the traditional dichotomy of masculine professional chefs and feminine domestic cooks (Hollows). Furthermore, from his earliest programs onward, Oliver placed emphasis on the gregarious nature of the culinary experience by chatting informally to the camera, to friends, to shopkeepers, or to fellow professionals.

It is interesting that Oliver's fatherhood is repeatedly emphasized in *Jamie's School Dinners.* Indeed, it is his status as a male chef that has given his persona distinction, for he has been able to occupy a niche between an older generation of unthreatening television chefs and a new wave of aggressive über-masculine figures such as Gordon Ramsay. Oliver came to prominence in the late 1990s, at a time when so-called lad culture loomed large in the British cultural imagination through, for example, men's magazine publishing, the unapologetically male-centered films of Guy Ritchie, and the music of Britpop bands like Oasis. This was perceived at the time as a backlash against the inroads of feminism (Moseley). Like the soccer star David Beckham, a man whose fashion and consumption choices supposedly show him to be in touch with his feminine side, however, Oliver's personality is perhaps more in tune with the ideal of the metrosexual man, whose gender attributes are fluid even though his sexual orientation is not.

A father, a millionaire, but also a man of social conscience, Oliver would come to be the role model for the modern British husband, which was evidently the reason he became only the second man ever to be featured on the cover of the women's magazine *Good Housekeeping* (in November 2006) in its eighty-four-year history (the first was King George IV on the event of his coronation). The fact that *Jamie's School Dinners* can be seen to advocate traditional gender roles—he takes charge of the career and campaigning, while his ex-model wife takes charge of raising the children—was rarely picked up by the media, however.

Able to move freely between realms of the "feminine" (the kitchen, the supermarket, the primary school) and more traditionally "masculine" activities (riding his scooter, swearing, talking to and about his "mates"), Oliver is an ideal vehicle for what Rachel Moseley has called the "daytime-ization of prime-time television (Moseley 32)" or the absorption of certain qualities generally deemed appealing to male audiences—narrative closure and stories of competition—into traditionally female-orientated lifestyle programming.[3] This negotiation between gendered spaces is given literal expression in *Jamie's School Dinners,* although the program could easily be interpreted as a critique of female authority figures—headmistresses, dinner ladies, mothers, teachers—and as a project to reinstate masculine authority in domestic spheres.

Although his restaurant is posited as a masculine realm, the school environments Oliver seeks to transform are mostly places of feminine authority, and particularly so in the case of the primary school he visits in County Durham (as is usually the case in the United Kingdom). The home of the children he visits is also female-centered, with emphasis on the role of the mother rather than the father. It is also notable that when Oliver is given control of a school class, he is keen to take them on a field trip that draws them outside and into the comfortably male realm of the nondomestic.

The Political Makeover Show and Educating the Underclass

Although it is in many respects an emblematic example of the contemporary makeover show, *Jamie's School Dinners* is also a logical extension of the sentiments of Oliver's earliest programs and books. Attention was initially focused mostly on his carefree, even self-indulgent persona, but his 2001 book, *Happy Days with the Naked Chef,* not only was dedicated to the "cooks of tomorrow," but contains advice on how to actively engage children in cooking (Oliver). As Helen Powell and Sylvie Prasad have noted, however, *Jamie's School Dinners* marks a turning point in Oliver's transformation from a celebrity chef cocooned in the comfy world of lifestyle television into a social reformer taking his message—and not just his recipes—into the world at large:

Positioning himself not as one of the lads but as a father and a trained chef who has significant cultural capital and expert knowledge, he has gained public credibility in seeking to improve the general health of a nation. Cast in this new role, he is an expert first and a celebrity second. That expertise is now recognized for what it is, something acquired over a long period of time through intense training and an ethic of deferred gratification that no lifestyle programming could ever reproduce, or even try to. Working towards the more realizable goal of adopting a healthier lifestyle rather than an overnight transformation into a kitchen maestro, the television expert can be seen in this case to be reverting to a more fulfilling traditional role, namely that of educator over entertainer. (65–66)

Although it is debatable whether Oliver the entertainer disappears altogether, Powell and Prasad are correct in speculating that politicized makeover programs like *Jamie's School Dinners* offer a very different kind of gratification from that of traditional lifestyle shows, where conversions and transformations unfold neatly within the confines of a single episode. The healthy lifestyle promoted by many contemporary cooking shows seems easily attainable, thus giving an empowering, reassuring message to viewers, but the nationwide transformation of school food provision and eating habits is a project far beyond the reach of a humble reality TV program.

A further paradox is that though *Jamie's School Dinners* fosters a sense of community through its interactive address to the viewers—instructing the audience to contribute to its narrative solution (by pressuring the government to intervene)—the program also communicates clear social divisions. Indeed, like other makeover shows of recent times, *Jamie's School Dinners* can be accused of perpetuating problematic stereotypes about the underclass—or, to use a more recent coinage, "chav" culture—and strategies for its education (or eradication).[4] And like other makeover formats that ultimately diagnose the ailing health of the family unit or express anxieties about class status, the program encourages "a 'them vs. us' dichotomy that constantly reinforces petit bourgeois attitudes, behavior and taste" (Morris 54).

In 2007 Prime Minister Gordon Brown spoke at the Labour Party Conference of 2007 about how a "class-free society [was] not a slogan but in Britain can become reality" (Glover). He was echoing the words of the Conservative Prime Minister John Major, who had set out his vision of a "classless society" seventeen years previously. But contemporary polls gauging perceptions of class difference tell a different story. According to research published by the *Guardian,* Britain's persistent social hierarchy is not simply a matter of income or status but of geographical location, the divide between the industrial (or postindustrial) north and the affluent south still being a force to be reckoned with.[5] Furthermore, in 2005, sixty years after the introduction of the welfare state, 2.7 million children across the United Kingdom were still living in poverty, and levels of illiteracy, infant mortality, and child obesity were among the highest in England (Leese 186, 190). At the same time, and somewhat paradoxically, the *Guardian* poll revealed that the "middle class's cultural influence—in particular on aesthetic lifestyle tastes—has never been greater than today" (Aitkenhead 35). This fact is exemplified by the vogue for organic produce, the growing obsession with carbon footprints, and the gentrification of traditional working-class activities such as soccer.

Jamie's School Dinners, as part of Oliver's wider campaign, makes the simplistic yet compelling case that a healthier diet will lead to greater intellectual performance by children and consequently prevent cycles of deprivation. The show thus makes explicit the cumulative message of the various makeover or swap programs of recent years, from *What Not to Wear* to *Ten Years Younger* (Channel 4, 2004–): namely, that the working class—or even those who have simply let themselves go in the appearance of their homes, their families, or themselves—are in need of nannying by middle-class "experts"; no wonder, then, that the program has been held up as the epitome of the British public service broadcasting, with its emphasis on education, information, and entertainment.

But if a proportion of the audience is likely to respond to the program's reforming message as intended, others may find Oliver's voyages around some of Britain's least lovely kitchens, homes, and landscapes to be similar to the exotic global travels of other cooks such as Keith Floyd. Here, Oliver heads to the north of England because statistics tell him that County Durham is an area of very high social deprivation, where the number of students with learning, behavioral, or communication difficulties is well above the national average (Ofsted iv, 1). But when he confides to the viewers that he has never been to County Durham and is unsure of what to expect, his ignorance of this former coalfield area will no doubt match that of much of his audience, whose knowledge of the area may well be confined to what they have learned from the locally set *Billy Elliot,* which provides a similar scenario of postindustrial transformation through *embourgeoisement* (Hill).

Indeed, Oliver's later campaigning program, *Jamie's Ministry of Food,* first broadcast on Channel 4 in 2008, would cause a degree of controversy for its representation of another northern industrial town. Continuing his crusade against junk food, *Jamie's Ministry of Food* described Oliver's attempt to teach a group of people from Rotherham (South Yorkshire) some of his recipes, which they would then pass on to others, and so on, until at least a quarter of a million people were cooking wisely. Oliver chose Rotherham as the starting point for this cellular enterprise after being incensed by reports of mothers in the town passing hamburgers to their children through school gates, in protest at the adoption of his healthy menus by the school kitchens. But following the broadcast of the first episode, there was concern by some residents of the town, and by other media observers, that *Jamie's Ministry of Food* was stereotyping northerners as ignorant and backward in their lifestyle choices. A representative of Rotherham Council complained that "the people [Oliver] put on television were pretty downmarket and he gave the impression that everyone living here is like that" (Alford). Writing in the *Sunday Times,* the journalist A. A. Gill spoke for the numerous commentators who were troubled by the implications of Oliver's voyage to the "unenlightened" north in his suggestion that Oliver had "begun to sound like St Columba, bringing the good cookbook to the heathen Picts" (Gill).

Although issues of class may have diminishing potency in contemporary television studies, *Jamie's School Dinners*—and *Jamie's Ministry of Food*—provides clear evidence of the persistence of class-related anxieties in the British cultural imagination. What is more, having risen to prominence at a time when New Labour had all but outlawed any acknowledgment of class difference, Oliver's evolving persona signifies a kind of reengagement with discourses hitherto suppressed. Indeed, at the start of his public career, the self-made millionaire Oliver had been criticized for his "mockney" delivery, deemed by some to be as emptily parodic as the dialogue and attitudes found, for example, in the gangster films of Guy Ritchie.

Endings and Beginnings

Because of the sheer scale of its reforming strategy, *Jamie's School Dinners* inevitably lacked the traditional gratifying ending of the more traditional makeover show. The one-off "catch-up" special, *Return to Jamie's School Dinners,* provided a partial resolution, informing the viewers of what Oliver had achieved politically since the original series. But by not participating directly in the program's new challenge (the provision of school meals by pub kitchen staff), Oliver reinforced the message that his project could be efficient only through follow-up grassroots activity, and that there was a great deal of campaigning and groundwork yet to be done.

A striking aspect of *Return to Jamie's School Dinners*—and arguably the payoff in narrative terms—was the sequence in which Oliver was granted an audience with Prime Minister Tony Blair. Although this was undoubtedly a coup for the program makers, Blair's association with the campaign—and with the young, passionate Oliver—can be understood strategically as a project to energize and rehumanize Blair in his final months of office. From the start of his reign, Blair had proven adept in exploiting the media for his cause, as witnessed famously by his carefully judged response to the death of Diana, the "people's princess." Upon his first election, Blair had been hailed as the figurehead of New Britain, or Cool Britannia, as it was sometimes called, a place that was no longer, in the words of Blair himself, "living in the world of a hundred years ago, when guys wore bowler hats and umbrellas, all marching down Whitehall" (Colebatch 40), but that was innovative, dynamic, and young. Oliver the "entertainer" was entering the political arena with his "Feed Me Better" campaign, but an aging Blair—his popularity plummeting, not least because of his uncritical alliance with U.S. foreign policy—was now showing an increasing willingness to temper his newfound reputation for aloofness through appearances on populist entertainment shows such as *The Simpsons* (Fox, 1989–) and *The Catherine Tate Show* (BBC1, 2004–).

More than just another entry in Oliver's already dense résumé, then, *Jamie's School Dinners* is an extraordinarily rich (and contradictory) document of British society, politics, and television in the late Blair era. Despite being, in essence, a mutated cookery show, its culinary lessons are ultimately pushed to the margins by its exposure of cultural tensions. *Jamie's School Dinners* may well support the case that the British have finally discovered their inner gourmet. But placed alongside other shows that seem to be about cooking but are actually about the intricacies of the class system—such as *Come Dine with Me* (Channel 4, 2005–), in which a group of strangers compete to be crowned the best dinner party host—*Jamie's School Dinners* makes a more compelling case for the currency of issues of class and gender in twenty-first-century Britain.

The relation between cooking and cultural identity has already been given attention by sociologists and media scholars, but it is notable that some of the most symbolic controversies in British broadcasting have been triggered by reality television programs with a cookery component. In Channel 4's infamous *Celebrity Big Brother* of 2007, one of the contestants, Jade Goody, a former runner-up on the program, became embroiled in an ugly row with Shilpa Shetty, the Bollywood actress and eventual winner. A hostile U.K. media focused on Goody as a symbol of the ignorant, uneducated underclass for her supposedly racist outbursts against Shetty, and her career as a reality TV star was threatened. (Goody died of cervical cancer in March 2009.) Tellingly, their row was set in motion by Goody's accusation of Shetty's "dirty" cooking habits and her discriminatory description of the actress as "Shilpa Poppadom." The underlying message of the ensuing debates about the incident was that Goody's fear of the foreign was the instrument of her downfall; evidently the "underclass" need to be educated about the (culinary) richness of multicultural Britain, the same point *Jamie's School Dinners* makes.

There was a comparable incident in the September 2007 run of *Hell's Kitchen,* the show in which celebrities working in a kitchen compete to impress a celebrity chef. One of the contestants, Brian Dowling, the openly gay winner of series 2 of the U.K. *Big Brother,* who had carved out a successful career as a television presenter, complained of homophobic harassment by Jim Davidson, a fellow contestant and comedian, notorious for his "unreconstructed" (i.e., racist, sexist, and homophobic) style of humor; bowing to public intolerance of Davidson's politically incorrect attitude, the makers of the show asked him to leave.

Although these programs showed the televisual kitchen—and by extension, the national consciousness—evolving into a far more inclusive place, British cooking shows continue to promote an ambivalent stance on notions of ideal masculinity. A notable development of recent years has been the vogue for shows such as *Ray Mears's Wild Food* (BBC2, 2007) and *The Wild Gourmets,* in which "foraging experts" and roving survivalists re-create the diets of prehistoric Britons, thus bypassing altogether the worlds of celebrity culture and politics, and leaving metrosexual men like Jamie Oliver back in the kitchen. Channel 4's miniseason of food-related programs in January 2008—trailed as the "Big Food Fight"—seemed designed to prove, however, that celebrity chef culture was still very much a boy's club. In keeping with contemporary anxieties about farming ethics and the vogue for organic produce, Oliver and Hugh Fearnley-Whittingstall presented separate programs about poultry farming (Oliver's contribution imaginatively titled "Jamie's Fowl Dinners"), and Gordon Ramsay, in typically combative form, presented a "Cookalong Live" (a one-off show that later became a series). Viewers may not have learned a great deal about the world of sauté, tapas, or al dente, for the menu was mostly given over to expressions of rugged, foul-mouthed masculinity, warnings about obesity, and challenges to the food industry to improve their ethical standards. British viewers could surely be excused their indigestion.

Notes

1. On the popularity of lifestyle television and cookery shows in the United Kingdom, see, for instance, Brunsdon, de Solier, and Morris.

2. For a brief history of Channel 4, see Harvey and Born.

3. The gulf between daytime and prime time is also negotiated by Oliver's frequent swearing, a trait shared by other "bad-boy" cooks such as Gordon Ramsay. Although originally aired after the 9 P.M. "watershed," complete with Oliver's impassioned but offensive language, *Jamie's School Dinners* has been repeated on British television during the daytime with the swearing removed; the DVD also gives the viewer the option to play the program without it.

4. The term *chav* is a derogatory slang term for the fashions and lifestyle of some members of the British working class. Broadly equivalent to the American term *white trash*, the term had entered the British national consciousness—and dictionaries—by around 2005, although it had been in circulation for some time before that. In British popular culture it is often associated with the characters found in comedic television programs such as *Shameless* (2004–), *Little Britain* (2003–), and *The Catherine Tate Show* (2004–).

5. See a poll conducted by the *Guardian* and ICM Research published in the *Guardian* on October 20, 2007, 1, 35–36.

Works Cited

Aitkenhead, Decca. "Class Rules." *Guardian,* October 20, 2007, 35–36.

Alford, Simon. "Jamie Oliver Faces Backlash over New Show." *Times,* October 4, 2008, www.timesonline.co.uk/tol/life_and_style/food_and_drink/article4880921.ece (accessed October 14, 2008).

Andrejevic, Mark. "The Kinder, Gentler Gaze of Big Brother: Reality TV in the Era of Digital Capitalism." *New Media & Society* 4.2 (2002): 251–270.

Bignell, Jonathan. *Big Brother: Reality TV in the Twenty-first Century.* New York: Palgrave Macmillan, 2005.

Born, Georgina. "Strategy, Positioning and Projection in Digital Television: Channel Four and the Commercialisation of Public Service Broadcasting in the UK." *Media, Culture & Society* 25 (2003): 773–799.

Brunsdon, Charlotte. "Lifestyling Britain: The 8–9 Slot on British Television." *International Journal of Cultural Studies* 6 (2003): 5–23.

Colebatch, Hal. *Blair's Britain: British Culture Wars and New Labour.* London: Claridge Press, 1999.

Collins, Richard. "The BBC—Too Big, Too Small or Just Right?" *Political Quarterly* 74.2 (2003): 164–173.

de Solier, Isabelle. "TV Dinners: Culinary Television, Education and Distinction." *Continuum: Journal of Media & Cultural Studies* 19.4 (December 2005): 465–481.

Fort, Matthew. "The TV Dinners: Chefs on the Box—a Recipe for Culinary Success?" *Guardian,* March 3, 1995, 22.

Frau-Meigs, Divina. "*Big Brother* and Reality TV in Europe: Towards a Theory of Situated Acculturation by the Media." *European Journal of Communication* 21.1 (2006): 33–56.

Gill, A. A. "Jamie Oliver's Army Has Lost Its Way." *Sunday Times,* October 5, 2008, http://entertainment.timesonline.co.uk/tol/arts_and_entertainment/tv_and_radio/article4867579.ece (accessed October 14, 2008).

Gillan, Jennifer. "From Ozzie Nelson to Ozzy Osbourne: The Genesis and Development of the Reality (Star) Sitcom." *Understanding Reality Television.* Ed. Su Holmes and Deborah Jermyn. London: Routledge, 2004. 54–70.

Glover, Julian. "Riven by Class and No Social Mobility—Britain in 2007." *Guardian,* October 20, 2007, 1.

Great Britain. Select Committee on BBC Charter Review. "Minutes of Evidence." April 5, 2005, www.publications.parliament.uk/pa/ld200506/ldselect/ldbbc/50/5040506.htm (accessed January 30, 2008).

Harvey, Sylvia. "Channel Four Television: From Annan to Grade." *British Television: A Reader.* Ed. Edward Buscombe. Oxford: Clarendon Press, 2000. 92–117.

Hill, John. "A Working Class Hero Is Something to Be: Changing Representations of Class and Masculinity in British Cinema." *The Trouble with Men: Masculinities in European and Hollywood Cinema.* Ed. Phil Powrie, Ann Davies, and Bruce Babington. London: Wallflower, 2004. 100–109.

Hollows, Joanne. "Oliver's Twist: Leisure, Labour and Domestic Masculinity in *The Naked Chef.*" *International Journal of Cultural Studies* 6.2 (2003): 229–248.

Jivani, Alkarim. "Channelling the Past." *Sight and Sound* 17.12 (December 2007): 28–31.

Leese, Peter. *Britain since 1945: Aspects of Identity.* Basingstoke: Palgrave Macmillan, 2006.

Liddiment, David. "Television: Providing a Popular Public Service." *Guardian,* March 14, 2005, www.guardian.co.uk/media/2005/mar/14/bbc .broadcasting1 (accessed January 23, 2008).

Morris, Nigel. " 'Old, New, Borrowed, Blue': Makeover Television in British Primetime." *Makeover Television: Realities Remodelled.* Ed. Dana Heller. New York: I. B. Tauris, 2007. 39–55.

Moseley, Rachel. " 'Real Lads Do Cook . . . but Some Things Are Still Hard to Talk About': The Gendering of 8–9." *European Journal of Cultural Studies* 4.1 (2001): 32–39.

Ofsted. Inspection Report for Eden Community Primary School. Inspection number 262859 (London: Ofsted, 2004), www.ofsted.gov.uk/reports/pdf/ ?inspectionNumber=262859&providerCategoryID=4096&fileName=\\ school\\133\\s10_133701_20040910.pdf (accessed January 15, 2008).

Oliver, Jamie. *Happy Days with the Naked Chef.* London: Michael Joseph, 2001.

Osborne, Alistair. "Ofcom: C4 Must Define Public Service Role before Cash Flows." *Telegraph,* June 15, 2007, www.telegraph.co.uk/money/main .jhtml?xml=/money/2007/06/15/cnofcom115.xml (accessed February 1, 2008).

Powell, Helen, and Sylvie Prasad. "Life Swap: Celebrity Expert as Lifestyle Advisor." *Makeover Television: Realities Remodelled.* Ed. Dana Heller. New York: I. B. Tauris, 2007. 56–66.

Spence, Des. "Jamie's School Dinners." *British Medical Journal* 330 (March 19, 2005): 678.

Thornham, Sue, and Tony Purvis. *Television Drama: Theories and Identities.* Basingstoke: Palgrave Macmillan, 2005.

CASSANDRA L. JONES

The Patriotic American Is a Thin American

Fatness and National Identity in The Biggest Loser

> We need a change
> Do it today
> I can feel my spirit rising
> We need a change
> So do it today
> 'Cause I can see a clear horizon
>
> What have you done today to make you feel proud?
> It's never too late to try
> What have you done today to make you feel proud?
> You could be so many people
> If you make that break for freedom
> What have you done today to make you feel proud?
>
> (excerpt from "Proud," *The Biggest Loser* theme song)

These words from the theme song of the television show *The Biggest Loser* are typical of depictions of fatness in American culture. The phrases "we need a change" and a "break for freedom" are typical in that fatness is constructed as a self-imposed prison that can be "cured" through altering one's diet or level of exercise. Joyce L. Huff's essay "A 'Horror of Corpulence': Interrogating Bantingism and Mid-Nineteenth-Century Fat-Phobia" finds in the Victorian era the flowering of the understanding of body fat as sediment that prohibits the body from functioning at full capacity. It was at this cultural moment that the construction of the body as object shifted to reading the body as "action" wherein fat becomes "the residue of certain inefficient or incorrect eating habits" (44). According to this model, fat is something exterior to the body, rather than something "belonging to and incorporated within" it. Large accumulations of fatty tissue then would act as a "symbolic pollution" of sediment, the building up of which

The contestants on *The Biggest Loser* (NBC, 2004–) listen intently, hoping that their fatness can be "cured" by altering their diet. Courtesy of NBC/PhotoFest. Photo by Dave Bjerke.

serves to shackle the body (44). Indeed, modern-day understandings of the psychological motivations for overeating include the idea of using fatness as a shield to protect oneself from relationships, happiness, and success in a bid to self-sabotage or cloak oneself in some manner, thus furthering the metaphor of self-imprisonment (Goodman 44). From the nineteenth century onward, immorality, excessive consumption, and the erring body have become linked. By remolding the body through diet and exercise, one might free oneself from the bodily prison, emerging proud and realigning the body with culturally prescribed norms of beauty and health.

The call to experience the pride of action, resolve, and freedom to determine one's very personhood through dramatic weight loss is present in the first two seasons of the series, but the third incarnation of *The Biggest Loser* marked a departure from the format of earlier episodes. Where previously only fourteen people competed for the $250,000 grand prize and the title "Biggest Loser," the 2006 season included a representative from each of the fifty states, and after a brief interview and workout with the trainers, these contestants were narrowed down to fourteen competitors who would remain on the ranch. The thirty-six others were sent home with a "secret." They would remain in the competition by working out at home, and the two at-home competitors who lost the most weight would return to the ranch and compete for the grand prize. Where previous contestants had expressed desire to lose weight to make their families proud, several contestants began to describe their weight loss not only as a source of personal or familial pride, but as a source of communal gratification for their entire states. The effect of this alteration was to construct the body and fat-phobic notions of health as a locus of state and national pride.

This essay explores the narratives employed by *The Biggest Loser* and examines how the bedrock American myths of the self-made man and the frontier inform our notions of fatness and weight loss. Examining the rhetoric of weight loss allows us to read these myths of land and nationhood as they interpret the American body and thereby produce hegemonic body and beauty ideals. To uncover the myth not only in the televised narrative but also in the contestants' feelings about their participation, I consider the construction of the television show, interviews with contestants after the season aired, and an interview with the trainers before the start of the third season.

The Biggest Loser

The Biggest Loser is one of several reality television shows that center the dramatic narrative on obese contestants' weight loss through diet and exercise. Each week the contestants are asked to lose as much weight as possible under the tutelage of their team's personal trainer, Bob or Kim, and with the help of two physicians and one nutritionist who remain nearly invisible for the duration of the show. Like those on *Survivor*, *The Biggest Loser*'s contestants face challenges, working as a team in the early stages of competition and later as individuals, to gain immunity from elimination. There are two types of challenges performed: physical and temptation. The former require contestants to perform competitive tasks that demonstrate endurance and strength, such as building a tower of wet sand carried from the ocean's edge. The temptation places the contestants, either singly or as a group, in a room with an elaborate spread of forbidden high-fat, high-calorie foods. The competitor who consumes the most calories in a timed period wins a highly valuable prize, such as a cruise with family members or home exercise equipment, but this gain comes at the expense of ruining his or her diet. The team winning the physical challenge also earns a prize, and the contestants proceed to weigh in. The team with the highest combined percentage of body weight lost is safe for the week, and the losing team is required to vote off a team member. In the case of a tie, the opposing team acts as the tie-breaker, making the strategic decision of whom to send home doubly important. After four months spent on the ranch, the remaining three contestants are sent home to continue their weight loss, returning for the live finale, in which the contestant with the highest percentage of body weight lost is declared The Biggest Loser and awarded the $250,000 grand prize.

Fatness as Spoiled Identity

The Biggest Loser, by removing the contestants from their homes and allowing them to "fix" their bodies on a ranch, enacts a narrative of de-contamination of the fat body and reinsertion of the thin body into main-stream society. As the tone of the theme song indicates, this reality show is framed differently from similar programs. Whereas television shows like *Survivor* pit contestants against each other and place the focus on a large cash reward, often by asking them to put themselves in dangerous situations (eating as little or as much food as can be caught or found near the campsite, for example), and to outwit, outlast, and outplay each other, *The Biggest Loser* places the focus on transformation, both psychological and physical, as well as teamwork. "Playing the game" is often frowned on by the contestants as well as the trainers, who see strategic voting, weight gain, and similar tactics dangerous both to the relationships the contestants have formed and to their health. The name of the show itself gestures to-ward its ultimate purpose, to change one's appearance the most through weight loss. This internal and external transformation is understood as more than a simple competitive makeover show. *The Biggest Loser* posits itself as the opportunity to grant the "freedom" to be "so many people." This framing is made possible by the already constructed notion of fat-ness as a spoiled identity. According to Le'a Kent, fatness is "an identity that can communicate only its own failure, an identity for which all other narratives are impossible" (132). The notion of spoiled identity neatly sets up the desirability of weight loss. When contestants believe that losing weight will liberate them, allowing any number of possibilities once they have remade themselves, they can begin the difficult road of weight loss. Building on this notion of spoiled identity, which is already in circulation in mainstream American culture, *The Biggest Loser* also contributes to the maintenance of that construction using the discourses of mental and physical health, morality, and sexuality. Without the notion of spoiled identity in place, the mythological frontier as a site of redemption for the repentant fat body could not operate.

Frontier Mythology

Richard Slotkin identifies four major components to the frontier myth as it functions in American culture: separation and regression (separation from the parent community and regression to a natural state), progress, and conflict (with enslaved Africans or Natives at each stage of Western expansion). Progress is characterized in differing ways: "The Puritan colonists emphasized the achievement of spiritual regeneration through frontier adventure; Jeffersonians (and later disciples of Turner's 'Frontier thesis') saw the frontier settlement as a re-enactment and democratic renewal of the original 'social contract'; while Jacksonian Americans saw the conquest of the Frontier as a means to the regeneration of personal fortunes and/or of patriotic vigor and virtue." Slotkin posits that by enacting these components (separation, regression to a primitive state, and regeneration through violence) one could achieve "the redemption of American spirit or fortune" (12).

In the context of the television show, this notion of escape to the West is clearly in the foreground. The contestants must leave their families, friends, and jobs behind as they travel to a ranch in California where they live with their trainers for four months. The ranch features Southwestern-style structures that evoke the West in the American imaginary as a place to rebuild oneself or one's relationship with America. In *The Biggest Loser,* however, there is a further complication: in addition to providing a site of escape, the ranch offers a decontamination zone, where the fatness of the contestants is contained, away from the larger (and supposedly thin) populace. At the completion of the filmed episodes, the bracketed space of the ranch functions as a way of reintroducing or reintegrating the reformed "outsider" back into mainstream culture.

Moral Failure and Fatness

Kathleen LeBesco argues that despite those that decry the decline of morality through the decentering of religion from American life, a renewed discourse that offers the means by which to arrange one's life, to judge one's own actions and those of others, has appeared to fill the vacuum. The discourses of health and morality have become so entwined as to be found in venues as diverse as the rhetoric of food-as-sin advertising to statements concerning the "deadly fattening of our youth" (Greg Critser quoted in Campos 235), which Paul Campos names as a site of the moral panic induced by our cultural fear and hatred of fatness.

Sloth and gluttony are the characteristics most often to be found in the representation of fatness as moral failure (LeBesco). Both are present in the narrative of *The Biggest Loser:* contestants often comment on how much more active they are now, which allows the audience to imagine the contestant as the slothful fat person he or she was before arriving at the ranch. As the season moves forward, the show juxtaposes the trimmer bodies of contestants with their earlier, fleshier selves using as flashbacks black-and-white footage of contestants moving in slow motion, thus furthering this perception of the slothful, corpulent body. Gluttony is also demonstrated in the competition for weight loss, particularly in the temptation challenges. This allows the audience a certain viewing plea-sure, as their assumptions concerning the gluttonous consumption of the corpulent is confirmed. Contestants are also asked to use their inherent greed for good instead of evil by turning the desire for food toward a more patriotic end, the lust for money and entry into the system of privilege attributed to the thin.

(A)Sexuality, (Un)Desirability, and Fatness

Representations of fat people operate according to mutually exclusive superlatives (Goodman 137). For example, fat women are seen as either "passive or rebellious, childishly compulsive or maternal, out-of-control or overcontrolling or domineering" (Goodman 138–139). The extremes concerning the desire and desirability of the corpulent woman, the notion that she is either asexual or hypersexual, finds a place in the representation of fatness in *The Biggest Loser.* The television show, despite the announced existence of the contestants' loved ones—family members, spouses, and children—participates in the construction of fat women (and men) as asexual by employing these relationships as rewards to be earned through effort, endurance, and ultimately weight loss.

While on the ranch, contestants are separated from family and friends and thus are removed from any preexisting romantic relationships. It is not until the contestants leave the ranch, either through elimination or through the "reveal" of the final three contestants to their family members after four months on the ranch, that we see them in the context of romantic relationships. Even phone calls home while on the ranch are allowed only when won as a challenge prize. Unlike other reality television shows, such as *Beauty and the Geek,* which seem to encourage dating between contestants, there has never been a publicized romance during the filming on the ranch.[1] Several of the contestants have been involved in romantic relationships, however, which actively dispels the construction of the spoiled fat identity. By denying the audience the ability to view a fat person in a romantic relationship, *The Biggest Loser* maintains the notion that fat bodies are undesirable, unlovable, or somehow spoiled. This echoes the discourse of the ranch as a decontamination zone, where the ranch manages this transgressiveness by isolating the potentially dangerous sexuality of the corpulent until they can be "cured" of their unlovability and be returned to mainstream society.

Double-Consciousness of the Fat Identity

In a preseason interview the two trainers, Bob and Kim, discussed their approaches to weight loss:

> BOB: And I think that my approach has always been the same, which is work it from the inside out. I get people to realize that it's how they feel on the inside. And when they feel good on the inside . . .
>
> KIM: Exactly.
>
> BOB: . . . they are going to look great on the outside. The body is going to follow where the mind leads them. (Harper and Lyons)

The notion of a thin person trapped in a fat body that forms a fat person's false double-consciousness, which exists solely in the construction of fatness itself, is one of the most often reoccurring tropes in the dominant narratives and representation of fatness. This thin persona locked behind walls of fat is assumed to be the "true" or "authentic" identity of the corpulent. *The Biggest Loser* relies heavily on this trope in its call to free this supposed authentic inner being, as is evidenced by Trainer Bob's reference to his inside-out technique, whereby "fixing" the fat person's mental state will result in weight loss. This notion of repair points to one of the ways in which fat is pathologized: fatness is an expression of a broken or somehow damaged mental state that requires mending. Once the "fix" is complete, the authentic (i.e., thin) self can emerge, healthy and happy. In the last episode before the live finale, the trainers take their team members to face their former selves. Dramatically revealed life-size cutouts of their bodies at their starting weights reduce several contestants to tears. Kim's words to the contestants Kai and Wiley ("You can't hide behind that girl anymore . . . no more" and "Say good-bye to this Wiley . . . and hello to the new Wiley") reveal both that the emergence of a "true" self has oc-curred and that the fragile and flawed states of "fat Kai" and "fat Wiley," their former selves, have effectively been slain.

What makes this particular occurrence of the discourse of fat double-consciousness different from other expressions of the notion, however, is its connection to the savage-civilized dichotomy of the frontier. Here, in the narrative of the television show, the drama of the frontier is both inscribed on the fat person's body and played out within that body's interior. That is to say that in this drama, the fat person is both savage and civilized. This mirrors quite markedly Richard Slotkin's interpretation of the hero of the frontier narrative: "Because the border between savagery and civilization runs through their moral center, the Indian wars are, for these heroes, a spiritual or psychological struggle which they win by learning to discipline or suppress the savage or 'dark' side of their own human nature. Thus they are mediators of a double kind who can teach civilized men how to defeat savagery on its native grounds—the natural wilderness, and the wilderness of the human soul" (Slotkin 14).

Whereas the ranch acts as the site of escape where the work of regen-eration can begin, it is the body that acts as the battlefield upon which the figurative West is won and the psyche in which the fat person and his or her authentic self, the thin person, make war in a schizoid battle for supremacy. Trainer Bob frames the struggle to free imprisoned fat people in the rhetoric of warfare: "I think using the fifty states is such a great metaphor, with *The Biggest Loser* showing we are battling this fight of obesity across our continent. And we are looking at people, one from every single state, and we are just trying to make a difference. We are trying to do something and pull this war on obesity down. We are trying to do something" (Harper and Lyons). The outcome of this terrific battle is predetermined by the show's format; after all, who would tune into a television show about fat people who could not or refused to lose weight? Indeed, this is what Trainer Bob's pre–season 3 interview proclaims: "I think what you're going to see in season 3 is just more of the same: big people trying to gain their lives again, gain control of their lives again and lose tons of weight in the process" (Harper and Lyons). Not only does Bob refer to the struggle to wrestle control from a supposed inner savage, but his slip that they will "gain their lives" implies that they are not in control of their lives, not even in possession of their own lives.

"Ambassadors to Our States"

Just as the hero of the frontier narrative offers a lesson to Everyman about how to conquer the "wilderness of the human soul," the "victor" of the battle between the barbaric fat woman and her civilized inner thin woman carries this instruction back to refined society. This is demonstrated clearly in the episode in which the three remaining contestants prepare themselves to leave the ranch. In the episode, two of season 2's contestants, Matt and Suzy, return to the ranch to give advice to Kai, Erik, and Wylie about how to maintain their weight loss after the show ends. As they leave, Wiley comments that Matt and Suzy have "passed the torch" to them and that they would soon be "go[ing] home and becom[ing] ambassadors to our states." In the process of becoming "ambassadors,"[2] the contestants attest to and reaffirm the effectiveness of the dominant narrative of fatness that prescribes diet and exercise as the cure for obesity, along the way supporting the underlying notions that fatness is a voluntary condition and that that condition is predicated on a particular laziness inherent in the corpulent body.

Reentry from the frontier marks a moment of celebration of the victory in the war on obesity, as the society that had once been "escaped" welcomes the return of the newly thin. The finale's reveal of the thin body provides enormous pleasure for the viewing audience and acts as an integral part of this process of reinsertion of the "outsider" body. The finale's dramatic display of the contestants' new appearances, wherein they burst through life-size pictures of themselves at their starting weights, initiates this moment of appreciative reception. Indeed, the live season finale acts as a sort of ticker-tape parade in which the victors are cheered by the audience and drenched in a sea of confetti; the fat savage is declared dead and the thin person released from P.O.W. status. The accompanying interviews conducted on national network television and local programming emphasize the reemergence of the body as a site of state and national pride. These expressions of pride are thinly veiled as references to the inspiration these dramatically changed bodies provide for the overweight viewing public.

Public Ownership of the Fat Body

An interview with a season 3 "at-home" contestant, Matthew McNutt, provides further insight into the extended reception of the newly emerged thin body as a source of local and state pride. McNutt was interviewed by *207,* a locally produced Portland, Maine, television show, and the conversation between him and the interviewer, Rob Caldwell, makes clear the ways in which his body was transformed not simply from fat to thin, but from hypervisible yet anonymous fat body to local celebrity, which impelled him toward a renewed public ownership of his body. "A few days from now, on the first of January, countless people will make a resolution to lose weight in 2007. To get in shape we usually need some inspiration, and there is no better example than a modest guy from Boothbay Harbor whose story is now known around the country" (McNutt). McNutt's dramatic transformation and his public display of his "new" body can be taken not only as an inspiration for the "countless people" grappling with an inner savage, but also as a body that acts for the public as a marker of that savage's perpetual and definitive defeat. This is indicated by the often-stated phrase "I'm not going back," which seems to act as a reassurance to the public of the stability of the newly freed and strengthened thin identity.

Despite McNutt's transformation and the fame it garnered, fat bodies are never entirely invisible. Melissa Jane Hardie notes that in the case of Elizabeth Taylor and her expanding and shrinking figure, hers is not simply a figure with "public" and "private" bodies; rather, "the public body, being, like all bodies, in the world, but also in the *limelight,* is also the body that betrayed her private habits (overeating)" (159). I complicate this by noting that like public ownership of the celebrity body, demonstrated by the public's fascination with famous figures such as Oprah Winfrey and Elizabeth Taylor, Americans' fascination with nonfamous fat bodies carries with it an everyday celebrity in which the "public" body is always marked with the supposed knowledge of "private" habits. Considering that the fat figure is often relegated to an asexual and undesirable space, the fat person, particularly women, are shunted to the position of the "fat friend." This unwelcome location, existing in relation to a thin subject, of not being the "star" of one's own life, is often cited in relation to the oppression of fat bodies. Indeed, we can see this rhetoric in the remark noted earlier by Trainer Bob that losing weight will allow fat individuals to "gain their lives." Despite this lack of subjectivity in an individual's own life, the hypervisibility of the fat body is undeniable. Drawing on Michel de Certeau's notion of the everyday, we might say that hypervisibility operating in conjunction with a lack of subjectivity amounts to a sort of "everyday celebrity," in which the mundane aspects of the everyday work in tandem with the spectacular aspects of celebrity to create a figure marked by a desire of the spectator simultaneously to control and to disavow its corpulence. One is compelled to look and yet cannot stand to be confronted with the "out-of-control" figure. This tension appears in an account of fat women by W. Charisse Goodman, who refers to this state as the "Full-Figured Phantom," defined solely by her weight and the cultural assumptions attached to her size and transformed into "an almost mythically unnatural and repulsive figure consumed by physical and emotional problems" (2). This ghostly figure, denied subjectivity, is seemingly contradictorily (as indicated by the word *phantom*) embodied as resistance and yet disallowed material form. Just as maps and other official documents create a "nowhen" that denies the existence of modes of resistance in the practice of everyday life (Certeau), so too might medical mappings that describe the contours of the obese body reject the fat body that resists this reading as unhealthy and morally corrupt. Yet where the maps representationally immobilize resistance, the everyday celebrity, as a projection onto the discursive body, cannot fully erase the presence of the material body that evokes horror and disgust.

This everyday celebrity attributed to the fat body and the conquest of the inner savage that occurs in the contestants of *The Biggest Loser* mark yet another way in which the mythology of the frontier circulates within the discourse of fatness. As I have already noted, the frontier functions as a site of separation and escape. Brian Roberts traces the trail of the forty-niners as they traveled from their middle-class homes in the East to their hoped-for fortunes in the West. Aboard ships these men took to their journals and created elaborate worlds of play for themselves, wherein "juxtapositions of nature and civilization, between the homes they left and this new, natural world of 'fantastic' shapes and things, were a continuing source of pleasure" (112). The gold-seekers he speaks of were taking delight in the escape from societal demands and expectations, using the in-between space of the ship en route as a site in which to re-create themselves and (temporarily) redraw gender performances (men performing the "woman's work" of washing clothes or transvestite "ladies" performing in ship dances). The ship itself functioned as transitional space between East and West, but it also formed a conduit in which the mythology of the frontier could begin its work even as the ship docked in an eastern harbor. That this world of play aboard the ship occurred before the forty-niners reached the frontier serves to illuminate the power of the frontier mythology as a site of modification, alteration, or release that can be indulged in without a geographical separation. This same flight occurs in the corpulent body in *The Biggest Loser:* the contestants escape not the middle-class societal expectations of success and manhood experienced by the forty-niners but rather the corporeal map of everyday celebrity, in order to free their inner thin persons, recover subjectivity in their own lives, and thus gain the ability to map their own bodies. Performing this remapping in the televised space of *The Biggest Loser,* however, produces a shift from one type of public bodily ownership, that of everyday celebrity, to public ownership of the spectacular celebrity body; the disgust associated with the state of everyday celebrity evolves into pride in the symbolic defeat of the frontier's savage. This transformation is quite precarious and is heavily invested with emotional baggage.

McNutt's trip from quasi-anonymity to celebrity is marked by fear and shame as his motivations. "When I first came home I was motivated purely by the sheer terror that in September my town was going to find out I was a part of *Biggest Loser* and all my starting weight, starting photos were going to be out there. And I've got to look different!" (McNutt). Should he have returned to his state not having lost a remarkable amount of weight, he would have "let his state down" and failed to live up to the frontier's potential to facilitate a dramatic transformation of self. This would serve not only as a moment of shame for McNutt, but also as a moment in which the myth of the frontier might be exposed as an illusion.

In discussing how much weight McNutt had lost, Caldwell noted, "You lost 176 pounds in all. Just to put that for what it's worth, not to be totally self-centered here, but that is three pounds more than what I weigh. So you lost, in effect, me" (McNutt). To which McNutt responded, "Yeah, I've been getting that from a lot of people." This seems to perform double duty in terms of significance. Not only have several people, in mentioning that McNutt has lost "them," expressed the notion of the doubly present fat person (an entire person—presumably the fat "savage" identity—is lost in the struggle to free the thin identity trapped within), but they have also articulated a particular ownership of his body by way of imagined participation in his weight loss. This sentiment of public participation and ownership of the corpulent body is reflected in the theme song's opening line, "We need a change." Not only does the lyrics' insistence on a collective serve to indict the viewer for his or her own risky health behavior, but it also encourages the identification of the viewer with the contestants as they move toward the release of their inner thin persons.

A follow-up show that aired September 4, 2007, revisited former contestants from the three seasons of *The Biggest Loser*. The show featured only nine of the ninety-four contestants that had been involved with the show. Among these returning former contestants were several who had changed their careers and were working as personal trainers, motivational speakers, or nutritionists. This return of triumphant inner thin persons served to reinforce the defeat of the inner savage as permanent. Their new careers as instructors in exercise, nutrition, and self-esteem simultaneously buttressed the notion of the knowledgeable victor returning to the refined society he or she had escaped. The reunion show acted as a further indicator of the effect of fame on the private sphere of their lives, opening up further public ownership of their transformed celebrity and celebrity-transformed bodies. Marty proposed to his season 3 fellow contestant Amy on the reunion show just at the moment she stepped on the scale to be weighed for the audience. This act not only reifies the notion of the "unlovable" corpulent body, but also fulfills the promise that weight loss will cure this condition: after a dramatic weight loss, love is sure to follow.

Naturalization of Eurocentric Beauty Ideals

Just as the narrative of the frontier naturalizes the oppression of Native Americans and justifies the removal of their lands, *The Biggest Loser* performs similar work of naturalization, in this case by the construction of fat as unhealthy and of collateral notions of thinness as the only desirable and desired body shape, a construction that occurs partially through the obfuscation of dieticians' and physicians' presence. Their absence silently reasserts the idea that fatness is unhealthy and that the loss of a significant amount of weight will confer the supposed health of the thin on the newly restructured body. After all, we do not need to be reminded of what we already know, so the presence of the physicians is unnecessary; their limited presence acts only as an authenticating backdrop against which the process of weight loss is deemed safe (despite the knowledge that yoyo dieting puts tremendous strain on the cardiovascular system, the health of which is a key indicator of longevity) (Campos).

When discussing the interplay between savagery and civilization, it is important to recall that the savage in frontier mythology is always racialized. In examining the racialization of the savage in conjunction with *The Biggest Loser,* two issues present themselves: the ways in which fatness and thinness are racialized in American culture and the naturalization of Eurocentric beauty ideals that the show performs.

Asking a person to lose weight to become more attractive adheres to Eurocentric beauty ideals, which, connecting patriotism to this process, reveals that this constructs the true American not only as a thin American, but as a white American or an American who can best conform to Eurocentric beauty ideals. Part of the process of containment and despoiling of the fat identity involves adherence to beauty ideals. Like most television programming, *The Biggest Loser* features few people of color. Success on the show depends on a body that can achieve the dramatic results demanded by the producers. The discourses of beauty and attractiveness present in constructing the fat identity as spoiled work then as a privilege, or bonus prize, to the contestants as they lose weight. The contestants who are able to lose the most weight in particular areas of their bodies (for women in the hips and thighs), those who can most closely approach Eurocentric beauty standards, are of particular importance in the notion of the infinite malleability of the human body.

When these naturalization processes collude with the narratives of pride for both the state and nation, what is achieved is the transformation of hegemonic body norms into more than a simple aesthetic. It becomes a moment in which notions of progress and patriotism police the borders of the body and call on the American public to perform their patriotic duty by conforming to this particular bodily aesthetic. This television show is not the only example of the phenomenon; indeed, the Presidential Fitness Challenge performed the same work for years before the creation of *The Biggest Loser.* The Presidential Fitness Challenge operates on a smaller scale, however, despite its national coverage. Where *The Biggest Loser* awards a cash prize and elevates the winner (and to a lesser degree other participants) to celebrity status, the presidential fitness test (despite its inclusion of high-profile figures such as Arnold Schwarzenegger and the president of the United States) amounts to little more than an elementary school gym teacher awarding certificates. It is the hypervisibility of that union of patriotism and health in *The Biggest Loser* that makes it such a dynamic text for examining the expression of patriotism through conformity to bodily borders.

The Biggest Loser employs the lasting American myth by "discovering" that the frontier does not exist simply in a particular space and time; it remains forever open and is the site of daily battle with our own "inner savage." In this narrative of displacement, containment, maintenance, and reinsertion, the normative body and the beauty ideals of dominant culture are further naturalized and reproduced through this wholly American myth of the country as a nation of continual progress, continually remaking itself in its own image.

Notes

1. Two contestants from season 2 of the show, the winner Matt and the third-place runner-up, Suzy, did date after the end of filming, and they were married in September 2006. Also, Marty proposed to his season 3 fellow contestant Amy during the reunion show that aired in September 2007, although their relationship was not publicized during filming.

2. The term *ambassador* and the notion of the Everyman status of the contestants bring an opportunity to discuss briefly the eliding of class issues in the framework of the show. Contestants are rarely seen without their team sweatsuits, shorts, and T-shirts, which obfuscate any potential class difference between the contestants. Though clothing and other class markers inscribed on the body are not the only ways in which we determine class, they are the most highly visible and are often used to determine class status. This erasure of class markers contributes to the maintenance of class invisibility and a continuing construction of American identity as decidedly middle class. Indeed, exercise often requires a certain amount of leisure time that is not always available to the working class, but in the framework of the show this fact is underemphasized, particularly when it comes to the fifty-state model of season 3. The thirty-six at-home players were asked to lose as much weight as possible without the benefit of leaving their jobs and family obligations to focus solely on weight loss. This supports the notions not only that the body is infinitely malleable, but also that the thin body is universally accessible.

Works Cited

The Biggest Loser. NBC. October 2004–December 2006.

Braziel, Jana Evans. "Sex and Fat Chics: Deterritorializing the Fat Female Body." *Bodies Out of Bounds: Fatness and Transgression.* Ed. Jana Evans Braziel and Kathleen LeBesco. Berkeley: University of California Press, 2001. 231–254.

Campos, Paul. *The Obesity Myth: Why America's Obsession with Weight Is Hazardous to Your Health.* New York: Gotham Books, 2004.

Certeau, Michel de. *The Practice of Everyday Life.* Trans. Steven Rendall. Berkeley: University of California Press, 1984.

Goodman, W. Charisse. *The Invisible Woman: Confronting Weight Prejudice in America.* Carlsbad, CA: Gurze Books, 1995.

Hardie, Melissa Jane. "'I Embrace the Difference': Elizabeth Taylor and the Closet." *Sexy Bodies: The Strange Carnalities of Feminism.* Ed. Elizabeth Grosz and Elspeth Probyn. London: Routledge, 1995. 155–171.

Harper, Bob, and Kim Lyons. Interview, September 2006, www.nbc.com/The_Biggest_Loser/video/.

Huff, Joyce L. "A 'Horror of Corpulence': Interrogating Bantingism and Mid-Nineteenth-Century Fat-Phobia." *Bodies Out of Bounds: Fatness and Transgression.* Ed. Jana Evans Braziel and Kathleen LeBesco. Berkeley: University of California Press, 2001. 39–59.

Kent, Le'a. "Fighting Abjection: Representing Fat Women." *Bodies Out of Bounds: Fatness and Transgression.* Ed. Jana Evans Braziel and Kathleen LeBesco. Berkeley: University of California Press, 2001. 130–150.

LeBesco, Kathleen. "Fat Panic and the Invisible Morality" (manuscript).

McNutt, Matthew. Interview with Rob Caldwell. *207.* NBC. WCSH, Portland, ME, December 18, 2006.

Roberts, Brian. *American Alchemy: The California Gold Rush and Middle-Class Culture.* Chapel Hill: University of North Carolina Press, 2000.

Shaw, Andrea. "The Other Side of the Looking Glass: The Marginalization of Fatness and Blackness in the Construction of Gender Identity." *Social Semiotics* 15.2 (August 2005): 143–152.

Slotkin, Richard. *Gunfighter Nation: The Myth of the Frontier in Twentieth-Century America.* Norman: University of Oklahoma Press, 1998 [1992].

PART II

Class, Gender, and Reimaging of Family Life

Disillusionment, Divorce, and the Destruction of the American Dream

An American Family *and the Rise of Reality TV*

The 1970s were a disturbing transitional period for many Americans. Decline of social institutions that formerly solidified and signified the American identity contributed to much of this turmoil. Politically, culturally, and economically the country was going through changes that were affecting it in adverse ways. Vietnam veterans were coming home from the war disillusioned and broken, the country was realizing that its political leaders were corrupt, and inflation had reached new heights. It was during these chaotic times that Craig Gilbert's *An American Family* (1973) aired on PBS. This series, the first of its kind, would later inspire the reality TV phenomenon of the late twentieth and early twenty-first centuries. *An American Family,* consisting of twelve one-hour episodes, featured an ostensibly "average" upper-middle-class family and presented many contemporary concerns to a broad viewing public. Those involved in the filming process understood its unique concept of following ordinary people and documenting their lives. In an effort to save a sinking station, James Day, the president of NET (PBS's New York affiliate) opted to create a show that would "address the vast changes that were occurring in American society, 'particularly with young people—their attitudes towards drugs, towards sex, towards religion'" (quoted in Ruoff 12). In the spirit of cinema verité[1] and its American counterpart, direct cinema,[2] Craig Gilbert proposed a series that would look at the institutions of marriage and family by following a "traditional" American family. Rather than adhering to the mandates set forward by cinema verité and direct cinema, however, Gilbert manipulated everything from casting to editing to publicity to assert that family and marriage were dying institutions and that the American dream was in decay.

Filming *An American Family* (PBS) in 1973. *From left:* Grant Loud, Pat Loud, Alan Raymond, Susan Raymond. Courtesy of PBS/PhotoFest.

Influences and Strategic Choices: The Making of An American Family

Craig Gilbert had a fixed thesis in mind as he began a search for "the quintessential American family." He drew inspiration from Allan King's *A Married Couple* (1969), Charles Reich's *The Greening of America,* Theodore Roszak's *The Making of a Counter Culture* (1968), and Ross Macdonald's *The Underground Man*—all of which attacked bourgeois institutions such as marriage, capitalism, and the American dream. His choice of the William C. Loud family (Bill, Pat, and their children, Lance, Kevin, Grant, Delilah, and Michele) allowed him to explore problems that festered below the surface of perfect facades.

The first book to influence the making of *An American Family* was Ross Macdonald's *The Underground Man* (1971). According to Jeffrey Ruoff, the novel "perfectly described" the type of family that Gilbert was looking for (17). Macdonald demonstrated how wealth alone could not provide happiness or balance to individuals with questionable morality. The Loud family of Santa Barbara, California, fit this mold. Its members were clean-cut, affluent, and attractive, yet the tension that was palpable between them from the first scene indicated to the audience that something was not right. The second influential book was Charles Reich's best seller *The Greening of America* (1970). This text analyzed the cultural revolution that overtook America in the 1960s and 1970s. Reich's book looked at the demise of the family and the disintegration of the dream, celebrating—as *An American Family* does not—the rise of a new consciousness of communal peace and love. Personal experience with a crumbling marriage and divorce further influenced Gilbert's interest in the project. When Curt Davis, Gilbert's supervisor, asked him to write up a proposal for a show that he had always wanted to do, "Gilbert thought about it during the weekend in which he 'drank a lot and wallowed in self pity' over his failed marriage. Somewhere, buried in the troubling question of why men and women have such a tough time maintaining relationships, was the germ of an idea for a show. He grabbed a pencil and began making notes. The result was the outline for *An American Family*" (Landrum and Carmichael 67).

Susan Lester, associate producer for the project, was also aware of the representational requirements. She knew that they were looking for "a family that sells Cracker Jacks. The kind of family you see on a television commercial, in a pretty house that has the best of what this country has to offer materially. . . . Material success was as important in what we were trying to say because we were trying to play around with the American dream" (Ruoff 17). Notes for the series were finalized *after* the Loud family had been settled on, which proves the importance the producer placed on locating the unscripted cast. The Loud family fit the filmmakers' agendas so well that, in spite of a concept that originally planned to concentrate on four families, the Louds became the only social unit central to the reality series.

Marriage, Kids, and Divorce: Living the Louds' American Dream

The William C. Loud family met all the series creators' requirements: they belonged to the upper middle class and lived in a luxurious ranch-style house; with four cars, three dogs, a pool, and the financial ability to take expensive vacations, they seemed to represent the American Dream. The family's perfect facade, however, hid many underlying problems. Bill and Pat Loud's marriage had steadily deteriorated over the years, so much so that Gilbert had the perfect opportunity to explore the troubled relationship between a man and a woman who typified this trend. The family could also perfectly illustrate the issues Charles Reich discussed in his book—the materialism of the old generation and the drug culture of the new generation, the decaying work ethic of the former and the unrepressed pleasure principle of the latter.

The traditional nuclear family in the United States (at least as depicted in the media) usually consists of a loving mother and father and perfect children. The Louds subverted this image of nuclear togetherness in every sense. Bill and Pat's divorce demonstrated that they were far from loving. Their differences and Bill's infidelity presented a more realistic portrayal, and the series played on their tension. When Bill and Pat were together, there was usually distance between them. When they talked, it was usually small talk, inconsequential. In the event that they did discuss their children, two completely different parenting styles emerged. An example of this estrangement appeared in episode 6, when Pat's comments about the children are countered with Bill's advice, "Life's too short to worry about all that jazz." It became clear throughout the course of the series that rather than simply studying the Louds, Gilbert wished to comment on them. The episodes presented Bill as a nonresponsive father. He continually told Pat that she should not worry about the children and that they should try to get them out of the house as soon as possible. Bill wanted his sons to follow his example, and he completely ignored their desire to find their own roles in life. Pat, on the other hand, wanted her children to be happy, claiming that she did not care what they did with their lives as long as they were content. Her behavior and apparent concern for the feelings of her kids had the added bonus of casting her in the role of the doting mother and the "star" of the series.

There were multiple reasons for the creative decision to give Pat Loud preference over her husband, but the most important seemed to be what each individual represented. During the late 1960s a counterculture began to emerge. This generation, notorious for rebelling against mainstream society, tried to illustrate how old ways of viewing relationships and institutions were no longer tenable. Out of this turmoil came Charles Reich's extremely popular study, *The Greening of America*, which became a driving force behind Gilbert's vision. *An American Family* capitalized on Reich's labeling of the different consciousnesses of members of society. A type II consciousness (Bill Loud) was often subject to ridicule. According to Reich, these individuals "are inclined to think of work, injustice and war, and of the bitter frustrations of life, as the human condition" (quoted in Landrum and Carmichael 68). Gilbert and Reich believed this consciousness was antithetical to 1970s sensibilities, and the individuals who embodied these characteristics should become figures with whom new consciousnesses struggled. Pat Loud differed from her husband. She bridged the gap between consciousness II and the next stage. Her children, as the younger, more rebellious generation, embodied Reich's consciousness III. They were interested in individuality and revolting against tradition. According to Reich: "The foundation of Consciousness III is liberation. It comes into being the moment the individual frees himself from automatic acceptance of the imperatives of society and the false consciousness which society imposes. . . . The meaning of liberation is that the individual is free to build his own philosophy and values, his own life-style, and his own culture from a new beginning" (225).

Because their values differed so drastically from Bill's, the children were in need of a mediator. In this role, Pat understood her children and tried to help her husband strengthen his relationships with them. The problem arose when Bill refused to change his ways of thinking. He remained distant and did not appear to care about the lives of his children. Bill's concern manifested itself only in his desire to help the boys find jobs that would make them self-supporting. Pat's acceptance of the children ensured her popularity among her offspring—as well as among the viewers. She very rarely tried to enforce rules, and she seemed to enjoy and encourage acts of rebellion. The series advanced the notion that, because Pat loved her children, she was able to do things as diverse as joining Lance at an avant-garde musical about transvestites in episode 2 or help Delilah with her costume for a dance recital in episode 3. As a consciousness II, Bill Loud never could perform these types of parenting feats.

The Loud children were rebellious teenagers who listened to rock music and used drugs and alcohol. Lance Loud, the oldest son, was a homosexual who apparently lived by taking handouts from others. *An American Family* attributed Lance's "outrageous" behavior to a deeper problem. In episode 8, Pat explains that she believes Lance would not have so many problems if "he had felt like his daddy loved him." Perhaps to explore a timely theme, the cameras focused on his struggles. Lance's decision to come out as a homosexual on national television, while extremely brave, was not all it appeared. According to Lance, though he had known he was gay for some time, he did not make a conscious decision to play up this aspect of himself. In a reunion episode taped ten years after the series aired on television, an older, more mature Lance explains that he thought his behavior was "extremely avant-garde." He discusses the idea that the promotional material outing him as a homosexual placed him in a very awkward role. For Lance, and the other members of the family, the exploitation of aspects of personalities and situations was extremely difficult. The Louds—like all families—had their quirks and foibles, but ordinary families lack a PBS film crew following and recording their every move.

Bill believed that his sons should want to find work to make money and start their own self-sufficient lives, but Grant Loud preferred to focus his time on his music rather than get a blue-collar job. Bill tried to instill a work ethic in his sons, but neither Grant nor Lance seemed to want to follow his father's example. In episode 7, Bill and Pat try to discuss employment with Grant, but he rebukes them. Grant is the stereotypical spoiled child, receiving everything he wants from his parents. When Bill and Pat force Grant to get a job with the "concrete king of California," he parties more than he works. As the first television series of its kind, *An American Family* aired footage of Grant Loud smoking what appeared to be marijuana and drinking copious amounts of alcohol. His behavior seemed to usher in the notion of the "Me Generation." Interestingly, Grant did not realize that his own behavior mirrored his father's. Even though Bill provided ample material possessions for his family, he did not seem to understand that his children and wife needed emotional support. Unlike Lance, Grant did not appear distressed by his father's detachment. In fact, he savored Bill's absence because it meant he could do what he wanted without reprimands.

Throughout the series, Gilbert returned to his thesis that the American family was broken, even when he filmed seemingly innocent conversations. In episode 7, one innocuous phone call between Bill and Pat's elder daughter, Delilah, and her boyfriend, Brad, becomes a commentary on the institution of marriage. She says, "My dad came home. Oh God, so embarrassing . . . they are arguing about whether you should put the cheese in the refrigerator or not. . . . I was so embarrassed. And then Nancy called me and her parents were fighting too." As she remarks that she cannot bear to be in the position her parents are in, the editing cuts to a shot of Bill and Pat in the kitchen. Bill sits at the table while Pat cleans up after a meal. There is a tense silence between them, and they clearly have nothing meaningful to say to each other; the lack of conversation is evidence of the sterility of their marriage. Although Pat says it in the next episode, it is clear that they "just [didn't] have any rapport at all anymore." Delilah's commentary about her friend's parents furthers the notion that the Louds are typical of many American families. To Pat and Bill, their home is not a comforting haven; it is a place of discontent and disharmony that they ultimately seek to flee. Furthermore, Delilah's schoolgirl confession of love for her boyfriend glaringly contrasts with the weary strain and futility of her parents' marriage. Gilbert went for the jugular by setting her seemingly sweet first teenage relationship against the crushing inevitability of the end of love, thus suggesting an unavoidable cycle of bitter disappointment.

Yet another instance of presenting the Louds as representative of all American families came with Bill and Pat's attendance at a cocktail party. In this scene Ross Macdonald's influence on Gilbert's thesis is revealed as characters seemingly stripped from Toulouse-Lautrec paintings swarm about in a daze of debauchery. As Ruoff observes, the claustrophobic cocktail party, "the careless party chatter, the sunglasses, the liquor, the leathered faces, the Hawaiian shirts, and the suggestion of extramarital affairs all combine to create an atmosphere of upper-middle-class subur-ban decadence, California style" (72). Bill asks about a woman's plans, and when a perturbed Pat replies, "Well, for the record, she is just pass-ing through," Bill chuckles anxiously, suggesting his past philandering. As the woman he is plying with liquor and flirting with chortles that he is "going through a very dangerous age," the camera continues to focus on Pat's studied effort to avoid observing Bill and his companions. Yet her tautness clearly demonstrates that she is well aware of her husband's wandering eye.

In addition to the uncomfortable cocktail party, Bill's own commentary on his unhappiness makes it clear that the series' thesis on the demise of the institution of marriage may not be inaccurate. Bill is quick to point out his dissatisfactions with his wife and family. In episode 12 he says that he objects to the family being a "twenty-four-hour deal." The belief that the family needs a man's total devotion and time was prevalent, according to him, because "somebody has sold society a bad bill of goods." Barbara

Ehrenreich writes, "According to writer William Iversen, husbands were self-sacrificing romantics, toiling ceaselessly to provide their families with bread, bacon, clothes, furniture, cars, appliances, entertainment, vacations and country-club memberships" (48). Bill feels that he has played the part of this unselfish, noble, and deluded romantic far too long and it is time for him to break out of that stultifying existence. The preceding scene shows Pat sitting down to have a discussion with her children and laying down some practical rules that they will have to follow after the divorce. Later she tries to rationalize with a less-than-enthusiastic Lance about his future hopes and vague aspirations. The editing of these scenes shows that it is Pat alone who is willing to take the role of interested facilitator in family affairs. Bill wishes to be free, enjoying vacations without familial obligations, leaving all the responsibility to his wife. Pat rightly says to her sister-in-law in episode 8, "He doesn't wanna be home very much." Bill even fails to understand the sacredness of marriage; he refuses to accept, let alone appreciate, the fact that marriage is a joint venture requiring an equal investment from both parties. Indeed, as Pat tells her brother and sister-in-law, Bill truly believes that his family should be a vital but small part of his life. He desires the role of occasional parent, a man simultaneously adored and left alone. Bill is bent on being a mere consumer and beneficiary of his family's goodness rather than an active worker in its more mundane but necessary business. Pat sums up their relationship when she observes, "When he says jump, you'd better believe we all stand up in a row and jump." If Bill is the figurehead and CEO of Loud Incorporated, then Pat represents the underappreciated manager whose efforts keep him free for vacations and chummy cocktails with female admirers.

In conjunction with the presentation of individual family members and their personal issues, the series employed effective editing to demonstrate that the institution of marriage was no longer a part of the American dream. From the opening sequence of the series, the music is upbeat at first as faces of the family members come onto the screen. The title evokes elements of the popular late 1960s–early 1970s television series *The Brady Bunch;* however, by the end of the sequence it is clear that the Louds are nothing like the Bradys. In the opening sequence of *An American Family,* the different members of the Loud family are separated from each other by a freeze frame that isolates each member in his or her own little square, much like the opening montage of the *Brady Bunch.* These squares soon swoop into place and fit together like so many puzzle pieces. The music becomes increasingly frenetic as the words *An American Family* appear on the screen. Finally, the word *Family* cracks, suggesting the institutional breakdown. This opening montage forewarns of the problems the Louds face.

If the title graphics do not sufficiently present the situation of the declining family, the series flashes forward to the last day of filming. A voiceover narration declares, "This New Year will be unlike any other that has been celebrated at 35 Wooddale Lane. For the first time, the family will not be spending it together. Pat Loud and her husband, Bill, separated four months ago, after twenty years of marriage." At the New Year's Eve celebration, a lonely Pat reads a book, watches her children dance, embraces her youngest child, and finally hugs a dog as the New Year needles its way into her miserable night. The film cuts to a shot of Bill Loud drolly dancing with his new girlfriend. The decision to begin this way heightened the dramatic effect of the reality series and further reinforced Gilbert's thesis about a dying American institution. At the outset he wanted to tantalize viewers with a chance to scrutinize a family scandal. The move was reminiscent of those found in any number of popular soap operas and prescient of those of more recent reality TV series. Gilbert, like fiction directors, teased the audience into tuning in for the next episode and begged for value judgments to occur in the interim.

Materialism and Capitalism: Disillusionment and the American Dream

According to the American dream, a man must, by dint of hard work, pull himself up by the bootstraps to acquire worldly possessions and position. Indeed, that was a work ethic that Bill Loud aspired to in every outward way. It was obvious he believed he was a sterling example of what can be achieved by tireless labor and clever dealings. According to Charles Reich, such men believe that "the individual should do his best to fit himself into a function that is needed by society, subordinating himself to the requirements of the occupation or institution that he has chosen. He feels it is a duty, and is willing to make 'sacrifices' for it" (72). Bill, illustrating Reich's argument, was constantly traveling to get more business, even though while traveling he did not have the comforts of home. He was a businessman

A scene from *An American Family* (PBS, 1973). Pat Loud is at center. Courtesy of PBS/PhotoFest.

to the core, and he considered such sacrifices necessary, since, as he tells his friend in episode 12, if his family expects to live the American dream he has to remain on the road. That is not to say that he feels himself an ennobled martyr for money; rather, he feels that his sacrifices, justified by his success, define him as a man.

Bill had financial success, but he did not have some of the ethical values that were inherent in the dream. According to Reich, "The American dream was not, at least at the beginning, a rags-to-riches type of narrow materialism. At its most exalted . . . it was a spiritual and humanistic vision of man's possibilities" (22). Bill completely failed to understand the greater potentialities; his version was limited to monetary success, and those admirable qualities that had made him a successful businessman were missing from his personal life. John G. Cawelti has pointed out that any "thought about the self-made man placed its major emphasis on the individual's getting ahead; its definition of success was largely economic" (5). Bill could well agree with Cawelti's definition of a successful self-made man. He was devoted to his job and to financial success, but not to his family, in effect resembling some flashier, more business-savvy, sexually predatory version of Arthur Miller's Willy Loman. He was a responsible and resourceful entrepreneur, but he shirked responsibilities at home, and though Lance mentions it jokingly in episode 11, he had indeed taken "the business of being a dad too lightly." In 1955 Manfred Kuhn wrote about eleven reasons men do not marry, and "unwillingness to take responsibility" is one of them (Ehrenreich 20). Because Bill had married but often wanted to live the unattached life of an irresponsible bachelor, he frequently felt his family was a burden. The most vital component of the American dream is the family, yet Bill did not have any inkling of that fact.

Bill's limited idea of success caused him to neglect elements of his life. He placed objects and wealth above family and marriage, and it was this characteristic that drew Gilbert's attention. Reich explained how financial excess had become an aim for many individuals when he wrote, " 'The money' is now being spent for consumer goods. It is being spent on all of the things, large and small, that make up the affluent American way of life—automobiles, appliances, vacations, highways, food and clothing. All of these things have reached beyond any standard of necessity to higher and higher standards of luxury" (164). For the Loud family and many like them, wealth became problematic. Bill worked to provide for his family, but the one thing the family needed was denied. Rather than forming bonds with his children and wife, Bill was aloof and at times disgruntled. He was an example of the dangers of striving for the American dream. On the surface his family appeared to have achieved a type of perfection, but the declining marriage and the breakup of the family provided a counterpoint to that outward positive appearance.

The Fallout: An American Family *and the Rise of Reality TV*

Perhaps the most overt manipulation of material came during the postproduction phase of the project. The press kit distributed with *An American Family* clearly demonstrated the director's underlying message of the death of the American dream and the destruction of the family. In much of the promotional materials the family was portrayed as less than ideal. In the reunion episode Pat Loud explains her frustration when she discusses the idea that her family was seen as degenerate, broken, and almost monstrous. She explains how WNET described events from the series and individual personalities and then asked the question, "Would you like to live next door to this family?" For Pat, as well as the other Louds, the promotional materials were extremely disheartening. The series gave them their fifteen minutes of fame, but they had to deal with the backlash from having their lives nationally televised. Even more discouraging than the promotional material was the public reaction. Most media and critics attacked the Louds themselves rather than the series. In one excerpt from the reunion episode, the distinguished anthropologist Margaret Mead argues with a group of critics who are insisting on criticizing the family without actually praising the new genre—reality documentary—Gilbert had invented. Mead insists on looking at the series as a new art form, but it seems that not many were able to do so. Separating the art form of reality TV from the personalities of its stars was nearly impossible. Perhaps examining the controversy surrounding both the Louds and the series could help explain the mid- to late-1990s reality TV boom. Looking at the contributions *An American Family* made to shows such as *The Real World* helps situate recent reality TV in the same genre as Gilbert's work. In this sense, Gilbert's legacy of thesis-driven documentary was the progenitor of today's most popular reality TV shows.

Audiences who neglected *An American Family*'s 1973 debut erroneously label MTV's *Real World* (1992) as the first reality television show. By comparing the two series, it is easy to see Craig Gilbert's influence. Though the idea of a thesis-driven documentary is nothing new, Gilbert's use of the form for television audiences has become a platform from which reality TV can dive into the public consciousness. The first season of *The Real World,* while garnering praise for its originality, did not do well in the ratings. Its producers, Mary-Ellis Bunim and Jonathan Murray, looked to the PBS series as a source of inspiration. The problem with the first season of *The Real World* lay in the fact that there was more documentary than drama. The producers did not follow Gilbert's example of building on an inherent thesis. Episodes that included the possibility of either romance or serious conflict were popular. Late into the first season, the producers realized that the viewing public wanted drama, so the next cast was more provocative; as the series progressed, it began showcasing more highly controversial individuals and issues. AIDS activism, gay rights, abortion, plastic surgery, physical abuse, politics, and even Lyme disease all found their forum on MTV. *The Real World* has gradually evolved into a series concerned with sex. Perhaps this change was inevitable, or perhaps the series creators, like Craig Gilbert, realized that drama is more effective than documentary when it comes to attracting the viewing public. The first season of *The Real World* tackled contemporary issues such as race, gender, and class, but recent seasons seem to take their cues from the more traditional dramatic soap opera form. Though these types of reality TV shows have their own niche in the entertainment industry, their bases in documentary or even thesis-driven documentary (à la *An American Family*) is almost nonexistent at this point. Furthermore, looking at new reality TV helps place *An American Family*'s own editorial and directorial decisions in perspective. With the PBS series Gilbert wanted to explore serious issues of the 1960s and 1970s, the kinds of problems identified by legitimate social observers. In contrast, contemporary reality TV has taken the ability to manipulate too far. In an industry where selling the series is of the utmost importance, reality TV must go to extremes to ensure that the shows are not pulled from the lineup before being aired. This climate of urgency encourages an industry focused on ratings and money rather than directorial integrity, originality, or insight. A series such as *An American Family* or the early years of *The Real World* would never survive more than one season in today's ratings-based climate.

Perhaps today's reality TV is the final, decadent stop for the genre. Shock and provocativeness are now the keys to success, and a series like *An American Family* or *The Real World* needed to incorporate elements of the fictional in order to continue. Gilbert understood that some manipulation is necessary. He recognized very early on that documentary television must also entertain. Landrum and Carmichael attest to as much when they quote Craig Gilbert as saying: "I feel very strongly that the television documentary, if it is to have any future, it must go in this direction. It must be in a series form—repetition and involvement with characters is what holds viewers—and it must be concerned with the events in the daily lives of ordinary citizens" (66).

Interestingly, Gilbert, with his own manipulations, seems to have opened the door for a modern cinema form that violates all the rules of the documentary. His insistence on illustrating the problems with the American dream and the institution of the family ensures that *An American Family* is more a social commentary than a study. Gilbert created his own meaning out of the material available, essentially setting the stage for today's reality TV producers. In an article Gilbert admits: "Yes, I am guilty. I had a point of view. . . . No, I did not think men and women were blissfully happy; no, I did not think relationships, by and large, were mature, mutually satisfying, and productive; no, I did not think family life was the endless round of happy mindlessness pictured in television commercials" ("Reflections II" 290).

Gilbert's thesis concerning the nation's basic social building blocks, then, found ample exploration in *An American Family*. It is undeniable that the series analyzed a number of social and cultural issues that were troubling Americans during the late 1960s and early 1970s. Rather than adhering to the mandates of cinema verité and direct cinema, *An American Family* chose to use the material available to tell the story of the dying American dream as documented by the disintegration of the William C. Loud family, and, in doing so, the series ushered in a new genre of television with a study of historic value.

Notes

1. New inventions in filmmaking ushered in new ways of looking at the documentary form. Directors began experimenting with the idea that filmmakers could speak truth with the images they film. Going back to the Russian idea of "Kino Pravda" (film truth), the Frenchman Jean Rouch in 1959 coined the phrase cinema verité. Like Dziga Vertov before him, Rouch believed that a director could use the camera as an eye for seeing real life. Rouch first applied cinema verité principles to *Chronicles of Summer* (1961), in which he let the interviewees and their opinions speak for themselves (Ellis 221). Rouch's idea of film truth is similar to a concept central to anthropological studies. To present an accurate portrait of a subject's life, time, and culture, the camera should essentially observe and record without overtly interfering. If done correctly, cinema verité becomes a tool for understanding, not a tool for promoting agendas.

2. Direct cinema, the American version of cinema verité, seems like a more idealistic form of documentary. Creators of this style came from a journalistic tradition and claimed that objectivity is possible. According to Jack Ellis, "An approach now called direct cinema was pioneered by Drew Associates in the *Close-Up!* Series on ABC-TV. . . . Its tenets were articulated most forcefully by Robert Drew and, especially, by Richard ("Ricky") Leacock. The Drew-Leacock approach falls within the reportage tradition, coming from Drew's background in photo-journalism and Leacock's experience as a documentary cinematographer" (223). Direct cinema differs from cinema verité in its assumption that a pure experience is possible. Direct cinema, as a type of journalism, looks for stories with an inherent beginning, middle, and end.

Works Cited

An American Family. PBS. WNET, New York. 1973.

Cawelti, John G. *Apostles of the Self-Made Man.* Chicago: University of Chicago Press, 1965.

Ehrenreich, Barbara. *The Hearts of Men.* Garden City, NY: Anchor/Double-day, 1983.

Ellis, Jack C. *The Documentary Idea: A Critical History of English-Language Documentary Film and Video.* Englewood Cliffs, NJ: Prentice-Hall, 1989.

Gilbert, Craig. "Reflections on *An American Family,* I." *New Challenges for Documentary.* Ed. Alan Rosenthal. Berkeley: University of California Press, 1988. 191–209.

———. "Reflections on *An American Family,* II." *New Challenges for Documentary.* Ed. Alan Rosenthal. Berkeley: University of California Press, 1988. 288–307.

"Lance Loud! A Death in an American Family." 2002. *PBS Online,* March 18, 2005, www.pbs.org/lanceloud/.

Landrum, Jason, and Deborah Carmichael. "Jeffrey Ruoff's *An American Family: A Televised Life:* Reviewing the Roots of Reality Television." *Film & History* 32.1 (2002): 66–70.

Macdonald, Ross. *The Underground Man.* New York: Alfred A. Knopf, 1971.

Reich, Charles A. *The Greening of America.* New York: Random House, 1970.

Ruoff, Jeffrey. *"An American Family": A Televised Life.* Minneapolis: University of Minnesota Press, 2002.

Shearer, Harry. Review of *An American Family: A Televised Life.* By Jeffrey Ruoff. *Wilson Quarterly* 26.3 (2002): 118–119.

The Real World. MTV. 1992–.

Su Holmes

"The television audience cannot be expected to bear too much reality"

The Family *and Reality TV*

> [Television has embraced] the fashionable "reality band-wagon": a crude construction that trundles ever forward, crushing anything "real" that pokes out through the scum of docusoaps and trivia. . . . Observation is largely out, scripting is hugely in. . . . In these vainglorious worlds of fabricated reality, only the cliché counts and the unsettling facts give way to the LCD [lowest common denominator] needs of entertainment. Grown producers have knowingly taken leave of their sensibilities—indeed, all sense of real life—in order to create a "reality world" that ideally troubles nobody. . . . Reality, a word I once thought I owned, has been reduced to a game show. . . . [But] yes, I am accused of being a hypocrite—"You created the stuff, and now you disown it." No. Just as any artist, I move on. (Watson 22)

Paul Watson produced the twelve-part documentary serial, *The Family* (BBC1, 1974),[1] which is widely regarded as the British counterpart to *An American Family* (PBS, 1973). Although speaking from his reluctant position as the "godfather of Reality TV" (Hoggart), Watson's comments invoke familiar dismissals of the form. Reality TV, seemingly cultivating an appetite for individualized narratives within self-contained "tele-scapes" of its own devising (Nichols, *Blurred* 31), is often seen as a regrettable popularization of the factual moving image and a further severing of the relationship between television and the public sphere. Given these negative cultural discourses, it is clear that Watson has a particular investment in distinguishing his work from reality TV. But his comments still raise important questions about how a historical genealogy of the form is being constructed—whether in the popular media or in academic discourse.

Television historiography has become a crucial part of television studies, yet when it comes to reality TV, the meeting of these spheres is still an evolving project. (This is doubtless hampered by reality TV's own obsession with "liveness" and "nowness," and the wider tendency to conceptualize it as an entirely new phenomenon.)

Both academic and popular discussions of reality TV have seized landmarks or flashpoints in mapping the unruly genealogy of the form—from *Candid Camera* to *An American Family* and *The Family*. For example, a recent British documentary on the history of "ordinary" people on television claims that, in *The Family*, viewers "watched real life as it happened. . . . The Wilkins family became our first Reality TV stars."[2] But this historical shorthand also emerges as problematic when, as is the case with *The Family*, the "milestone" itself has never really been analyzed. Although liberally cited, *The Family* has been referred to rather than examined. On a scholarly level, it has perhaps been overshadowed by interest in the spectacularly controversial *An American Family*, which featured the breakup of the Loud family (specifically, the divorce of Mr. and Mrs. Loud) as part of the serial itself. But until Jeffrey Ruoff's *"An American Family": A Televised Life* in 2002, the American show had also received little sustained attention since its original broadcast in 1973. It seems that, implicitly or otherwise, these programs have not been deemed serious enough for the province of documentary scholarship, yet they have perhaps been considered too serious (and too old?) to capitalize on the current scholarly energy surrounding reality TV (Holmes). In this regard, *The Family* seems to have slipped through the analytic cracks.

Although some of its innovations are seen to reside in the text itself (its serial form, the unprecedented access to and focus on "ordinary" people), many of the assumed connections between then and now can really be explored only at the level of extratextual discourse—perceptions of genre, privacy, or ordinary people as performers. We always map the past from the vantage point of the present, so the positioning of *The Family* is no exception here. But in the eagerness to forge a relationship between now and then, what gets lost is the sense of "newness" and the debate that attended *The Family*'s first airing. After all, critics and viewers at the time did not know that *The Family* would later be positioned in popular memory and cultural history as the gateway to a whole range of popular factual programming. This is vividly encapsulated by a critic's blunt assertions in the *Daily Telegraph* in 1974: "It is sadly unlikely that *The Family* will be seminal. . . . The television audience cannot be expected to bear too much reality."[3]

The aim of this essay is not to mount an overriding argument for or against *The Family*'s status as a precursor to reality TV (which would negate the complexities involved in television historiography). But in seeking to come to a more nuanced understanding of this relationship, I explore what might be termed pockets of comparison, drawing on original archival research[4] in a bid to reconstruct aspects of *The Family*'s popular circulation.

"New Real-Life Documentary Serial for BBC"

In deciding to produce *The Family*, Watson was influenced by the success of *An American Family* in America the previous year, and he engaged in a dialogue about the production with the BBC's office in New York.[5] On April 3, 1974, after Watson had interviewed many potential families, *The Family* introduced viewers to the Wilkinses. The family comprised Terry Wilkins (thirty-nine), a bus driver, Margaret Wilkins (thirty-nine), a part-time greengrocer, and their children Marion (nineteen), a hairdresser, Gary (eighteen), a bus driver and conductor, Heather (fifteen), and Christopher (nine). Gary's wife, Karen (eighteen), and their baby son, Scott, as well as Marion's boyfriend, Tom, also lived with the family, and they occupied a rented flat above the greengrocer shop where Margaret Wilkins worked.

There is little doubt that *The Family* was seen at the time as a landmark program—as suggested by press headlines (the surprise expressed at the fact that a "BBC serial stars real people") and by the manner in which critics reflected on its influence and significance when it came to an end. But in regard to questions of social content and aesthetic form, the emphasis on innovation was also shored up by the producer Paul Watson and the BBC. In this respect, the BBC was apt to foreground aesthetic innovation. Their press release, titled "New Real-Life Documentary Serial for BBC," drew attention to how *The Family* exploited "new microphone techniques" as well as the latest lightweight cameras, which allowed "interior filming without artificial lights."[6] In comparison, Watson's discourse about the program took a broadly Marxist stance in the face of questions of class, social access, and representation and emphasized the importance of giving the "ordinary" people a voice. *The Family* also emerged at the same time that the BBC was exploring "access" programming, which evolved into their series *Open Door* (1973–1983). Part of the international growth of access TV, the series featured programs made by various marginalized groups, ranging from black teachers to the "transex liberation group."[7] But in terms of making a connection with Watson's program, there is clearly a tension here insofar as the very idea of "the family" (and a white, working-class family at that) suggests a central, rather than marginalized, social concept. (In fact, in the early 1970s at least, nearly 70 percent of the population could still be classified as working class; see Marwick 143). As I discuss below, the program's claim to typicality was hotly contested. But the fact that the discourse surrounding *The Family* ascribes an inter-textual connection with access programming makes clear how limited the opportunities were for ordinary people to appear on television at this time (and in the British context, the concept of the ordinary is often equated with the working class).

The terms *direct cinema, cinema verité,* and *fly-on-the-wall* are often used (problematically) in interchangeable ways (see Corner, *Art*). But despite the claim that *The Family* was probably more responsible than anything else for the popularization of the concept of fly-on-the-wall pro-gramming,[8] this term did not have an especially wide currency in 1974. Much of the debate, about direct cinema at least, had been associated with key figures in the United States (Wiseman, Leacock, Pennebaker). This was acknowledged by *Sight and Sound* when it noted how "very little of this debate has been heard [in the United Kingdom]. And right into the middle of it drops *The Family.* What were critics going to make of it? What were the viewers supposed to think?" (Young 210). Watson did have Roger Graef's *The Space between Words* (1972) on which to draw (this was also interested in the inner life of the family, albeit within a "communication experiment" setting) (Corner, *"American Family,"* 8). But in the BBC's own categorizations of documentary forms, there is no distinct listing for observational or fly-on-the-wall in the mid-1970s; neither appears until the end of the decade.[9]

There is also the question as to how the program might have related to the documentary culture of the time. Although observational filmmak-ing, once transferred to television, has been seen as particularly suited to intimate subjects (Kilborn and Izod), it is not the case that the BBC's documentaries had previously dealt only with "public," metanarrative issues. We know relatively little about routine British documentary produc-tion in this period, and celebrated high points—such as *Civilisation* (BBC,

1969) and *The Ascent of Man* (BBC, 1974)—tend to be emphasized above all else. The main placing for the genre was in the Tuesday documentary strand (a regular slot for documentary screenings on the BBC), as well as in series such as *Omnibus* (BBC1) and *Horizon* (BBC2). In 1973 the Tuesday strand ranged across *The Group* (alcoholism), *The Press We Deserve, The British Empire,* and *A Place of Your Own* (house prices), to titles on sport, the film industry, and film stars. *Omnibus* featured titles such as "Born Black," "Born British," "Artists in Wartime," and "Marcel Marceau," and *Horizon* offered "Sex Can Be a Problem," "The Making of the Natural History Film," and "How Much Do You Smell?"[10] We can add to this occasional series such as *One Pair of Eyes* (a collection of "personal films") and *Larger Than Life* (a series of half-hour documentaries on unusual people). It is also possible that *The Family* owed as much, if not more, to current affairs programs such as ITV's *This Week* (1956–1992) and the BBC's more populist and personal *Man Alive* (1965–1982). As Anita Biressi and Heather Nunn describe: "Examining 'problem' issues around social and sexual life, *Man Alive* conducted highly personal interviews with ordinary people and provoked tears often enough to attract the label 'sob-umentary' " (65).

It is true that *The Family* provoked debate about questions of privacy and television's role in mediating, and often reshaping, the boundary between public and private (something that has historically been divided *by* the family). From the initial descriptions of the program as a "much-heralded peepshow," to the clear distaste expressed for the "doubtful privilege of displaying [one's] sordid life to the public gaze,"[11] the very idea of Watson's experiment was seen as offending bourgeois sensibilities. When later comparing *The Family* with *Big Brother,* Margaret Wilkins (now Margaret Sainsbury) reminds us how there was "no love-making" and no "filming in the toilet" in 1974.[12] But what is perhaps most striking, from today's perspective at least, is the absence of a confessional tone in *The Family.* For example, Margaret Wilkins's revelation (episode 1) that Christopher was fathered by another man was greeted with outright disgust in the press, with regard both to acceptable sexual morals and to the televisual display of such intimate details. Yet this revelation is imparted as factual information ("now I'll tell you this . . ."), and rather than emerging from a to-camera confessional, it materializes in the course of a kitchen conversation between Margaret Wilkins and Marion's boyfriend, Tom. It was also actually included in a bid to *circumvent* a sensationalist exposé, although this was later undermined by the Wilkinses' prolific extratextual circulation. Margaret Wilkins's ghostwritten book, *A Family Affair,* was serialized in the tabloid newspaper the *Sun,* and it filled in (in the manner of a spicy romance novel) the various infidelities on both sides of the marriage during the years before *The Family* began. But though this may have been a narrative strand woven by the tabloid press, *The Family* itself did not broach intimate sexual matters in the manner of *Man Alive.*

Based on the evidence of *The Family,* this is not, therefore, a culture in which "feeling and emotion have lost much of their private character"—as Frank Furedi describes with respect to the rise of a confessional or therapeutic culture (40). Indeed, the traditional British script of personhood still pivoted on notions of "stoicism, understatement, the stiff upper lip and of fortitude" (Furedi 19). Although there was very little about the Wilkinses that critics and viewers found understated (they often generated hyperbolic reactions), the family still became famous for what was perceived as their ability to deal with the public pressure the serial generated—frequently described as "bearing up." This emphasis emerged largely through comparisons with the American version. Although British critics and viewers and the Wilkinses had not actually seen *An American Family,* it played an important role in the discursive circulation of the British program. The fact that the American version was positioned as instigating the breakup of the Loud family was constantly referred to in British press reports, and the Wilkinses mentioned it often onscreen. The invocation of *An American Family* with such comments as "after television took them apart, the family fell apart"[13] seemed to perform certain functions here. For one, and despite the PBS origins of the American show, it initially produced a reassuring contrast between the apparently excessive and intrusive values of American television and culture and the British sense of public service, restraint, and hardiness. The first *Radio Times* article on *The Family* ran the headline "The Family That Stars Together Sticks Together," which was surely a direct reference to the narrative climax of the American show.[14] The American press dubbed the Loud family "affluent zombies" (Ruoff 12), but it was also predictable, in the context of British popular culture and identity, that *The Family* sought to locate the "ordinary" and the "real" in the context of the stoic and no-nonsense working class. In terms of the perpetual emphasis on the Wilkinses' bearing up in the face of the filming and the fame, we might also note the greater tendency to position television visibility as a trial as much as a privilege. Reflecting on the rise

of the self-reflexive individual (Giddens), Furedi argues that therapy culture did not begin to permeate mainstream British culture until the 1980s,
and in the 1960s and 1970s "Britain was frequently contrasted with the
let-it-all-hang-out ethos of the US" (18). With respect to *An American
Family*, Ruoff indeed outlines how some critics saw the Louds' willingness to share their private lives "as representative of a therapeutic society
thriving on a 'compulsion to confess,' an indication of the weakening of
America's moral fiber" (106).

Although the rise of therapy culture, in which discourses of confession
or therapy are no longer confined to religious or institutionally specific
contexts, was also still in its early stages in the United States, it is certainly
the case that *The Family* still bears the marks of a more traditional conception of the relationships among society, family structure, and identity.
In the individualization thesis, "Stripped of tradition, time/space, class
categories and so on, the basic unit of social reproduction is now claimed
to be the individual" (Adams 7). But as I will show, *The Family* is still
very much entrenched in markers of an older modernity—particularly the
relations among the family, social class, and the State.

A "Serious" Film? Perspective, Performance, Agency

Like *An American Family*, *The Family* was a "blend of seriousness and
sensationalism" (Ruoff 62). That is not to imply that this curious mix
differs from the political possibilities of reality TV today (which can and
does engender heated debate about questions of identity, power, and the
world around us).[15] But the difference lies in the extent to which the social
and political address of the program is actively encoded in the text itself, as
well as in the relationship between the *particular* (the Wilkinses) and the
general (society). What gets flattened out in the positioning of *The Family*
as a precursor to reality TV is the very self-conscious nature of its social
intentions—what Nichols may call its recourse to documentary "discourses
of sobriety" (*Representing* 2)—and the context into which these are placed.
Watson maintained that he "wanted to try and make a serious film about
people contending in an urban society."[16] He hoped that contemporary
political and social events, such as mentions of the recent miners' strike,
the three-day week, and a closely fought election, could be examined in the
context of the Wilkinses' family life (Young 208). In fact, what has been

lost in the recent invocations of the serial as a precursor to reality TV is how it spoke to the social and political context from which it emerged.

Popular constructions of Britain in the 1970s often paint a particularly bleak picture. As Peter Leese puts it, "The fabric of post-war society, which had often been patched up through the first full decade of the post-war age, began to appear threadbare" (67), and notions of consensual collectivism had truly eroded. As was the case elsewhere in the world, Britain was struggling to come to terms with high rates of inflation, and the mid-1970s brought the most severe economic recession since the war (Moore-Gilbert 2). As unemployment increased and British citizens encountered serious threats to their living standards, industrial conflict emerged on a scale unparalleled since the 1920s (Moore-Gilbert 3). (Most notable were the miners' strikes of 1972 and 1973–1974, which effectively brought down Edward Heath's Conservative government.) This represented a sharpening of class divisions and attitudes, and fragmentation could also be seen at the level of gender and race, given that emergent forms (feminism and the women's movement, multiculturalism) clashed with traditional discourses and structures (patriarchy and racism) (Whannel 194).

With respect to class, we have already seen how Watson emphasized the importance of giving the working class a television voice. But the BBC production files indicate how he intended to make a more explicit connection with the resurgence of organized trade union action than actually transpired. According to one memo, Watson was looking for a family with a father "working in industry and subject to collective bargaining for his pay . . . possibly involved in union activities,"[17] and the initial *Radio Times* introduction described how Watson would be using "news and current affairs [programs] to spark off the Wilkinses' comment[s] about what is going on around them"[18] (this never actually happened). Neither Watson nor the Wilkins family professed to specifically left leanings (a Labour government was voted into power in 1974). But it is interesting to speculate about the extent to which Watson's original intentions were shaped, or perhaps circumscribed, by the BBC's long-standing institutional concerns surrounding objectivity and impartiality. After all, the BBC's "Principles and Practice in Documentary Programmes" (1972), which was operative at the time *The Family* was made, was characteristically contradictory: it acknowledged how directing or producing inevitably involved the construction of a point of view, while it also insisted that for a documentary filmmaker "to express his views would be a total abuse of the power platform he controls" (21). In this regard, *The Family,* like any BBC documentary, worked within particular institutional constraints.

References to the wider political context were either brief or indirect. In episode 6, for example, Marion's boyfriend, Tom, comes in from the local pub keen to tell Margaret Wilkins a joke he has heard: "Eh Margaret, you should have been in the pub this morning, when they were on about the politics and that—the state of the nation, now that [Harold] Wilson's got in and that. Some matey came out with a great one. He is the only bloke who, when he goes to the toilet, wears his underpants. . . . That way he doesn't have to look down at the unemployed [they all laugh]" (May 12, 1974). At the same time, given the program's constant emphasis on the housing shortage, questions of welfare provision were implicitly or explicitly present. The Labour government, which was in office from 1974 to 1979, set out to implement its Social Contract agreement. The crux of this was that in recognition of the sacrifice of wage increases, there would be enhanced welfare benefits (Marwick 136). Yet in *The Family* emphasis was constantly placed on inadequate and bureaucratic structures where housing, or more specifically, council housing, was concerned. The emphasis on overcrowding was also aesthetically and formally present in the serial insofar as the observational filming style, and the close proximity between camera and participants, often accentuated the vision of a cramped domesticity. In *An American Family,* the camera frequently left the affluent Louds' "ranch," so spacious and open, to move into different geographical and physical spaces. Yet trips outside the Wilkinses' flat were more brief and infrequent—which further contributed to a sense of physical and social claustrophobia.

A key narrative in the first half of the serial focuses on the efforts of young Gary and Karen to secure a council house, which would enable them to move out of the Wilkinses' cramped flat. Although the officials whom Karen meets at Reading Council are not presented in the same sharply negative light as those in the previous decade's famous documentary-drama, *Cathy Come Home* (BBC, 1966), she is told that they don't have enough points to qualify. (The only way for her to rise up the scale would be to have another child.) Margaret Wilkins then tells Karen that you have to "worry the living daylights out of [the] . . . council these days to get anything," and she goes on to pinpoint further flaws in a system that allows people coming "in from other towns" to usurp homes needed by the residents of Reading.

Perhaps some viewers took heed of Margaret's suggestions. A headline in the *Daily Express* later reported: "Housing row over TV's Wilkins family. A young couple barricaded themselves into their flat after watching the BBC real life television series." Their demonstration protested against Reading Council's insistence that they did not qualify for a council house.[19] But given that despite the pessimistic outlook cast in the early weeks of the serial, Gary and Karen *do* get a council house in episode 6, a debate about the influence of the camera on the events portrayed inevitably ensued. (Did they get the house only because they were on TV?)

But when compared to *Cathy Come Home,* which engendered a national debate on the subject of housing, which in turn led to social reform (see Corner, *Art*), *The Family* did not generate this kind of overtly politicized discourse, which was not central to its circulation and reception. As one critic summed up, the show was often seen as simply being "burdened with the trivial chit-chat of domestic routine," which had "no interest at all to any outsider."[20] I will return to this judgment shortly, but this description now seems particularly striking, given that (compared to popular factual programming today), its discursive relationship with social observation and comment is narratively explicit.

The Family articulated the Wilkinses as subjects who represented social as well as individual identities. This was most apparent in the use of voiceover to frame the background and social position of the family members, especially in the first two episodes. While referred to as observational, Watson's work mixes styles or, rather, demonstrates how television has rarely used observational filmmaking in its "pure" form.[21] In episode 2 we are given more information about Gary's wife, Karen, when Watson explains, "There are many like Karen—ensnared within the trap of low wages, inadequate education, and early marriage" (April 12, 1974). Such moves from the particular to the general were often accompanied by a still shot of the family member. Though perhaps intended to reinforce the sense that the audience is being offered a snapshot of the life of *one* social subject, the aesthetic impression, when the person is caught in the frame, reinforces a kind of ideological containment—especially when compared to the boisterous and vocal identities displayed by the family in the observational sequences. Watson often positioned himself as the omniscient voice of God, the origin of meaning, and the possessor of superior social knowledge. Witness, for example, the events in episode 3, when Heather bluntly rejects the advice of her school careers officer by stating how "half the girls in my class . . . get fed up" (April 19, 1974). (This episode prompted debates in the press about the education system and the age at which youths could leave school.) After we fade to a still of Heather, Watson narrates: "Heather . . . must take her chance in the growing ranks of unemployed youth, for without the certificate she will be prey to every cheap-labour employer. It could be a bleak future." Not only does Watson appear to occupy a superior temporal position (he knows Heather's past, her present, and apparently her future), but he also knows best.

The description of the serial as being "burdened with the trivial chit-chat of domestic routine" privileged the observational sequences—which did represent the program's dominant aesthetic and narrative mode—whereas other critics thought it displayed a clash of styles. Watson's expository contextualization ("There are many like Karen") could abruptly shift to a sequence displaying a domestic squabble, Margaret doing the housework, or young Christopher watching TV. But the judgments cast on the apparent triviality of the domestic routine, as well as the wider perception that Watson's serial was not a serious documentary (which failed to live up to its original aims), are also inflected by a gendered public-private dichotomy. This takes on a particular resonance in relation to contemporary television when we consider how this dichotomy has shaped the perceived relationship between reality TV and the documentary. The terms of discussion—hard/soft, public/private, social/personal, objective/subjective—have often been gendered, and the positioning of the documentary as a "masculine" genre, especially in terms of its relation with the public sphere, is often implicit. In fact, Liesbet van Zoonen has argued that reality TV has been both derided and controversial in part *because* of its flagrant disregard for the historical, gendered division of private-public realms. We might also speculate whether the focus on the domestic has shaped the lack of real scholarly engagement with *The Family*. (And documentary criticism in Britain has in many respects been primarily a male preserve.)

Indeed, this was precisely the time when second-wave feminism was proclaiming that the personal was political, and in watching the serial today, it is difficult not to note the power struggles surrounding the gender roles in *The Family*. As the most dominant member of the family, Margaret

Wilkins tended to be framed as a timeless working-class matriarch, one that might be found in a British soap opera. But the younger relationships (Marion and Tom, Karen and Gary) offer fascinating insights into changing gender expectations, as well as the continued constraints placed on gender roles.[22] In comparison, feminism and the women's movement represented a more explicit discourse in *An American Family*—as can be seen in the narrative impetus of the Louds' divorce. As Ruoff describes it, Pat Loud emerged "as a foil to discuss general issues related to the women's movement," and the release of her autobiography capitalized on this connection, exploring issues of divorce, single motherhood, and sexual liberation (123).

The emphasis on family cohesion in the British program did not lend itself to discussion of gender issues. In fact, when the Scottish Women's Liberation Group proclaimed that, as a strong matriarchal figure, "Mrs. Wilkins has done more for the movement than Germaine Greer or anyone else," she promptly replied, "Look, I don't want to be a celebrity and I'm certainly not one of these women's libbers."[23] This may reflect the extent to which radical feminism in particular was often perceived as an attack on the very concept of the family (which obviously sat uneasily with the focus of Watson's serial). But it may also offer insight into the relationship between feminism and class here. In her weekly column in the *Evening News*, Margaret Wilkins spoke about issues raised by the program, such as sex before marriage (Marion and Tom), the "colour problem" (Heather's boyfriend Melvyn was of mixed race), and the role of the mother-housewife. As she muses in one column:

> Now, I genuinely believe that a housewife can be a great job. It can be much more rewarding for you and your family than if you have to go out to work each day. So many things affect our everyday lives at home—like rising prices, rising rates, house shortages. Just because we are housewives, we don't have to sit at home and let politicians and councillors make decisions to alter our lives without us having any say in them. Look at the great job those housewives in Cowley [Oxford] did in stopping the strike and getting their husbands back to work. I really admire them.[24]

It is tempting to simply read this in hegemonic terms; we don't even know if she wrote the column, and the emphasis on wanting to be an ordinary housewife also seems at odds with her class status and the family's economic position. Nevertheless, her direct reference to the political and economic contexts of the time speaks to how feminism was cut across, and shaped by, discourses of class. The popular image of the bourgeois feminist emphasized the pursuit of individualism, but working-class women (and women in the unions) recognized the importance of solidarity with male class allies, so that their relationship with these discourses was uneasy (Bolt).

In this regard, the extent to which *The Family* engaged with its political context, and what this might mean, could clearly benefit from more debate. This is especially so in light of its perceived relationship with reality TV, and the similarities and differences this comparison might reveal. This seems to be particularly important given that the dominant themes in the critical reception of the program in 1974 were more myopic—focused on the contested "typicality" of the Wilkinses and questions of mediation and performance.

With regard to *An American Family,* Ruoff comments how "critics failed to recognize the mediation involved . . . and talked about the Louds as if they were next-door neighbors" (xxiv). When issues of mediation were recognized, there was generally more emphasis on the significance of mediation at the shooting stage (the effect of the filming on the family's performance) than there was on the postproduction construction of meaning through editing. Although questions of mediation were hardly a marginal concern in the reception of the British serial, it was nevertheless also the case that emphasis was placed primarily on questions of performance rather than postproduction. As the *Times* critic Christopher Dunkley observed, if the "intention is to deliver a certain 'truth' . . . it is succeeding. It is telling the truth about the way an overcrowded family behaves when it has a BBC television crew living in the house for 18 hours a day."[25] Though it might be easy to assume that viewers in this period were less critical and savvy when navigating their way through the complexities of the real, 52 percent of the BBC's viewers apparently rejected the very idea of observational television, agreeing with the statement that "this sort of programme will never work because no matter how often they say they forget the cameras [are there] it just isn't true."[26]

When compared to access programming, *The Family* was evidently not authored by the Wilkins family—something that was occasionally debated by certain critics in the press. But the fact that this strand of debate was subordinate to the emphasis on the family as dramatic agents and performers reflects the extent to which the media debate militated against their association with the role of victim. (This is despite the fact that, as I mentioned earlier, Watson's voiceover often gave this impression). Existing work on *The Family* has noted the often vitriolic reception of the Wilkinses (Corner, *"American Family"*). A filmmaker and supporter of *The Family,* Roger Graef, attributed the reception of the Wilkinses to the fact that to "present British families other British families . . . is to confront them most uncomfortably. And they panic, lest the box turn into a mirror" (773). But as Corner observes, the emphasis on *The Family* as an uncomfortable mirror underrates the extent to which class difference (and distance) pervaded the responses it received (*"American Family,"* 9). The language of the reviews bespeaks a tapestry of class prejudice, and critics discussed sequences in ways that conflated an aesthetic and class distaste. For example, in episode 3, "the camera sniffed around the Wilkinses' establishment, Heather's boyfriend helped her wash her hair (close-up of him ogling her well-developed bosom) while Tom . . . swayed in from the local clutching his pint").[27] It would be something of an understatement to suggest that the Wilkinses became one of the first and most visible constructions of what Corner has since called "the bad ordinary" on television, "one part of the assumed badness of which is the belief that the depiction will encourage a further slide in standards of behaviour and values of living" (Foreword xvii).

Although middle-class critics clearly did not see the serial as a mirror, part of the controversy that surrounded *The Family* did revolve around what was perceived to be its apparent claim to typicality where family life was concerned. Christopher had been fathered by another man, Marion was cohabiting with Tom, Gary had entered into a shotgun wedding with Karen, and Heather had a boyfriend of African and Caribbean descent. Letters and columns debating the typicality of the Wilkinses were plentiful; still more objected to the "real" language used. One viewer, for example, wrote to the BBC to insist that "the average working-class family does not regard illegitimate children as something to be found in every . . . home. . . . Most of all, the women folk in the average working-class family do *not* intersperse most of their conversation with expressions such as 'piss off' and 'arseholes.'"[28] Despite (or perhaps because of) Britain's declining empire status, there were still more anxieties about the image the program would project of Britain overseas.

Watson perpetually maintained that he had never laid claim to a representation of typicality, although it is not difficult to see that this concept was crucial to his project in at least two ways. It established the social ("public") basis for the serial, and it directed attention away from the possibility that the Wilkinses had been selected with their dramatic, or rather sensational, potential in mind. As Margaret Wilkins notes nearly ten years later in the follow-up, *The Family: The After Years* (1983) (screened the same year that the American version was also revisited): "I know why you picked us—because you were bloody lucky. You had everything in one family, didn't you? A girl living with a boyfriend. A couple who were pregnant when they got married. Heather, a teenage young woman . . . going with a coloured fella, and then there was Christopher. So what else did you want?" (December 17, 1983). But times had changed, and what Margaret paints as scandalous was no longer perceived as such. First, when the serial was rescreened in 1983, some critics felt that the boundaries of privacy had been pushed back to such a degree (renegotiated, of course, by television itself) that *The Family* could no longer be of any real interest to the TV audience.[29] Second, although *The Family: The After Years* presented a far less cohesive picture of the family than the 1974 serial, critics hardly batted an eyelid when it came to its ideological implications. All three of the marriages featured in *The Family* had broken down, Heather was a single mother of two, and young Christopher was a jobless teenager in Thatcher's Britain.

But although Margaret Wilkins (now Sainsbury) later described how "being on a documentary like this brings you fame—but of the worst kind. You don't get all the trappings—like money and status," she also insisted that they didn't "regret doing it."[30] Furthermore, as was not the case in the debate surrounding *An American Family*, television itself was not viewed as contributing to the breakdown of the family unit. In fact, the Wilkinses have been far more compliant documentary subjects in this regard, rarely complaining about their representation or television experience. As I noted earlier, certain members of the family (Margaret, Marion, and Heather) have since achieved renewed recognition by appearing in television documentaries or press articles about reality TV. Although this has sometimes contributed to Watson's bid to differentiate the program from recent popular factual programming ("It really was 'reality TV' in those days, but what you see now is not what I call 'reality TV' "),[31] the family's conception of the show is still framed in terms of social access and representation—as set up by Watson and the program itself in the mid-1970s. As Marion comments in a 2005 documentary about ordinary people on television: "We have been part of history, and that's something we never would have been—and we're proud of it."[32]

Framing *The Family*: Generic Discourses and Evaluation

If the Wilkinses were seen as slightly more typical in 1983 than they were in 1974, this perception engages a debate about documentary epistemology (rather than simply ideological constructions of family life). Given that documentaries claim to offer access not to "*a* world, but to *the* world" (Kilborn and Izod 211; emphasis in original), debates about typicality go to the heart of the genre's attempt to produce meaningful accounts of its social environment (Kilborn and Izod 211). In this regard, the initial response to *The Family* would appear to reflect Nichols's conception of a documentary mode of engagement. In *Representing Reality* Nichols famously argues that the distinction between documentary and fiction resides less in markers of textual difference than in the frameworks of viewing brought to the text (24). The viewer of fiction employs "procedures of fictive engagement," whereas the documentary viewer employs "procedures of rhetorical engagement," becoming involved in constant conjecture about the denotative authenticity of the indexical bond between image and reality (28). This represents a practical testing of "subjective responses" ("Life *is* like this, isn't it?" "This is so, *isn't* it?") (114), which is precisely what *The Family* dramatized.

But the advent of popular factual programming has compelled scholars to revisit the question of the aesthetic and cultural distinction between the documentary and fiction. The apparent increase in the fictionalization of factual programming, in which the primacy of "narrative design virtually assumes a life of its own" (Kilborn and Izod 9), is not only seen as a consequence of importing the techniques of fictional drama into factual output; it is also seen as reflecting the shift away from exterior referents in favor of those that are "snugly relocated within the realm of television itself" (Corner, "A Fiction" 92). But this argument cannot easily be separated from the more general sense that television's influence on documentary production has represented a fatal downward spiral in itself. Furthermore, to posit this as a recent shift downplays the long-standing difficulty of defining the documentary as a coherent genre (Kilborn and Izod), while it also ignores the extent to which television genres have always been negotiated on an intertextual level, in relation to surrounding program culture.

Well before there was a need to explore the possibility of a "post-documentary" culture (Corner, "Documentary"), critics in the mid-1970s were discussing the documentary as a somewhat elastic category. As the newspaper critic Christopher Dunkley outlined when *The Family* was released: "The word 'documentary' has become so overworked since television took to the air that it has become almost useless. . . . Even if we limit our pool to what is proclaimed as a documentary, one finds, during the last month, works differing wildly."[33] The BBC Documentary Department also recorded in one meeting in 1973 (commenting on the BBC's own document "Principles and Practice in Documentary Programmes") that documentary producers "work . . . in a changing world. To many, 'Drifters' . . . now appeared to be fiction rather than documentary. If the BBC were to try and formalise a distinction between a documentary programme and a fiction programme, it would have to take account not only of this sliding scale of audience expectations but also of social, cultural and aesthetic considerations on which such a distinction would have to be based."[34] In going on to address the importance of labeling (how programs are promoted, for example, in the *Radio Times*), the discussion at the BBC acknowledges how genres are discursive categories that are not simply the product of inherent textual elements.

Indeed, I began this essay with a quote in which Watson, fighting against popular constructions of reality TV history, seeks to distinguish his work from this devalued generic label. This reflects the extent to which, as recent work on television genres has made clear, generic categories are political: bound up with relations of power. Jason Mittell's *Television and Genre: From Cop Shows to Cartoons* was not the first intervention to argue for a discursive approach to genre (see Neale), but he drew attention to the political significance of generic categories. Far from arriving at a "proper" definition, the goal of genre analysis should be to "focus on the breadth of discursive enunciations around any given instance, mapping out as many articulations of genre as possible and situating them within larger cultural *contexts and relations of power*" (Mittell 174; emphasis added). This reveals how generic discourses are also practices of evaluation (and such judgments are themselves often related to wider discourses, such as gender and class).

The Family was a highly visible cultural site for such a discursive struggle, and it was through this framework that myriad issues, ranging from the social function of the program to the authenticity of its performances, were further negotiated. The BBC's preferred term, used in the *Radio Times,* was "documentary serial," and this label was always applied when the corporation was seeking to shore up its status. For example, the *BBC Handbook of 1974* (an annual publication) emphasized how *despite* the controversy the show had caused, "many viewers took the programme seriously—seeing it as an important social documentary" (7). At the same time, the situation is more generically complex than this at the level of discourse. As Ruoff elaborates, *An American Family* was rarely perceived in relation to the heritage of nonfiction film, and it was only those writing for specialized film magazines who "cited non-fiction precedents with greater frequency" (109). This was also true in the United Kingdom, where publications such as *Sight and Sound* constituted one of few spaces where *The Family*'s relationship with, and significance for, the documentary form was interrogated and explored. Otherwise, *The Family* was compared to and discussed through other generic frames, principally those of soap opera and sitcom.

One of reasons that *The Family* has been positioned as a precursor to the explosion of popular factual programming lies in its serial narrative design, and it is clear that for critics in 1974, serial narrative meant soap. Although British television also screened *Emmerdale Farm* (ITV, 1972–) and *Crossroads* (ITV, 1964–1988), the principal reference point for the British soap was undoubtedly *Coronation Street* (ITV, 1960–), which similarly promised access to the domesticity of working-class life. In explaining how Watson "wanted to do more than real-life soap opera," or how "the Wilkinses got *sud-all* from their real life soap,"[35] the generic category of soap is used to dismiss the form, to pass judgment on its domestic triviality, or to imagine its addicted and emotionally invested viewers. Cementing the generic association with low cultural value, BBC audience research also revealed that, like soap operas, *The Family* was more popular with female viewers than male.[36]

When it came to the reception of *An American Family,* Ruoff observes that, for many critics, the perception of tightly organized stories and narrative drive "grated against the realism of handheld camera and direct sound" (110). The nature of narrative construction in *The Family* was similarly a topic of debate, and the penultimate episode, featuring the wedding of Marion and Tom, undoubtedly focused these discussions: Watson overlaid Tom's last bachelor hours with the song (and the theme) "High Noon," and a deadline—"get him to the church by 3:30." The camera cuts between the separate activities of Marion and Tom, marked by the ticking of a clock. (Watson later described this as a mistake and likened it to a music video).[37] Although the ending of the serial was seen as being unwritten (unlike the American version, the U.K. version continued to be filmed while the first episodes were being broadcast), Marion and Tom's wedding is set up as a key narrative and temporal arc from the start. In episode 2, Marion is pushing Tom to confirm a date for their wedding, which she insists must be "within the next seven weeks." When Tom keeps resisting, she admits, "Apart from [wanting to do it soon] I want it on television. That would mean more to me than anything else" (April 12, 1974). Thus, the serial's narrative climax was all but written.

Critics certainly expressed an antipathy for the serial by invoking its bid to exploit narrative enigmas, whether with regard to an ongoing narrative strand ("Can Marion land superbachelor [Tom]? . . . Why does . . . 15-year-old Heather, so animated outside the home, stand self isolated in a corner whenever the family gathers?"),[38] or its use of cliff-hanger endings. Episode 2, for example, which had tracked the so-far-futile efforts of young Gary and Karen to secure a council house, ends with a letter falling through the mail slot and Watson's voiceover: "A week later, Karen's faith is rewarded. The council reply . . . [credits roll]." But the emphasis on a narrative affinity with soap should be qualified. From today's point of view, and especially when the show is compared to the tightly edited docusoap, it is worth recognizing what Corner describes as *The Family*'s "expanded durations of domestic time," which offer a "relaxed, spacious approach and an engagement with the inconsequential" (*"American Family"* 9). With fades marking out the beginning and end of sequences, it is not always easy to predict its forms of "over-looking and overhearing" (*"American Family"* 9), and there is a greater use of the observational documentary's investment in what elsewhere would be seen as dead time. In light of this, it does not seem that surprising that a good number of critics and viewers were simply bored.[39] But though they reflect a lack of cultural familiarity with texts that depart from the expository style of the documentary, these responses also foreground how fictional expectations were also in operation.

Just as some American critics found that the much-heralded separation of the Louds at the end of *An American Family* fell short of expectations as the narrative climax of the serial, principally because it lacked the "sharp emotional clarity of fiction" (Ruoff 114), so there were complaints that any "interesting narratives" in *The Family* were too quick to "sag into a structureless amble."[40] These judgments also shaped interpretations of *The Family*'s aesthetics. Despite the long heritage of realist television drama in Britain (and *Coronation Street* also provides a reference point here), *The Family* was just as likely to be criticized for lacking the dramatic certainties and aesthetic polish of fiction. It was, for example, apparently "badly lit and poorly photographed" (Young 207).

But fiction entered the interpretative framework here in multiple ways—including assessments of character. Though Watson had aimed to deactivate the referent of fiction by claiming that the program was intended as more than a "real-life soap opera,"[41] he also encouraged it at the level of character construction. The first reviews often quoted Watson's suggestion that he was launching "real-life rivals for the fictional families who inhabit *Coronation Street* and *On the Buses*" (the latter was a popular sitcom of the early 1970s).[42] This invocation of "high" and "low" generic referents may further speak to the serial's aim to expand its potential audience. The opening sequence of *The Family,* which uses snapshots of the participants, may claim to capture the "reality of the time" (Biressi and Nunn 65). But for a good number of critics, it immediately conjured up a fictional referent: it seemed to deliberately ape the opening titles of *Coronation Street*. In both shows the camera moves in, swooping over rows of rooftops before focusing on the domestic existence of particular characters inside.

Comedy was also a highly visible genre by which *The Family* was framed. In comparison with other generic referents, however, this was a framework that was often used to praise, rather than to dismiss, the program. As a critic in the *Guardian* noted early on: "An unexpected thing about the BBC's fly-on-the-wall series is that it is extremely funny. . . . The Wilkinses are in a pure and lineal line of descent from *The Glums* through the Garnets [featured in the sitcom *'Til Death Do Us Part*]. They are an incorrigible, resilient, irresistible lot clouted and comforted by their mother, Margaret Wilkins."[43] The *Daily Mirror* article "Fun in the Family Way" agreed, suggesting that "one of the things that has made the family consistently watchable has been that . . . they have been comic. Not dreary . . . but bouncy, combative, cheeky and funny."[44] In terms of the use of comedy as an interpretative as well as evaluative frame, critics frequently recalled and quoted comic scenes, including dialogue excerpts, punch lines, and self-directed "audience" reaction. This is certainly not separate from the class prejudice that structured the critical reception of the program, as such comments pivot on the tradition of treating "the working classes [on television] as though they are inherently amusing" (Root 96). But though the difference between laughing *at* and laughing *with* is inevitably blurred here, it would be rash to dismiss these generic discourses as simply further evidence of the class prejudice directed at the family.

According to BBC audience research, and in stark contrast to those who were simply bored, some claimed to watch "merely to see what hilarious situations this maniacal family will get into this week."[45] Given the centrality of fiction here, we might have expected the emphasis on comedy to increase the concern about authenticity and performance in *The Family*. But this was not the case. Recurrent critical comments such as "we have to pinch ourselves to remember that this is not the figment of some scriptwriter's imagination"[46] demonstrate how the interpretative frame of comedy was used to bolster the emphasis on an authentic spontaneity, at the same time expressing an appreciation of its entertainment possibilities. Watching *The Family* is like watching comedy, but it is *better*—funnier—because the material is seen to emerge from "real life." Despite the sitcom's often low cultural status as a genre, comedy was specifically invoked to express an approval for the authenticity of the program; its relation to the documentary was cited to suggest just the opposite. After all, "documentary truth" in *The Family* was described as "the way an overcrowded family behaves when it has a BBC television crew living in the house for 18 hours a day."[47]

In his piece "Finding Data, Reading Patterns, Telling Stories: Issues in the Historiography of Television," Corner describes the "double dangers" of television historiography—the pitfalls of an "over-distanced approach" (in which the past is "another country"), and the problem of an "undue proximity" (the past as "today with oddities") (277). In terms of popular constructions of reality TV's genealogy, it was the potential for an "undue proximity" that provided the impetus for this archival excavation of *The Family*. Of course, in approaching the serial with this discursive weight in mind, we are predisposed to ask certain questions of *The Family* (questions of the "real," of ordinary people and agency, of generic hybridity). This is thus very far from what Jason Jacobs, in his discussion in "The Television Archive: Past, Present and Future," describes as the importance of "blind searching, rogue searching, or 'chancing it' in the hope that something relevant will turn up" (18). Indeed, in terms of understanding what is new about reality TV (and perhaps what is not), an alternative approach might involve scouring TV schedules and newspaper reviews for the unexpected and the forgotten. But it is precisely in such sites of reception that we can see and feel changing attitudes to the television themes mentioned above, which are rarely available in the text itself.

This essay has also used *The Family*'s extratextual framework to think about the historical specificity of generic discourses and their functions. When Ruoff observes that *An American Family* was infrequently discussed in relation to nonfiction film, a situation paralleled by the reception of *The Family*, the implication is that this demonstrated a lack of critical recognition (109). This is certainly a possible interpretation, but especially when examined in relation to debates surrounding reality TV, it also reifies a generic hierarchy that relies on an idealized conception of the documentary form (and sees apparently fictionalizing attributes as a regrettable slide toward trivialization). If *The Family* is indeed to be seen as a precursor to contemporary popular factual programming, then there may be much to learn from the deft interpretative maneuvers it solicited between fact and fiction, as well as its rejuggling of the traditional generic hierarchies that circulate in and around reality TV.

Readers may well have made up their own minds about *The Family*'s historical positioning, and about Watson's reluctant status as "the godfather of Reality TV." But at the level of historiography and reality TV scholarship, I hope that few would argue with the premise that an "enriched sense of 'then' produces, in its differences and commonalities combined, a stronger and more imaginative sense of 'now'" (Corner, "Finding Data" 275).

Notes

1. The first episode of the serial can be viewed at www.screenonline.org.uk/tv/id/444743/index.html.

2. "I'd Do Anything to Get on TV," Channel 4, broadcast April 20, 2005.

3. *Daily Telegraph,* July 1, 1974.

4. This was undertaken at the BBC Written Archive Centre, Caversham, Reading, U.K. The research involved consulting internal BBC documents, such as production memos and audience research reports, as well as an extensive collection of press reviews and articles.

5. Paul Watson to David Wheeler in BBC's New York Office, October 18, 1973, TV Central: Documentaries: The Family: General, BBC Written Archive Centre (WAC).

6. "New Real-Life Documentary Serial for BBC," BBC press release, March 11, 1974, WAC, T66/55.

7. "Public Access Television," *Australian Financial Review,* June 29, 1973.

8. See "Joe Sieder, 'Fly on the Wall' TV," www.screenonline.org.uk/tv/id/698785/index.html.

9. *BBC Handbook, 1979,* 3.

10. Ibid.

11. Richard Afton, "The Family," *Evening News,* July 4, 1974.

12. "I'd Do Anything to Get on TV."

13. "Family of Six to Star in New TV Series," *Times,* March 12, 1974, 16.

14. "The Family That Stars Together Sticks Together," *Radio Times,* March 28, 1974, 9.

15. In January 2007 the British version of *Celebrity Big Brother* prompted a near-global debate about racism (in the wake of the apparent racist bullying of the Bollywood star Shilpa Shetty), and *Hell's Kitchen* provoked a furor over homophobia (and the apparent bullying of the reality star Brian Dowling).

16. Transcript of *Speakeasy* radio show, July 6, 1974.

17. BBC Families Project, undated note, TV Central: Documentaries: The Family: General, WAC.

18. "The Family That Stars Together."

19. *Daily Express,* June 16, 1974.

20. Peter Knight, "The Family," *Daily Telegraph,* June 14, 1974.

21. This was also following the pattern of *An American Family;* see Ruoff 45.

22. Karen's domestic and familial isolation emerges as a constant narrative undercurrent in the serial.

23. "The Woman Who Became the Best Known Mother in Britain Overnight," *Daily Mail,* April 5, 1974.

24. Margaret Wilkins, "If Only I Could Be an Ordinary Housewife," *Evening News,* May 10, 1974.

25. Christopher Dunkley, "What Is Truth?" *Times,* May 1, 1974.

26. "The Family: How Viewers Reacted and What Functions the Viewing of It Performed for Them," survey conducted by BBC, WAC, 6.

27. William Marshall, "Nice One Heather . . . and Mum," *Daily Mail,* April 18, 1974.

28. *Radio Times,* July 13–19, 1974, letter held in WAC, T66/155/1.

29. *Daily Mail,* September 17, 1983.

30. "Where Did the Family Go?" *Sunday Mirror,* February 2, 1986, 9.

31. "I'd Do Anything to Get on TV."

32. Ibid.

33. Dunkley, "What Is Truth?"

34. Colin Young, extract from minutes of meeting, July18, 1973, "Principles and Practice in Documentary Programmes," BBC file R78/2,623/1.

35. Ben Thompson, *New Musical Express,* July 30, 1988, 23 (emphasis added).

36. "The Family: How Viewers Reacted," 22.

37. "I'd Do Anything to Get on TV."

38. *Daily Mail,* April 4, 1974.

39. "The Family: How Viewers Reacted," 24.

40. "The Family," *Daily Mirror,* May 29, 1974.

41. Thompson, *New Musical Express.*

42. "Stars of New TV Family Series—A Family," *Guardian,* March, 12, 1974.

43. "The Family," *Guardian,* April 4, 1974.

44. "Fun in the Family Way," *Daily Mirror,* June 27, 1974.

45. Audience research report on *The Family,* June 17, 1974, WAC.

46. *Daily Telegraph,* June 5, 1974.

47. Dunkley, "What Is Truth?"

Works Cited

Adams, Matthew. *Self and Social Change.* London: Sage, 2007.

Biressi, Anita, and Heather Nunn. *Reality TV: Realism and Revelation.* London: Wallflower Press, 2005.

Bolt, Christine. *Sisterhood Questioned? Race, Class and Internationalism in the American and British Women's Movements, 1880s–1970s.* London: Routledge, 2004.

Corner, John. "*An American Family* and *The Family.*" *Fifty Key Television Programmes.* Ed. Glen Creeber. London: Arnold, 2004. 6–10.

———. *The Art of Record.* Manchester: Manchester University Press, 1996.

———. "Documentary in a Post-Documentary Culture? A Note on Forms and Their Functions," www.1boro.ac.uk/research/changing.media/John%20Corner%20paper.htm.

———. "Finding Data, Reading Patterns, Telling Stories: Issues in the Historiography of Television." *Media, Culture and Society* 25 (2003): 273–280.

———. "A Fiction (Un)Like Any Other?" *Critical Studies in Television* 1.1 (Spring 2006): 89–96.

———. Foreword. *Big Brother International: Formats, Critics and Publics.* Ed. Ernest Mathijs and Janet Jones. London: Wallflower Press, 2004. xii–xvii.

Furedi, Frank. *Therapy Culture: Cultivating Uncertainty in an Uncertain Age.* London: Routledge, 2004.

Geraghty, Christine. *Women and Soap Opera.* Cambridge: Polity, 1991.

Giddens, Anthony. *Modernity and Self-Identity.* Cambridge: Polity, 1991.

Graef, Roger. "Skeletons on the Box." *New Society,* June 27, 1974, 772–773.

Hoggart, Paul. "Through a Glass, Darkly." *Times,* November 18, 2006, http://entertainment.timesonline.co.uk/tol/arts_and_entertainment/tv_and _radio/article632954.ece (accessed October 10, 2007).

Holmes, Su. " 'Riveting and Real—A Family in the Raw': (Re)visiting *The Family* (1974) after Reality TV," *International Journal of Cultural Studies* 11.2 (June 2008): 193–210.

Jacobs, Jason. "The Television Archive: Past, Present, Future." *Critical Studies in Television* 1.1 (2006): 13–20.

Kilborn, Richard, and John Izod. *An Introduction to Television Documentary: Confronting Reality.* Manchester: Manchester University Press, 1997.

Leese, Peter. *Britain since 1945: Aspects of Identity.* Basingstoke: Palgrave Macmillan, 2006.

Marwick, Arthur. *Culture in Britain since 1945.* Oxford: Basil Blackwell, 1991.

Mittell, Jason. *Television and Genre: From Cop Shows to Cartoons.* London: Routledge, 2004.

Moore-Gilbert, Bart. "Introduction: Cultural Closure or Post-Avant-Gardism? *The Arts in the 1970s: Cultural Closure?* Ed. Moore-Gilbert. London: Routledge, 1994. 1–28.

Neale, Steve. "Questions of Genre." *Screen* 31.1 (1990): 45–66.

Nichols, Bill. *Blurred Boundaries: Questions of Meaning in Contemporary Culture.* Bloomington: Indiana University Press, 1994.

———. *Representing Reality: Issues and Concepts in Documentary.* Bloomington: Indiana University Press, 1991.

Root, Jane. *Open the Box: About Television.* London: Comedia, 1986.

Ruoff, Jeffrey. *"An American Family": A Televised Life.* Minneapolis: University of Minnesota Press, 2002.

Thomas, James. " 'Bound in by History': The Winter of Discontent in British Politics, 1979–2004." *Media, Culture and Society* 29.2 (2007): 263–283.

van Zoonen, Liesbet. "Desire and Resistance: *Big Brother* and the Recognition of Everyday Life." *Media, Culture and Society* 23.5 (2004): 669–677.

Watson, Paul. "The Slow Death of Inquiry." *New Statesman,* December 4, 2006, 22.

Whannel, Garry "Boxed In: Television in the 1970s." *The Arts in the 1970s: Cultural Closure?* Ed. Bart Moore-Gilbert. London: Routledge, 1994. 177–197.

Young, Colin. "The Family." *Sight and Sound* 43.4 (Spring 1974): 206–211.

LEIGH H. EDWARDS

Reality TV and the American Family

Reality television shows are reframing ideas of the family in U.S. culture. The genre titillates by putting cultural anxieties about the family on display, hawking images of wife swapping, spouse shopping, and date hopping. Its TV landscape is dotted with programs about mating rituals, onscreen weddings, unions arranged by audiences, partners testing their bonds on fantasy dates with others, family switching, home and family improvement, peeks into celebrity households, parents and children marrying each other off on national television, and families pitching their lives as sitcom pilots. Though obviously not the only recurring theme pictured, family is one of the genre's obsessions. Scholars have begun to draw attention to certain questions surrounding family, gender, and sexuality, but we have yet to address fully how the genre debates and reshapes the family or to account for the centrality of that theme in reality programming. This discussion of the family is important, since TV has always played such a vital role in both shaping and reflecting fantasies of the American family.

Using historicized textual analysis, this essay demonstrates how the reality TV genre both reflects and helps shape changing "American family" ideals. A significant number of reality shows picture a seemingly newfound family diversity. For every traditional "modern nuclear family," with its wage-earning father, stay-at-home mother, and dependent children, we see a panoply of newer arrangements, such as post-divorce, single-parent, blended, and gay and lesbian families. What is the significance of this family diversity as a recurring theme in factual programming? Concurrent with images of demographic change, we also see a familiar rhetoric of the "family in crisis." Witness the emergency framework of *Nanny 911* (a British nanny must save inept American parents who are at their breaking point) or *Extreme Makeover: Home Edition* (a design team must renovate the home of a family otherwise facing disaster). Their premise is that the American family is in trouble. Many scholars have noted how the family has constantly been described as being in crisis throughout its historical development—with the calamity of the moment always reflecting contemporaneous sociopolitical tensions (Gordon 3). The idea of crisis has been used to justify "family values" debates, which usually involve public policy and political rhetoric that uses moral discourses to define what counts as a healthy family.

I would argue that reality programs focused on the familial settings and themes implicitly make their own arguments about the state of the American family, entering long-running family values debates. In their representation of family diversity (which different series laud or decry) and in their use of family crisis motifs, reality narratives capture a sense of anxiety and ambivalence about evolving family life in the United States. Reality TV markets themes about our current period of momentous social change: the shift from what sociologists term the "modern family," the nuclear model that reached its full expression in the context of Victorian-era industrialization and peaked in the postwar 1950s, to the "postmodern family," a diversity of forms that have emerged since then. Indeed, a key theme in reality TV depictions is that family is now perpetually in process or in flux, open to debate. Social historians define the modern family as a nuclear unit with a male breadwinner, female homemaker, and dependent children; its gendered division of labor was largely only an option historically for the white middle class whose male heads of household had access to the "family wage."[1] This form was naturalized as universal but was never the reality for a majority of people, even though it was upheld as a dominant cultural ideal.[2] Diverse arrangements have appeared since the 1960s and 1970s, constituting what the historian Edward Shorter termed "the postmodern family." New familial forms have emerged, spurred by increases in divorce rates and single-parent households, women's entrance into the labor force in large numbers after 1960, the decline of the "family wage," and the pressures on labor caused by postindustrialism and by globalization.[3]

Taken as a whole, reality series about the family alter some conventional familial norms while reinforcing others. I would agree with critics such as Tania Modleski and Sherrie A. Inness, who argue that popular culture texts that address issues such as gendered roles and the real contradictions in women's lives often both challenge and reaffirm traditional values (Modleski 7–9, Inness 178–179). These reality programs picture some updated norms (frequently, the edited narratives validate wider definitions of familial relations or urge men to do more domestic labor). The genre's meditation on the shift in norms is not radical, however, because it occurs within TV's liberal pluralism framework. Various programs construct their own sense of the contradictions of family life, such as tensions involving women juggling work and child care, gender role renegotiations, further blurring of public and the private "separate sphere" ideologies, racialized family ideals, and fights about gay marriage. Such shows celebrate conflict, spectacularizing fraught kinship issues as a family circus in order to draw more viewers and advertising, but they most often resolve the strife into a liberal pluralist message by episode's end (for example, using the liberal discourse of individualism to represent racism as an interpersonal conflict that can be resolved between individuals through commonsense appeals rather than as a structural social issue).[4]

I would contextualize these themes both in terms of television's long history as a domestic medium and in reference to ongoing family values battles. The new household models and demographic changes, such as increased divorce rates, sparked a political backlash beginning in the 1970s: the family values media debates that have intensified since the 1990s. These skirmishes, such as Dan Quayle's attack on the sitcom character Murphy Brown as a symbol of unwed motherhood in the 1992 presidential debates, are an important sociohistorical context for the current reality programming trend. For my purposes here, I date the full advent of the current genre to the premiere of MTV's *The Real World* in 1992, although related forerunners like police and emergency nonfiction series emerged in the late 1980s, and factual programming has, of course, been around since the medium's origins.[5] Though critics debate the looseness of the term *reality* TV as a genre, I use it to refer to factual programming with key recurring generic and marketing characteristics (such as unscripted, low-cost, edited formats featuring a mix of documentary and fiction genres, often to great ratings success).

The links between TV and the family are foundational, as long-running research on television and the family has established. The television historian Lynn Spigel has shown how early TV developed coextensively with the postwar suburban middle-class families that the medium made into its favored topic and target audience. The historian Stephanie Coontz has noted how current nostalgia for the nuclear family ideal is filtered through

All in the Family (CBS) ran from 1971 to 1979. Shown here are Carroll O'Connor as Archie Bunker and Sammy Davis Jr. in a guest appearance on the show. The series was known for its socially relevant programming targeted to middle-class white audiences. Courtesy of CBS/PhotoFest.

1950s domestic sitcoms like *Leave It to Beaver.*[6] As critics have illustrated, family shows comment not only on society's basic organizing unit but also on demographic transformations by tracing their influence on the family. Ella Taylor traces a family crisis motif in 1970s series such as *All in the Family, The Jeffersons,* and *One Day at a Time,* noting network efforts to generate socially "relevant" programming to grab a targeted middle-class demographic as well as to respond to social changes prompted by the women's and civil rights movements (2–3). Herman Gray, likewise, in *Watching Race,* has detailed assimilationist messages, reflecting prevailing social discourses, in portraits of black families in the 1980s, like *The Cosby Show.* I demonstrate how reality TV opens a fresh chapter in TV's long-running love affair with the family—the medium has birthed a new genre that grapples with the postmodern family condition.

Reality TV mines quarrels about family life, producing, for example, gay dating shows (such as *Boy Meets Boy,* 2003) at the precise moment of national deliberations over gay marriage. The genre sinks its formidable teeth into these controversies. Much as domestic sitcoms did in the 1950s, it gives us new ways of thinking about familial forms in relationship to identity categories like gender and sexuality or to larger concepts like citizenship and national identity. It does so in part by illuminating the cultural tensions underlying family values debates, such as the family's contested nature as a U.S. institution that legitimates social identities, confers legal and property rights, and models the nation imagined as a family, whether a "house united" or a "house divided."

Tracing recurring tropes in reality programs about the family, I would argue for four key narrative stances toward social change: nostalgia for the traditional modern nuclear family; promotion of a new, modified nuclear family norm in which husband and wife both work outside the home; a tentative, superficial embrace of family pluralism in the context of liberal pluralism; and an open-ended questioning of norms that might include a more extensive sense of family diversity. These narrative trends are particularly evident in some specific reality subgenres: family-switching shows (*Trading Spouses, Wife Swap, Black.White, Meet Mister Mom*); observations of family life (*The Real Housewives of Orange County; Little People, Big World*); celebrity family series (*The Osbournes, Run's House, Meet the Barkers, Being Bobby Brown, Breaking Bonaduce, Hogan Knows Best*); home and family makeover programs (*Extreme Makeover: Home Edition, Renovate My Family*); family workplace series (*Dog the Bounty Hunter, Family Plots, Family Business*); family gamedocs (*Things I Hate about You, Race to the Altar, Married by America, The Will, The Family*); parenting series (*Nanny 911, Supernanny, Showbiz Moms and Dads*); and historical reenactment programs with family settings (*Colonial House, Frontier House*).

These programs watch middle-class "average joes," perhaps the viewer's friends and neighbors, navigate the shoals of domesticity, grappling with cultural problems such as the tension between kinship and chosen bonds, the effect of the media on the family, and the state's efforts to define "family" as a matter of national concern and to legislate access to marriage rights. Ultimately, these shows convey a kind of emotional engagement, what Ien Ang would term "emotional realism," regarding changes in family structures in the United States, capturing a recent shift in middle-class attitudes toward the American family, a change in what Raymond Williams would call that group's "structure of feeling" (Ang 47).

Narrative Tropes

Reality TV spectacularizes such issues as a family circus in order to draw viewers and sell advertising. Part of its vast ratings appeal stems from the fact that it portrays real people struggling with long-running cultural problems that have no easy answers: tensions in the ties that bind, between kinship and chosen bonds, between tradition and change; personal versus social identity; and competing moralities. The genre explores angst about what "the American family" is in the first place.[7] Such widespread worries are not surprising, given that this unit is a social construction that is notoriously difficult to define, particularly since it has historically encoded gendered roles and hierarchies of class, race, and sexuality that define ideas of social acceptance, a crucible for selfhood and nationhood. Critics have noted the regulatory nature of the modern nuclear family model, and official discourse has traditionally framed that unit as a white, middle-class heterosexual norm to which citizens should aspire (Chambers).

Reality TV does not explicitly solve those family values disputes. Instead, it concentrates on mining the conflict between the two familial forms, one residual and one emergent. Rather than answering questions about what the postmodern family will become, it rehearses sundry arguments about how the familial unit is getting exposed, built up, torn down, and redefined. Some programs offer wish-fulfillment fantasies, smoothing over rancorous public squabbles and social changes but not resolving those tensions.

For example, Bravo's *Things I Hate about You* (2004), reflecting this panoply, turns domesticity into a sport in which snarky judges determine which member of a couple is more annoying to live with and partners happily air their dirty laundry on TV (sometimes literally). One week we see an unmarried heterosexual couple with no children, the next a gay domestic partnership. No one model dominates. The series fits all these groupings into the same narrative framework: a story about family and the daily irritations of domesticity. Other reality programs chart a fading modern nuclear family ideal. The dating show subgenre continues to spawn a vast number of formats and high audience ratings. While series like *The Bachelor* romanticize young people trying to find their "true love," marry, have children, and embody the traditional family ideals of their parents' generation, they also implicitly register the shifting of those norms, not least because the cast members also see the overwhelming majority of these arranged TV couplings and engagements dissolve, just as more than 50 percent of marriages in the United States end in divorce.[8]

Trends in Reality TV's Textual Representations of the Family

Drawing on the sociopolitical and media history of the family values debates, reality TV offers viewers the voyeuristic chance to peer into other people's households to see how all this cultural ruckus is affecting actual families. As the genre takes up the modern and postmodern family in various ways, it often explicitly engages with public policy and media discussions. The way reality serials address familial life illuminates an uneasy shift from modern nuclear family ideals to the postmodern reality of diverse practices.

One main trend in reality programming is for series to look backward with a nostalgia for the modern nuclear family that reveals the instability of that model. Some series revert to older concepts, such as the sociologist Talcott Parsons's mid-twentieth-century theories of functional and dysfunctional family forms. He argued that the modern nuclear family's function under industrialized capitalism was to reproduce and socialize children into dominant moral codes, as well as to define and promote norms of sexual behavior and ideas of affective bonds associated with companionate marriage. Dysfunctional families that deviated from norms were functionalism's defining "Other," and some critics argue that this paradigm still influences sociological research on family life (Stacey, *In the Name of the Family;* Chambers 1–32; Every). Pop psychology concepts of functionalism and dysfunctionalism certainly circulate widely in today's mass media, and we see their influence in reality shows.

A particularly apt example is the spouse-swapping subgenre, which includes shows like ABC's *Wife Swap.* The titillating title implies it will follow the wild exploits of swingers, but the show instead documents strangers who switch households and parenting duties for a short period. Similarly, on Fox's *Trading Spouses: Meet Your New Mommy* (the copycat show that beat ABC's to the air), two parents each occupy the other's home for several days. Both series focus on the conflict between households, revealing a fierce debate among participants as to whose family is healthier, more "normal," or more "functional." On *Trading Spouses,* one two-part episode swaps mothers from white suburban nuclear families, each comprising a husband, a wife, two kids, and a dog ("Bowers/Pilek"). Both clans want to claim modern nuclear family functionality for themselves, but economic tensions ensue, even though each woman describes her family as middle class. A California mom with an opulent beach house judges her Massachusetts hosts, with their modest home and verbal fisticuffs, as unkempt, whereas her outspoken counterpart deems the beach household materialistic and emotionally disconnected. Each woman characterizes the other family as dysfunctional. Their conflict reveals not only the degree to which many people still use these older ideals as their own measuring sticks, here staged as issues such as tidiness or appropriate levels of emotional closeness, but also the tenuousness of those ideals, given the intense contradictions between two supposedly functional families.

Through the premise of swapping households or roles for several days, these programs explore Otherness by having participants step into someone else's performance of kinship behaviors. In so doing, they illuminate identity categories that are performed through the family. This dynamic was perhaps most notably executed on the series *Black.White,* which used makeup to switch a white and black family for several weeks and staged racial tensions between them. In this subgenre more generally, participants reproduce a version of their counterparts' social identity. Thus, the switch highlights the arbitrariness of such identity performances. Since the shows allow the participants to judge each other, family appears as a topic of open-ended debate.

These programs depend on conflict generated by social hierarchies of race, class, gender, and sexuality, and they privilege white male heteronormativity. Their narratives often focus on gender, encouraging men to take on more child care and domestic chores. Yet they still rely on ideologies of gender difference to explain household units and to reaffirm the mother's role as nurturer-caregiver. By absenting the mother, the wife-swap series imply that husbands and kids will learn to appreciate the woman of the house more.

These series encourage a liberal pluralist resolution to conflicts, one that upholds an easy humanist consensus, or what critics term "corporate multiculturalism," which markets diversity as another product rather than picturing and validating substantive cultural differences. The framing narratives resolve competing ideas, most often by defining as normal a modified modern nuclear family (two working parents). In shows about alternative households, for example, the narratives sympathize with the single mom or the lesbian couple but uphold the intact nuclear family as more rational and functional. Yet the narratives also often critique participants' overly intense nostalgia for the bygone modern nuclear ideal, and they sometimes allow for some validation of alternative models, such as an African American extended family. They depend on sensationalism and conflict over values to spark ratings.

This open warfare over functional and dysfunctional families includes a huge helping of nostalgia, as epitomized by a series like MTV's *The Osbournes*. This hit show supports the sense that if the modern nuclear ideal has been replaced by a diversity of family forms, U.S. culture still has an intense nostalgia for the older norm. Is nostalgia for the fantasy nuclear unit actually a defining characteristic of the postmodern family? It is for *The Osbournes*. Viewers flocked to the show because it juxtaposes a famously hard-living, heavy-metal family with classic sitcom family plotlines, edited to emphasize the irony of seeing the cursing, drug-abusing rock star Ozzy and his brood hilariously butchering *Ozzie and Harriet*–style narratives.

The entertainment press dubbed them "America's favorite family," and a series of high-profile magazine cover stories tried to explain the show's wild popularity by pointing to how the Osbournes "put the fun in dysfunctional." The show garnered MTV's highest-rated debut at that time and enjoyed some of the strongest ratings in the channel's history during its run from 2002 until 2005.[9] Part of the appeal lies in how the Osbournes seem to capture on videotape a more accurate sense of the pressures of family life, ranging from sibling rivalry to teen sex and drug use to a serious illness (such as Sharon's cancer diagnosis and treatment). Even though their fame and fortune make them unlike home viewers, the family can be related to because of the struggles they confront openly. Likewise, they reflect current family diversity because they are a blended family; their brood includes their son and two daughters (one of whom declined to appear on the series), Ozzy's son from his first marriage, and their children's teen friend whom they adopted during the show after his mother died of cancer. Ozzy himself suggested that he did the series in order to expand understandings of the family: "What is a functional family? I know I'm dysfunctional by a long shot, but what guidelines do we all have to go by? *The Waltons*?" (Hedegaard 33). Ozzy here is both arbiter and agent; he notes TV's power to define a range of meanings for the family, whether through the Waltons or the Osbournes.

Yet even while the program's narrative meditates on entertaining dysfunctionality and new family realities, it also continuously tries to recuperate the Osbournes as a functional nuclear family. Story arcs are edited to frame them as dysfunctional (cursing parents, wild fights, teenage drug use), but also to rescue them as functional; there are sentimental shots of the family gathered together in their kitchen or clips of them expressing their love and loyalty despite the titillating fights. Even though Ozzy tells his family they are "all f—ing mad," in the same breath he says he "loves them more than life itself" ("A House Divided"). The edited narrative purposefully emphasizes the bonds of hearth and home, sometimes trying to establish functionality by cutting out serious family events that would have made Parsons blanch: Ozzy's drug relapse, severe mental illness, and nervous breakdown during taping; trips to rehab by Jack and Kelly, the son and daughter; and Sharon's temporary separation from Ozzy over these issues. Press coverage of the show and fan response likewise emphasized a recuperative dynamic, both looking for the loveable, reassuring nuclear family beneath the rough exterior. As an *Entertainment Weekly* cover story noted, Ozzy Osbourne went from being boycotted by parents' groups in the 1980s for bat biting and supposedly Satanic lyrics to being asked for parenting advice from men's magazines (Miller). Thus, even while registering the limitations of Parsons's model, the series still tries to rehabilitate this celebrity family as functional. As a result, this program and others like it explore the postmodern family, but at the same time they look back wistfully on the old modern nuclear paradigm.

The Osbournes is also a prime example of a program that explicitly comments on the influence of television on family ideals. Part of the show's insight comes from registering how much the media, whether the popular music industry or television, have shaped this family unit. Brian Graden, then president of MTV Entertainment, described the program's draw as "the juxtaposition of the fantastical rock-star life with the ordinary and the everyday"; summarizing one episode, he laughed, "Am I really seeing Ozzy Osbourne trying to turn on the vacuum cleaner?" Graden noted that after they collected footage on the Osbournes, producers realized that "a lot of these story lines mirrored classic domestic sitcom story lines, yet with a twist of outrageousness that you wouldn't believe" (Miller).

Watching footage of their daily experiences, Graden immediately views them through the lens of earlier TV sitcoms; everywhere he looks, he sees the Cleavers on speed. And the show Graden's company makes of this family's life might one day comprise the plotlines other viewers use to interpret their own experiences in some way. After their smash first season, the Osbournes were feted at the White House Correspondents' dinner and managed to parlay such national attention into more entertainment career opportunities, with a new MTV show, *Battle for Ozzfest* (2004–), hosted by Sharon and Ozzy and featuring bands competing to join their summer tour; Sharon's syndicated talk show that ran for one season (2003–2004); and their children's slew of TV, movie, and music ventures growing out of their exposure from the reality program.

Though most families could not follow the Osbournes into celebrity, what many do share with the rockers is the knowledge that TV significantly shapes familial ideals. This media awareness marks a parenting trend. In their recent audience study of family television-viewing practices, Stewart M. Hoover, Lynn Schofield Clark, and Diane F. Alters found that parents had a highly self-reflexive attitude toward the media. They were well conscious of how the mass media both reflect and shape social beliefs, and they worried about the daily influence of television in their children's lives. Hoover et al. identified this media anxiety as part of what they term "self-reflexive parenting" behaviors stemming from increased concerns about child rearing since the 1960s. They see this model of parenting as part of what Anthony Giddens calls the project of self-reflexivity in modernity, in which people are reflective about their interaction with the social world as they continually incorporate mediated experiences into their sense of self (Hoover et al., Giddens).

The two most prominent parenting shows, *Nanny 911* and *Supernanny,* portray a severe tension between modern nuclear ideals and postmodern variations. They suggest that threats from within and outside the American family are destabilizing it to the extent that it must be saved by the no-nonsense child-rearing philosophies of its colonial parent, dispatched in the form of a Mary Poppins–style nanny. They implicitly refer to nineteenth-century domestic science ideals as well as mid-twentieth-century sociological theories, such as Talcott Parsons's schema of functionalism and dysfunctionalism. As a case study, these shows clarify how anxiety about expertise and professionalism contributes to consumer behavior (hire a nanny to fix your unruly children, buy the series' tie-in books as magic talismans). They relate to other programs, such as the Learning Channel's suite of shows about parenting and childbirth, all of which resort to expert advice and affirm conventional modern nuclear family forms. They demonstrate how reality programming can be framed as a pedagogical site. As Annette Hill has found, many viewers see reality TV as an opportunity for social learning. Ron Becker has shown that these nanny programs also display neoliberal rhetorics because they focus on the need for the family to be autonomous to help legitimate the shift to post-welfare-state governance in contemporary America.

By way of contrast, there is a more marginal satire of parenting found in Bravo's suite of shows *Showbiz Moms and Dads, Sportkids Moms and Dads,* and *Showdog Moms and Dads.* These programs follow parents whom the edited narratives present as overly protective or controlling. They spend too much on consumer goods, live their dreams vicariously through their kids, suffer from intractable generational tensions, and sometimes treat their pets like children to an extreme extent. The shows denaturalize parenting behaviors and elucidate them as performative roles. This ironic treatment fits Bravo's marketing and target audiences.

Moving from parenting to a different element of domestic science rhetoric, home makeover shows establish an ideological tie between a rationalized home and a healthy family, a connection further blurring the traditional public-private split. In the blockbuster *Extreme Makeover: Home Edition* and its short-lived imitator, *Renovate My Family,* teams of experts evaluate family life, advising participants and home viewers alike in family values as they anxiously gauge new household forms. On both series, it is families that depart from the modern nuclear norm that need assistance (single-parent, blended, impoverished, orphaned).

Instead of advocating government aid in the form of low-income housing or social welfare safety nets, these series perform a kind of neo-liberal privatization and outsourcing, which speaks to a diminishing public sphere. Through the largesse of their corporate advertisers, these programs will provide needy families with domestic palaces and consumer goods that will effortlessly heal any family troubles. In the case of *Renovate My Family,* the program uses pop psychology (and the kind of therapeutic address Mimi White reads as saturating television in general) to counsel families on problems like alcoholism, threats of divorce, or withdrawn children. It is no surprise that the host is Jay McGraw, son of famous TV "life coach" Dr. Phil McGraw, tough love guru. In this reality format, as critics have shown, the moment of revealing the new home is supposed to spark emotional realism in the family, the weeping moments of "authenticity" Hill has noted viewers look for in reality programs. Neoliberalism reaches new heights in *Extreme Makeover* when First Lady Laura Bush appears on one episode to laud their work, and a series of other episodes sends the design team to hurricane-ravaged Gulf Coast areas to "help out" where the government has not. In this discussion I join a conversation of scholars such as John McMurria, Gareth Palmer, and Jennifer Gillan, who have begun illuminating the neoliberal political economy in these home makeover programs. Gillan asserts the *Extreme Makeover* series models neoliberal citizenship for viewers by invoking American frontier mythology and an idea of "neighborliness" when, in the season 2 finale, it helps build a new home and a community center for the family of the rescued POW Jessica Lynch's fallen Navajo comrade, Lori Piestewa, assuaging guilt over more Native "vanishing Americans."

Another main trend in reality TV is a push forward to an uncertain present and future, an exploration of emergent models of the postmodern family, following single parents and patchwork households as they try to negotiate interpersonal relationships and constant redefinitions of the family. A program like Bravo's *Showbiz Moms and Dads* follows several single mothers (along with other family types) as they pursue the dream of fame and celebrity for their children, achieved to some degree for these families by being on the series. Another high-profile single-mom series is a reality take on *The Sopranos,* A&E's *Growing Up Gotti.* Cameras follow Victoria Gotti, daughter of the deceased crime boss John Gotti, as she mothers her three rowdy teenage sons. She launches the show by pointing out, in case there was any question, that they are "not your typical family." The show plays on the ironic juxtaposition of the mafia "Family" background with the daily toil of home life with teenagers.

As part of a similar critique of older family ideals, some programs simply meditate on threats to the continued survival of the nuclear family, tapping into fears for the sake of ratings. These programs imagine the threat to the nuclear ideal in terms of divorce (programs pairing divorcees for another tilt at the marriage wheel, such as *Who Wants to Marry My Dad?* and *Who Wants to Marry My Mom?*), infidelity (*Temptation Island, The Ultimate Love Test*), lack of commitment (*Paradise Hotel, Forever*

Eden, Love Cruise), the lure of money over romantic entanglement or family bonds (*For Love or Money, Joe Millionaire, Mr. Personality, The Family*), or the pressures of fame (*Newlyweds: Nick and Jessica, 'Til Death Do Us Part: Carmen and Dave, Meet the Barkers, Diary Presents Brandy: Special Delivery*).

Some programs turn the instability of the nuclear family into sensationalized plot twists. One season of *Big Brother* included the surprise gimmick of having a half brother and half sister as contestants in the house together; the two did not know of each other's existence, since the sister grew up with their father and the brother had never met him. Producers, upon realizing their connection when both applied to the show, put them in the house together, then used the newfound blood bond to generate high drama in the Machiavellian competition game as the two discovered they were siblings. Fox turned the search for one's birth parent into reality fodder with *Who's Your Daddy?* which had an adopted daughter attempt to pick out her biological father from a group of men. That program incited protests from adoption groups for trivializing the process, and the poor taste quotient reached a new high on CBS's *The Will*, where cutthroat relatives competed for a patriarch's inheritance, which also sparked protests for insensitivity and was canceled after one episode (Smith).

It is notable that several key reality programs historicize the development of familial ideals and their inequities. "Historical experience" programs till this ground. Linking family history to a broader framework of U.S. history, this subgenre sends participants back in time to reenact earlier lifestyles and pinpoints the exclusionary nature of white patriarchal family models and the social institutions founded on them. On PBS's House series, for example, many of the female, African American, or gay and lesbian participants become frustrated with the historical roles they had to fit into on *Colonial House* or the Victorian-era *Frontier House* (as they materially register in some way what it would have been like to be disenfranchised women, enslaved blacks, or sexual dissidents facing a penalty of death). As they explore a different epoch and its material conditions, these series often examine how the family unit came to be seen as the fundamental unit of social organization, an instrument for colonization and imperialism, or a model for the modern nation-state (witness CBC's *Pioneer Quest* in Canada as well BBC/PBS House programs set in England: *Manor House, 1900 House,* and *The 1940s House*).

Cultural Histories and Family Values Media Debates

I would argue that reality TV is the popular media form with the most to say about the current status of the American family. The television historian Lynn Spigel has shown that early TV developed coextensively with the post–World War II suburban middle-class family—a specific kind of modern nuclear family model the medium made into its favored subject and audience. As Spigel notes, while sociologists like Talcott Parsons were arguing in the 1940s and 1950s that the modern nuclear family is the social form best suited to capitalist progress, the new electronic TV medium targeted the postwar white, middle-class families flocking to the suburbs, encouraging the development of the modern family as a consumer unit.

As a new genre now exploring the self-conscious imbrication of family and the media as one of its main themes, reality TV raises vital issues of marketing and consumerism. If television enters the home to become, as Cecelia Tichi has shown, "the electronic hearth" around which the family gathers, so too does the family envision itself through the tube. TV addresses the family as ideal viewer, imagined community, and the basis for democracy mediated through mass communication; the nation is figured as a collective of families all watching their television sets (a collective that can now exercise its democratic rights by calling in to vote for a favorite singer on *American Idol*). If the domestic sitcom was like an electronic media version of a station wagon trundling the modern family along in the 1950s, reality TV is the hybrid gas-electric car of the postmodern family today.

As reality programs ponder the status of American families now, they also enter into the family values media debates in ways that speak to the politicization of the family. Coontz has proven that the family has been seen as the moral guide for the nation ever since the late nineteenth century, from Theodore Roosevelt's insistence that the nation's future rested on the "right kind of home life" to Ronald Reagan's assertion that "strong families are the foundation of society" (94). As the media studies critic Laura Kipnis notes in her recent witty polemic against modern coupledom, alternative models of organization trouble the social contract, so it is no mistake that "the citizenship-as-marriage analogy has been a recurring theme in liberal-democratic political theory for the last couple of hundred years or so, from Rousseau on" (23–24).

Since family opens such a space of performed social identity, often articulated through narrative, it is not surprising that television has always been one of the key battlegrounds for familial ideas. In her study of how 1970s television responded to the perceived cultural crises of the time, the historian Ella Taylor argues that TV families of the 1950s and 1960s were largely portrayed as harmonious, the building blocks of society and a consensus culture (*Ozzie and Harriet, Leave It to Beaver*), whereas 1970s families appeared under siege and in crisis because of significant changes, such as a spike in divorce rates during that decade (*All in the Family, One Day at a Time*). For Taylor, 1980s TV witnessed a variety of family forms but was dominated by a retreat to nostalgic intact nuclear families (*The Cosby Show, Family Ties*) (2–3). As other critics have since noted, 1990s TV families continued in the 1980s vein (*Home Improvement, Seventh Heaven*) but also satirized family ideals through dysfunctional family sitcoms (*The Simpsons, Married with Children*). Meanwhile, popular fictional shows in the early 2000s seem more explicitly to debate the variety of family forms emerging with recent demographic trends. Witness ABC's popular nighttime soap, *Desperate Housewives* (2004–), which initially garnered more than 20 million viewers and top ratings; it depicts women struggling with their roles in a range of settings, including intact nuclear families, post-divorce families, single-parent households, and childless families.[10] In terms of audience reception of these TV images over time, a series of pioneering "family television" studies since the 1970s has shown how many families actually use television in diverse ways to help shape subjectivity (Morley, *Family Television, Home Territories*).

Reality TV itself has always been a remarkably familial genre, though the earlier examples of unscripted programming that display a similar obsession with the family do so in a different sociohistorical context. As Jeffrey Ruoff notes, *An American Family* is still the most widely circulated direct cinema documentary in U.S. history. It aired just as large-scale social movements such as women's liberation, civil rights, and gay rights were generating upheavals, and it put social changes like the soaring divorce rate into focus by charting an individual family's response to its time period. Earlier formal precursors also include the long-running madcap Chuck Barris game shows such as *The Newlywed Game* (first aired in 1966) and *The Dating Game* (premiered in 1965), which turned aspects of marriage and dating into farce.[11]

Not surprisingly, recent public arguments about family and marriage often turn reality TV into prime fodder. Conservative groups frequently protest reality fare. Most spectacularly, complaints made by conservative activists from the Parents Television Council prompted the Federal Communications Commission (FCC) to threaten Fox with a fine of $1.2 million, the largest to date, for *Married by America* when it was on the air. The show had audiences pick mates for couples who could have gotten married on air (though none did and all the arranged couples stopped dating after the show). The protestors found it a vulgar trivialization of the institution of marriage (Rich).

On the flip side of the coin, progressive thinkers have used reality TV to make public arguments advocating a greater diversity of marriage and household arrangements. The cultural theorist Lisa Duggan, in a 2004 *Nation* article, explores public policy about state-sanctioned marriage in the context of the debates over gay marriage, critiquing, for example, "marriage promotion" by both the Clinton and the Bush administrations as a way to privatize social welfare. Duggan calls for a diversification of democratically accessible forms of state recognition for households and partnerships, a "flexible menu of choices" that would dethrone the privileged civic status of sanctified marriage and "threaten the normative status of the nuclear family, undermining state endorsement of heterosexual privilege, the male 'headed' household and 'family values' moralism as social welfare policy." She uses reality TV as an example of current dissatisfaction with gendered, "traditional" marriage and a marker of its decline, describing "the competitive gold-digging sucker punch on TV's *Joe Millionaire*" (which tricked eager women into believing they were competing to marry a millionaire) as an entertainment culture indicator of the statistical flux in marriage and kinship arrangements. She argues that the franchise confirms social anxiety that "marriage is less stable and central to the organization of American life than ever" (1). Notably, Duggan pairs her *Joe Millionaire* example with the pop singer Britney Spears's rapidly annulled 2004 Las Vegas wedding (to a high school friend, Jason Alexander) as similar social indexes; the celebrity life and the reality show plot represent similar kinds of evidence, both equally real (or equally fake) in current entertainment media culture.

Regardless of the different ways the genre enters into existing political discussions, what is striking is that it continually becomes a site for family values debates. A case in point is how a couple competing on the sixth season of CBS's *The Amazing Race* (2005) made headlines because critics accused the husband of exhibiting abusive behavior toward his wife in the series footage. The couple, Jonathan Baker and Victoria Fuller, made the rounds of talk shows to protest that characterization, but the main dynamic of press coverage has been to turn them into a teaching moment. Both went on the entertainment TV newsmagazine *The Insider* and were asked to watch footage of themselves fighting and answer the charge that it looked abusive; Baker responded: "I'm a better person than that. I have to say I had a temper tantrum, you know, I pushed her, I never should have, and you know, I regret every moment of it and you know what, hopefully that experience will make me a better person. That's our story line, you know, that's who we were on television. That's not who we are in real life" (*Insider*).

Such a framing of that reality TV footage is emblematic: the show is perceived as somewhat mediated and constructed but still real enough to warrant a press debate. Through a bit of internal network marketing, Dr. Phil actually made them the topic of one of his CBS prime-time specials on relationships. Noting that the show sparked reams of hate mail and even death threats toward the couple, Dr. Phil explicitly argues that America was watching the couple and wants to debate them in TV's public sphere. At the outset of the interview, he invokes and calls into being an imagined national public, saying, "America was outraged and appalled by what they've seen." After he exhorts the husband to correct his behavior, he concludes, "So America doesn't need to worry about you?" (*Dr. Phil Prime-time Special*). Dr. Phil does not completely buy Baker's argument that he was only acting aggressively for the camera or that the editing heightened his behavior, and he admonishes the man for exhibiting bad behavior in any context, mediated or not. Dr. Phil is well aware of the construction of images that he himself perpetuates, and he even draws attention to how Baker tries to manipulate this on-camera interview by coaching his wife, yet he insists on a substantial component of actuality in all these depictions. In the press and popular response, the gamedoc show couple becomes a paradigmatic reality TV family example that can be used to analyze the state of the American family more generally.

Ultimately, reality programs add a new wrinkle to television's family ideas. The genre illuminates how the current definition of the family is up for grabs, and reality TV enters the debate arena in force. Instead of having nostalgia for the Cleavers as a model of the modern American family, viewers might one day have nostalgia for the Osbournes as a model of the postmodern American family. The amplified truth claims of reality TV comment on the social role of television itself as an electronic medium offering "public scripts" that, as the medium evolves, viewers increasingly want to interact with on the screen and participate in themselves.

Notes

1. Historians now question how far back to date the nuclear family. Many assert the need to nuance the long-held theory of a total family revolution from premodern to modern families between the 1780s and 1840s as a consequence of industrialization. Coontz argues the conventional idea that industrialization ushered out the extended family does not hold true when one considers that the highest numbers of extended families occurred in the mid-nineteenth century. What most scholars do agree on, however, is that the white, middle-class, nuclear family model became idealized and codified in the Victorian period, even when the reality of people's lives differed drastically, and that it has been used to regulate ideas of family and behavior since then (Coontz 12).

2. Two-parent households were the majority only from the 1920s to 1970s, and the modern nuclear family represented only a minority of those households (Frey et al. 123–124).

3. See Stacey, *Brave New Families* 3–19; Cott. Stacey notes that more children now live with single mothers than live in modern nuclear families (*In the Name of the Family* 45).

4. Jon Kraszewksi has provided a helpful analysis of the discourse of liberalism that, for example, MTV explicitly promotes (Kraszewski 192).

5. Though we know unscripted programming has been around since television's earliest days, the date of the current reality trend's onset is a matter of critical debate. To cite representative examples, Kilborn dubs *America's Unsolved Mysteries* (1987) the original impetus for current reality TV, whereas Jermyn points to *Crimewatch UK* (1984–) (Kilborn; Jermyn 75).

6. Coontz and other historians have demonstrated that the 1950s fantasy family was not only the product of a statistical anomaly (unusually high rates of marriage and childbearing after World War II), but was also rooted in damning contradictions and inequities, such as the imperative for women to return to the home after wartime labor and wholly subordinate their needs to those of their husbands and children, which sparked the original desperate housewives and high rates of alcoholism (Coontz 37; see also May 11).

7. I use *American* to refer to the United States specifically, though I am well aware of problems with this shorthand; as Jan Radway notes, *America* more properly refers to all the Americas.

8. Census data indicate that 50 percent of first marriages and 60 percent of second ones are likely to end in divorce within forty years (Coontz 3).

9. The March 3, 2002, debut had a 2.8 household rating, and the show's ratings eventually exceeded 5 million viewers in the first season, though parts of the subsequent seasons have had lower ratings (Deevoy).

10. The show has at times averaged 13.9 million viewers ("Top 20").

11. *The Newlywed Game* aired 1966–1974, 1977–1980, and, as *The New Newlywed Game*, 1984–1989. *The Dating Game* ran 1965–1986 and, as *The All-New Dating Game*, 1986–1989 and 1996–1999.

Works Cited

Ang, Ien. *Watching Dallas: Television and the Melodramatic Imagination.* London: Routledge, 1985.

Becker, Ron. " 'Help Is on the Way!' *Supernanny, Nanny 911,* and the Neoliberal Politics of the Family." *The Great American Makeover: Television, History, Nation.* Ed. Dana Heller. New York: Palgrave Macmillan, 2006. 175–192.

"Bowers/Pilek." *Trading Spouses: Meet Your New Mommy.* Fox. August 3, 2004, August 10, 2004.

Chambers, Deborah. *Representing the Family.* London: Sage, 2001.

Coontz, Stephanie. *The Way We Never Were: American Families and the Nostalgia Trap.* New York: BasicBooks, 1992.

Cott, Nancy F. *Public Vows: A History of Marriage and the Nation.* Cambridge: Harvard University Press, 2000.

Deevoy, Adrian. "Ozzy's Summer of Love." *Blender* (June–July 2002): 90–96.

Dr. Phil Primetime Special: Romance Rescue. CBS. February 15, 2005.

Duggan, Lisa. "Holy Matrimony!" *Nation,* March 15, 2004, www.thenation.com/doc.mhtml?i=20040315&s=duggan.

Every, Jo Van. "From Modern Nuclear Family Households to Postmodern Diversity? The Sociological Construction of Families." *Changing Family Values.* Ed. Gill Jagger and Caroline Wright. London: Routledge, 1999. 166–179.

Frey, William H., Bill Abresch, and Jonathan Yeasting. *America by the Numbers: A Field Guide to the U.S. Population.* New York: New Press, 2001.

Giddens, Anthony. *Modernity and Self-Identity: Self and Society in the Late Modern Age.* Stanford: Stanford University Press, 1991.

Gillan, Jennifer. "*Extreme Makeover Homeland Security Edition.*" *The Great American Makeover: Television, History, Nation.* Ed. Dana Heller. New York: Palgrave Macmillan, 2006. 193–210.

Gordon, Linda. *Heroes of Their Own Lives.* New York: Viking, 1988.

Gray, Herman. *Watching Race: Television and the Struggle for "Blackness."* Minneapolis: University of Minnesota Press, 1995.

Hedegaard, Erik. "The Osbournes: America's First Family." *Rolling Stone,* May 9, 2002, 33–36.

Hill, Annette. *Reality TV: Factual Entertainment and Television Audiences.* London: Routledge, 2005.

Hoover, Stewart M., Lynn Schofield Clark, and Diane F. Alters. *Media, Home, and Family.* New York: Routledge, 2004.

"A House Divided." *The Osbournes.* MTV. March 5, 2002.

Inness, Sherrie A. *Tough Girls.* Philadelphia: University of Pennsylvania Press, 1999.

The Insider. CBS. January 19, 2005.

Jermyn, Deborah. " 'This *Is* about Real People!' Video Technologies, Actuality, and Affect in the Television Crime Appeal." *Understanding Reality Television.* Ed. Su Holmes and Deborah Jermyn. London: Routledge, 2004. 71–90.

Kilborn, Richard. "How Real Can You Get? Recent Developments in 'Reality' Television." *European Journal of Communications* 9 (1994): 421–439.

Kipnis, Laura. *Against Love: A Polemic.* New York: Pantheon, 2003.

Kraszewski, Jon. "Country Hicks and Urban Cliques: Mediating Race, Reality, and Liberalism on MTV's *The Real World.*" *Reality TV: Remaking Television Culture.* Ed. Susan Murray and Laurie Ouellette. New York: New York University Press, 2004. 179–196.

May, Elaine Tyler. *Homeward Bound: American Families in the Cold War Era.* New York: Basic Books, 1988.

Miller, Nancy. "American Goth: How the Osbournes, a Simple, Headbanging British Family, Became Our Nation's Latest Reality-TV Addiction." *Entertainment Weekly,* April 19, 2002, 25.

Modleski, Tania. *Feminism without Women: Culture and Criticism in a "Postfeminist" Age.* New York: Routledge, 1991.

Morley, David. *Family Television: Cultural Power and Domestic Leisure.* London: Comedia, 1986.

———. *Home Territories: Media, Mobility and Identity.* London: Routledge, 2000.

Radway, Janice. " 'What's in a Name?' " *American Quarterly* 51.1 (March 1999): 1–32.

Rich, Frank. "The Great Indecency Hoax." *New York Times on the Web,* November 28, 2004, www.nytimes.com/2004/11/28/arts/28rich.html?ex=1102397227&ei=1&en=9736fb1bcb36aee1.

Ruoff, Jeffrey. *"An American Family": A Televised Life.* Minneapolis: University of Minnesota Press, 2002.

Shorter, Edward. *The Making of the Modern Family.* New York: Basic Books, 1975.

Smith, Lynn. "Fox Show 'Daddy' Draws Ire." *Los Angeles Times,* December 22, 2004.

Spigel, Lynn. *Make Room for TV: Television and the Family Ideal in Postwar America.* Chicago: University of Chicago Press, 1992.

Stacey, Judith. *Brave New Families: Stories of Domestic Upheaval in Late Twentieth Century America.* New York: Basic Books, 1990.

———. *In the Name of the Family: Rethinking Family Values in the Postmodern Age.* Boston: Beacon Press, 1996.

Taylor, Ella. *Prime-Time Families: Television Culture in Postwar America.* Berkeley: University of California Press, 1989.

Tichi, Cecelia. *Electronic Hearth: Creating an American Television Culture.* New York: Oxford University Press, 1991.

"Top 20 Network Primetime Series by Households: Season-to-Date 09/20/04–11/28/04." *Zap2It,* December 4, 2004, http://tv.zap2it.com/tveditorial/tve_main/1,1002,272|season||,00.html.

SARAH A. MATHESON

Shopping, Makeovers, and Nationhood

Reality TV and Women's Programming in Canada

As has been the case in a number of countries, the emergence and rapid proliferation of reality TV in Canada has prompted a variety of critical responses. For some, reality TV appears to have initiated a decline in quality on television as more expensive (and seemingly more culturally valuable) domestic dramas are increasingly being replaced with cheaply produced reality shows, lifestyle programming, and celebrity news shows. For others, the arrival of "franchise" series such as *Canadian Idol, Canada's Next Top Model,* and *Project Runway Canada* signal a continued erosion of "distinctively" Canadian programming in favor of standardized formats that mimic the style and content of popular American television. Discussions surrounding the cultural value of reality-based formats therefore frequently express disdain for the form and for the ways it has changed the landscape of television in Canada. This debate has also had specific resonance in discussions about women's programming in Canada; it has offered speculation about how the trend toward reality-based television has affected the style, content, and ideological underpinnings of women's television. This essay examines the discourse surrounding reality TV in women's programming in Canada, considering its positioning on the two main cable channels aimed at a female viewership: W Network (formerly the Women's Television Network, WTN) and Slice (formerly Life Network). Both channels have been recently rebranded, and part of their reinvention has been a turn toward reality and lifestyle programming, which are now the mainstay of their schedules. Canadian-produced makeover, home renovation, and family and relationship series are typically scheduled alongside similar series imported from the United States and Britain. I situate this turn toward reality-based formats in the context of the history of debates and policies surrounding women's programming

Stacy London and Clinton Kelly provide the typical fanfare for finding female beauty through the application of consumer products and "attitude" on the U.S. version of *What Not to Wear* (TLC). Courtesy of TLC/PhotoFest.

and the representation of women on television in Canada. I consider the different ways these channels frame reality TV in relation to women's issues and investigate how specific programs may reflect tensions between the political and commercial objectives associated with women's TV. As case studies, I examine the popular consumer-advice program *The Shopping Bags,* currently airing on W, and *Plastic Makes Perfect,* a makeover series about cosmetic surgery currently being broadcast on Slice. The series I've chosen represent interesting responses to reality formats; they take up familiar subject matter but offer unique perspectives on consumerism and beauty. Although women's programming in Canada has indeed undergone a significant transformation, and reality television has been an important part of these changes, I argue that the critical discourse that associates reality TV with its decline needs to be reconsidered. My analysis will reveal that while these programs are in dialogue with American and British series, they also potentially complicate or disrupt dominant discourses surrounding gender, nation, and television.

Reality Television in Canada

In 2006 the Canadian Broadcasting Corporation (CBC), Canada's national public network, announced its decision to preempt its popular news program *The National* to simulcast a new American reality series entitled *The One,* which was an *American Idol*–style talent contest that also followed the drama of contestants' offstage lives. The airing of the series anticipated the Canadian version that would follow, as the CBC had purchased the franchise rights to produce its own installment of the program. This proved to be an immensely controversial decision that prompted an unprecedented outcry from the public, many of whom objected to a national newscast being bumped for an American reality show. The uproar was exacerbated by the dismal ratings of *The One,* which was canceled after only two episodes. As Derek Foster has discussed, this incident sparked a public debate about reality television in Canada, not only raising issues about quality, but also linking it to American programming's influence on Canadian television: the revered cornerstone of Canadian TV was threatened by cheap U.S. fare.[1] The airing of *The One* also conflicted with statements made by CBC President Robert Rabinovitch less than one year earlier. Rabinovitch told the House Commons Heritage Committee that reality programming did not fit within the mandate of a public broadcaster. He said, "There are certain types of programming that we don't have to do or should do. For example, we don't do reality television. . . . If we only were chasing rating points we could do reality programming" (MacDonald and Tuck). Since then the CBC has introduced a number of new reality shows (including *Dragon's Den, Making the Cut,* and *The Week the Women Went*), which has prompted critics to suggest that this reflects a decline of standards at the CBC and raises questions about the status and relevance of the nation's public broadcaster.

This incident highlights some of the discourses surrounding reality television in Canada. Not only is it aligned with notions of a decline in quality, it also replays anxieties about cultural imperialism (two things that seemingly go hand in hand). This controversy is part of a wider popular dialogue that has followed changes in programming and policy. In 2004 the Canadian Radio-television and Telecommunications Commission (CRTC), the broadcasting system's regulatory body, made changes to Canadian content regulations, expanding the definitions of priority programming to include genres such as entertainment magazine and current affairs programs. This has been seen as a move that initiated the decline in the production of domestic dramas, which are more expensive to produce and generate less advertising revenue than the reality-based forms. Historically, in Canada scripted drama has been framed as a more culturally valuable form, and its erosion has been linked to the trend toward reality programming, which has been supported in part by these policy changes. Therefore, the dialogue about reality TV in Canada has often been framed in terms of its negative effect on the Canadian system generally (as part of a decline in quality) and in terms of its threat to national culture as well.

These discourses have been important in discussions of women's television as well. The rebranding of both WTN and Life was met with harsh criticism in the press. In both instances, the association of reality-based genres with trashy and superficial television was evoked as evidence of the deterioration of women's programming on these channels. It becomes clear that much of the critique about the changes on both networks is framed as a matter of taste, expressing contempt for reality television (and its supposed questionable cultural value), and for the ways it has become intertwined with so-called traditional or stereotypical female genres and subject matter (which are seemingly in conflict with feminist values).

Women's Television Programming in Canada

The emergence of women's television programming in Canada needs to be understood in relation to the history of debates about women and television that unfolded in the context of second-wave feminism. As Julie D'Acci points out, "Early research on gender and television had its beginnings in the worldwide second-wave feminist movements" (378). Within these movements, the representation of women on television and in other media was identified as a factor contributing to the oppression and inequality of women. The academic research undertaken in Canada, as in the United States, was focused on quantitative content analyses of sex-role stereotyping. Initiated in the context of 1970s mass communications research, its underlying theoretical assumptions, according to Sue Thornham (summarizing the work of Gaye Tuchman) are as follows: the mass media "firstly *reflect,* in the form of images or representations, society's dominant values. Hence content analyses can be used to reveal a predominance of traditional and stereotypical images of women across all media forms. Secondly, they act as agents of *socialization,* transmitting stereotyped images of sex-roles, particularly to young people" (Thornham 55; emphasis in original). This research, Thornham notes, further assumed "a direct relationship between media organization, content and social effects." Therefore, if women do not occupy positions of power in the media, this fact influences content, which results in distorted images of women and their social roles and further contributes to wider negative social effects, including impeding women's success (56).

This type of research has since been criticized for its limited consideration of how media texts are interpreted by viewers and how their social effects may be understood. The conclusions of research into sex-role stereotyping, however, had an immense influence on how discussions of women's television would unfold in Canada. The 1970 report of the Royal Commission on the Status of Women provided guidelines and recommendations for combating discriminatory practices and for improving opportunities for women in Canadian society. As Linda Silver Dranoff points out, the commission report "also expressed concern about the stereotyping in the mass media" (61–62). In 1974 the CBC produced its own report on discrimination in broadcasting and outlined fifty recommendations designed to improve employment opportunities for women at the corporation (Dranoff 62). A host of studies followed that conducted content analyses of gender portrayal in the media. For example, in 1978 the Canadian Advisory Council on the Status of Women also commissioned a report on sex-role stereotyping in advertising, and similar studies were undertaken by the performers' rights union, ACTRA, the CBC, and the feminist watchdog group MediaWatch (Spears and Seydegart 3).

In 1979 the federal government devised a national action plan intended to "promote equality of women in Canadian society and eliminate discrimination" (Public Notice CRTC 1992-58). Following the publication of its report, "Towards Equality for Women," the CRTC formed its own task force to develop policies and guidelines designed to eliminate sex-role stereotyping in broadcast media. During its first meeting the task force reportedly agreed to "address the issue as a problem of injustice and inequality, rather than as one of 'poor taste' " (Public Notice CRTC 1986-351). What followed were a series of studies, public meetings, and hearings that culminated in the 1982 publication of *Images of Women,* which summed up the task force's findings and recommendations. In its summary of concerns, the report identifies a range of key issues, including the need to avoid demeaning or degrading representation, to avoid presenting women only in traditional roles (such as housewife), to include women as experts and authorities, to present a diversity of family life, to avoid portraying women as "either excessively concerned with youth and beauty or neurotically afraid of aging" and presenting women with predominantly negative traits (such as "catty, bitchy, dependent, incompetent, subservient, submissive," or unintelligent) (CRTC 29-31). The report also addressed commercial advertising, raising concerns about how women are represented as both buyers and sellers. The report states that as buyers, women should not be, among other things, represented as "exclusive buyers and users of products for the home," and "products such as cosmetics, fragrances, jewellery, and clothing should be presented as personally beneficial, not as a means to catch or please a man" (CRTC 34). As sellers, it states, "women should be presented as experts and authorities as well as men. . . . Voice-overs on TV and announcers on radio should be female as well as male. . . . Women should be shown selling a wider range of products and services, not only those assumed to be for women" (CRTC 34). Interestingly, the report expresses concern not only about negative and demeaning representations of women, calling for a break from traditional or stereotypical portrayals of women's roles and characteristics, but also about stereotypical portraits of women consumers: it suggests particular ideas about what constitutes appropriate or desirable modes of consumption for women (a notion that I'll return to).

These policy discussions and the public debate surrounding them addressed two main issues: representation (the portrayal of women in the media) and employment equity (participation of women on and off the air), the underlying logic being that improvement in the latter would help alleviate problems in the former. According to Shirley Anne Off, in the early 1990s a number of women's groups (including the National Action Committee on the Status of Women, Toronto Women in Film and Television, and the Royal Commission on the Status of Women) called for the establishment of a women's television channel designed to address these content and employment issues (106, 111). She situates WTN in the context of these discussions about sex-role stereotyping and in relation to Canada's 1991 Broadcasting Act, which introduced an equity clause.[2] The fragmentation brought on by cable and the quickly expanding choices available to viewers opened up an ideal space for programming targeting a niche market of women viewers. The prospect of a women's television channel was also framed as a potential means of addressing some of these pressing political issues surrounding gender discrimination in Canada.

The Arrival of the Women's Television Network (WTN)

The plan for a new women's television channel, therefore, emerged in an era marked by two decades of politically charged discussions about the need for alternative women's television. In 1993 the CRTC received fifty applications for the seven broadcasting licenses that were set to be approved. Two proposals for women's channels were submitted. One, awkwardly named T'elle'vision, was backed by CanWest Global Communications in Toronto, and the other, Lifestyle (later to become WTN), was backed by Winnipeg's Moffatt Communications. Both promised to address employment issues by placing women in key positions at the networks and to offer programming by and for women that resisted negative or stereotypical representations (Pearce). Lifestyle was successful in obtaining its license in 1994 and was scheduled to launch on January 1, 1995. The channel was described as television "for, by, and about women and their worlds," which evoked the notions both of employment equity and of programming for and about women. And, as Off points out, its application proposed programming that would highlight information shows for women and entertainment programming that "would challenge sex-role stereotyping, would feature strong lead female characters, would not portray gratuitous violence, would ensure that dramatic violence was viewed within a context of social reality, and would focus on issues of importance to women" (108). Its license stipulated that 70 percent of its schedule would be dedicated to "Information" programming and 30 percent to "Entertainment" (Van Den Broek 20). Clearly framing itself within this wider dialogue about sex-role stereotyping, proposed programming on this new channel highlighted nontraditional genres as well as series that showcased women's perspectives on current affairs. An article in *Herizons* summed up some of what Lifestyle promised to offer women viewers. For example, *POV Women* was described as a program that would "look at world events from women's point of view and ask what one woman can do to change the course of events"; it would "identify the most appropriate action in terms of community, politics, healing, compromise and standing up for one's rights" ("Proposed TV Channel"). Another suggested program, *The Women's Network*, emphasized a similar activist orientation. It was described as "providing women's groups around the country with an opportunity to communicate with one another about their activities and agendas" ("Proposed TV Channel"). Other projected shows included *Girl Talk* (a discussion forum for girls age twelve to sixteen), *The Creators* (focused on women's contributions to art and culture), *A Different Voice* (showcasing documentaries by "women of color and Aboriginal women"), and *Sharing the Wisdom* (focused on "developments in math, science, history, biology and business"). In addition, the channel would air "classic and contemporary movies geared to women" ("Proposed TV Channel"). The channel, therefore, purported to dedicate itself to programming that departed from conventional or mainstream women's programming. Forms typically associated with a female audience—melodrama and romance, soap opera, cooking, fashion, and things associated with the domestic realm—were not emphasized in the proposed programming. Genres perceived to be more "serious," such as public affairs and documentary shows, were emphasized, as were matters seemingly aligned with "public" concerns (world events, math, science, history, biology, business, and so on). The notion that women's television could be a platform for political and community activism also seemed to evoke a clear connection with a liberal feminist agenda.

When the newly named Women's Television Network (WTN) was finally launched in 1995, its programming schedule roughly conformed to what had been proposed in its licensing application. *POV, Girl Talk,* and *Sharing the Wisdom* appeared during the first season. Other original programs offered female takes on traditionally male genres, such as *Car Care* and *Natural Angler.* Other shows presented critical and comedic takes on traditional women's programming. For example, *Go Girl!* was a spoof of women's talk shows in which the superficial subjects of women's television (beauty, fashion, fitness, and the like) were mocked and parodied. And the documentary miniseries *Double Talk* was a "hard-edged" look at stereotypes of women in the media.

WTN also routinely aired popular Movies of the Week (probably the most traditionally "feminine" genre represented on the channel) in its series *Open for Discussion.* These were framed by panel discussions featuring professionals and experts, however, who would provide further information on the issue portrayed in the film, interview women dealing with similar situations, and debate the accuracy and realism of the fictional representation (often taking issue with the way problems were being depicted in the films). The inclusion of these expert voices, personal reflections, and critical analyses seemingly worked to balance the melodramatic, emotional presentation of women's issues found in more traditionally female genres with a more didactic, often scientific, and explicitly feminist framework.

The early programming on WTN therefore was a fascinating attempt to fashion a women's channel in ways that attempted to resist reinscribing the historical gender base of television described by Patricia Mellencamp (Fiske 179). By offering nontraditional programming and reframing traditional female genres from a feminist perspective, WTN's schedule appeared to be explicitly shaped by the larger debates and discourses that surrounded discussions of sex-role stereotyping, debates that had been unfolding since the 1970s. It appeared that the social and political goals of women's television were initially given priority over the commercial. WTN therefore was framed not only as a service offering entertainment for women (and generating profits) but as a channel that, through its articulated public service mandate, would fulfill larger social and political objectives. As Shirley Anne Off points out, "WTN embraced two contradictory mandates. One mandate was political—to respond to the argument put forth by feminist organizations and scholars that women are objectified and stereotyped by the popular media. The other was commercial—to establish a privately owned, profit-oriented cable television channel squarely targeted at the female audience" (106).

Despite the arguably innovative programming on WTN, the channel struggled to secure viewers and received the lowest ratings of the newly launched channels: its audience shares were more than 70 percent below its target (Urlocker). Derided as "Tampon TV," it also faced harsh criticism in the press. Predictably, some reacted negatively to what was perceived to be an overtly feminist tone. Joe Chidley, reviewer for *Maclean's* magazine, described WTN as the "most-discussed new channel and the least watched" and suggested that its low ratings may have been a result of its "feminist perspective" and "women-only" focus (Chidley). In his review, Michael Urlocker of the *Financial Post* wrote, "While other new channels serve up Twin Peaks repeats, non-stop videos, or the history of helicopters, WTN might feature an informal discussion about sensitive men, a documentary on female circumcision in Africa or a speech written by writer Betty Friedan at a geriatric centre." Other critics questioned who was being addressed by WTN, seemingly drawing distinctions between "feminist" television and television for women. For example, in an *Alberta Report* article, the writer stated: "A *women's network* is not an inherently bad idea, but tuning to *WTN* is disheartening. Watching it, it rapidly becomes clear that the *network* is burdened by the intellectual portmanteaux of modern feminism: the exaltation of victimization, the weepy white guilt over the fate of the Third World, the wild revisions of history. *WTN* is in jeopardy of becoming self-parody, and it cannot be successful until it really fulfils its stated mandate—to become a *network* for all *women,* and not just for hothouse-bred liberal feminists" ("Real Women" 35).

Though these reactions to the feminist tone of the channel are not surprising, given the backlash against feminism that reached popular discourse in the mid-1990s, it was clear that the fledgling ratings of WTN indicated that it was not successful in its appeal to women viewers through these innovative programming strategies. Within months changes were being introduced that, critics argued, began to move WTN away from its original mandates. Reruns of mainstream American and British comedies were introduced, such as *The Mary Tyler Moore Show, Rhoda, French and Saunders,* and *Kate and Allie.* Ironically, the 1970s liberal feminist heroine Mary Richards became the channel's biggest ratings draw. And critics noted a general "softening" of the WTN schedule as "soft lifestyle shows such as Flare TV, The Painted House and Metro Café" were introduced (Van Den Broek 20). Interestingly, this shift from "information" to "lifestyle" programming suggested an increasing emphasis on popular genres and entertainment over education and awareness. In her detailing of the first few seasons of WTN, Off comes to the conclusion that the channel's feminist values were ultimately compromised for commercial success. She argues that the channel eventually abandoned its risky and innovative original programming in favor of more stereotypical female genres such as fashion, cooking, and talk shows (106, 110).

Rebranding of WTN: W Network

In 2001 Moffatt Communications sold WTN to Shaw Communications' Corus Entertainment Ltd. The channel was moved from Winnipeg to Toronto and was subsequently rebranded as the new W Network (W). This was accompanied by drastic changes in personnel: most of the original WTN staffers were let go. The arrival of W is typically characterized as representing the end of WTN's feminist mission: the channel embraced a schedule of lifestyle-oriented reality programming and moved firmly toward a commercial, mainstream entertainment–focused format. In promoting the recast channel, the new general manager, Wendy Herman, talked about the network's redirection as an attempt to overcome its reputation as a "do-good" channel with "heavy" programming. In an interview in the *Ottawa Citizen* she says, "The research tells us that what women want is entertainment. . . . At the end of the day they want to be entertained, they want to relax, they want to escape. That's where you'll see the shift in our network . . . toward more of an entertainment focus" (quoted in Atherton). W's new "unscripted" drama *elove*, a program about women searching for love online, was used as an example of original programming that viewers could look forward to. Some critics reacted strongly to W's abandoning WTN's original premise. For example, Antonia Zerbisias of the *Toronto Star* used W as an example of the CRTC's inability to enforce broadcasters' licensing agreements. She wrote: "Consider W was originally licensed as WTN, The Women's Television Network with a primo place on the dial, to give the 'women's perspectives' on 'health, job options, women's history, current events, family relationships, law, science and technology, parenting, financial planning, travel and women in the arts.' The original applicants . . . even promised they'd deliver 'the voices of women from Latin America, women from Africa, women from Asia.' Check its schedule, decorating and shopping shows, movies and dramas. None of the promises have been kept." Similarly, the *Globe and Mail*'s critic John Doyle criticized the channel's new focus on consumerism, using the Canadian lifestyle shows *The Shopping Bags, Take This House and Sell It,* and the British series *You Are What You Eat* as examples of the "cheesy, air-headed garbage" that now fills its schedule: "When W went on the air, it was WTN, the Women's Television Network. Its mandate was to offer intelligent programming for women, made by women. . . . A few years ago Corus Entertainment swallowed up WTN. . . . Soon, WTN became W and, now, W is, like, totally about shopping" ("CRTC Finally Does Something").

Most of the original programming on W has been replaced by reality and lifestyle shows. Design programs (*Divine Design, Take This House and Sell It, Save Us from Our House, Colour Confidential*), makeover shows (*Style by Jury, Queer Eye for the Straight Girl*), cooking shows (*What's Cooking, Cook Yourself Thin*), and British lifestyle series (*How Clean Is Your House, You Are What You Eat, How to Look Good Naked*) occupy much of W's daytime and prime-time schedules.

The narrative of W's rise in the ratings and decline in terms of its social value has therefore been structured as a kind of heroic yet failed feminist experiment. It suggests that the original ideals underpinning the network, informed by decades of communications research on gender and media, were gradually compromised as the commercial constraints of television, the realities of the media marketplace, and the demands of advertising and ratings were revealed to be incompatible with these larger feminist goals. Lifestyle programming and reality-based shows (as apparently distinct from "information" genres) are implicated as markers of this corruption and as agents contributing to the demise of more important, meaningful, or serious television for women.

Rethinking the Rise and Fall of Feminism on Canadian Television

Rarely mentioned in this dialogue are the viewers themselves. Focusing on commercial pressures alone ignores the basic reality that few women watched WTN in these early years; why didn't women prefer this programming, which was supposedly more adequately serving their interests? Was this a case of women not knowing what kind of television was good for them and, as "cultural dupes," mistakenly choosing programming that did not meet their needs? Have they been so completely socialized that they are unable to recognize how they are oppressed by these less valuable, more vulgar forms? It is unclear how the critics account for the fact that WTN failed to attract a sizable viewing audience despite its assertion that it had fashioned the channel on sound market research about what women want from TV.

Throughout this dialogue about WTN's promises and failures, a specific bias is revealed. WTN's original programming was deemed important in part because of the ways it departed from how women had been addressed and represented by conventional, mainstream television. This attitude proposed a distinction between television that serves women and television that doesn't. The rejection of "popular" women's genres in favor of more "serious" formats provided programming that was deemed "good for" women. What becomes clear are the ways that the network and the studies that informed it reinforced an existing bias against things aligned with traditional notions of femininity: so-called feminine genres, traditionally feminine roles, and those things associated with traditional feminine realms (such as the domestic). While feminist media critics in the 1980s and 1990s were conducting research and devising theories that sought to reconsider the cultural significance of previously devalued women's genres such as the soap opera and talk shows, WTN was positioning itself in opposition to these forms.[3] What I would argue, then, is that one possible reason WTN failed to engage women was that it was informed by a limited and perhaps less relevant feminist discourse that conflicted with the values and tastes of the audience it was attempting to address. Moreover, its rejection of genres traditionally popular with women discounted the pleasures associated with them and reinscribed a gender bias about what constitutes valuable or important programming. The introduction of lifestyle programming, and its association with reality TV as a generally less esteemed form, offered subject matter more aligned with the personal, the emotional, and the private (all aspects that evoke the notion of traditionally feminine concerns). Commercial pressures undoubtedly had an effect on how W's schedule shifted, however its move toward genres more traditionally identified as female may reflect more than just a privileging of profit over public service.

It is tempting to frame this shift in programming around a turn toward postfeminism in popular culture. The arrival of W in 2001 corresponded to increasing discussions of postfeminism in women's television. Angela McRobbie describes postfeminism as "an active process by which feminist gains of the 1970s and 80s come to be undermined" (255). In positing the birth of W as signaling the death of feminism on the channel and as a process that initiated a turn toward programming seemingly in conflict with the WTN's original feminist ideals, this narrative certainly suggests that it can be read through a postfeminist frame. In her analysis of cosmetic surgery on television, Sue Tait situates popular makeover programs as "part of a broader cultural post-feminism expressed through media texts which figure women's empowerment and access to public culture, but which render this through individualist and consumerist frames, such as the 'girl power' feminism of the 1990s or the libertarian celebration of sexuality, fashion, and careers in the popular *Sex and the City*" (122). The new consumer ethos on W noted by Doyle, along with programming occupied by makeover narratives and postfeminist dramas such as *Ally McBeal* and *Sex and the City* (both of which have aired on W), further suggests the relevance of postfeminist discourse to examining these shifts.

I would like, however, to propose another way of examining women's television in this context. Rather than offering a monolithic discourse on women's issues and subjects traditionally associated with the concerns of women, W (and Slice, as I argue below) presents conflicting narratives and representations. These channels offer a wide range of different perspectives on beauty, consumerism, fashion, motherhood, and so on; some perhaps are informed by postfeminist ideas, whereas others may question, disrupt, and complicate dominant discourses. In viewing these channels as ambivalent spaces and places of conflict that offer potentially contradictory discourses on women and women's culture, my analysis seeks to identify specific programs that prompt a rethinking of the typical way the narrative of women's television in Canada has been framed.

The Shopping Bags *and the Female Consumer*

The characterization of the popular W series *The Shopping Bags* as an example of the "cheesy, air-headed garbage" found on the network serves to support the notion that it should be disregarded as empty, frivolous fare. In his critique John Doyle also suggests that the program's focus on shopping makes it no different from the commercials that surround it ("CRTC Finally Does Something"). The notion that it is about consumerism seems here to negate the possibility that it has anything of value to offer women. It is, however, a program that invites a consideration of how women are addressed as consumers and what image W provides of the female consumer. The CRTC's *Images of Women* report expressed concern about how the media were representing women consumers in the 1970s and 1980s. It was not that women being aligned with consumption was found to be problematic, but rather the manner in which their relationship to consumption was being defined. In particular, the report took issue with defining women as passive consumers, as purchasers only of products for the home, and with the linking of products with women's desire to "catch a man." Further emphasis was put on presenting women as sellers as well as buyers and on their status as experts (CRTC 34). This suggests that popular portraits of women consumers are considered significant vehicles that convey ideas about femininity and women's positioning in society. As Maggie Andrews and Mary M. Talbot have argued, consumption is "a sphere where femininity is performed, where versions of femininity are legitimated and negotiated, or contested and rejected" (1). This speaks to the need to look more closely at the images of consumption that women's television offers. *The Shopping Bags* presents the ideal opportunity for such analysis.

The show is a consumer-advice program hosted by journalists and two self-confessed "shopaholics," Kristina Matisic and Anna Wallner. The women provide information about products (what to look for, how to assess quality) and conduct their own consumer tests of various goods. In addition, they also provide challenges to claims made about "As Seen on TV" merchandise advertised through infomercials. These products range from those typically marketed to female consumers (detergent, tampons, baby food, maternity clothes, lingerie, jewelry, cosmetics, cleaning products) and those aimed at a more broadly imagined consumer (car tires, computers, camping gear, pets, food). They also offer tips on negotiating the best price for a product or service. In describing her experience hosting the show in an interview, Wallner speaks enthusiastically: "It feels incredible . . . it's doing what I love to do. It's telling stories, making television and shopping, and empowering consumers. . . . It makes me feel good about what I do when I get up in the morning" (Blakey). The notion of empowerment through shopping seems to support the postfeminist notion that women's empowerment has been refigured through consumerism. The type of empowerment advocated in *The Shopping Bags*, however, complicates this notion.

As Sue Thornham has pointed out, "Women's relationship to consumption and to consumer culture has been a central issue in feminist cultural theory" (126). In the context of the 1970s women's liberation movement, feminists saw the feminine "'fashion and beauty' system of consumer culture" as "the product of patriarchal ideology" (133). Thornham writes, "Women's positioning within an ideology of consumption, like their confinement to domesticity and 'full-time mothering,' was seen as part of their political oppression in the sphere of the personal" (134). She outlines how this linking of consumption and women's oppression relied on a specific portrait of the female consumer (passive, victim) that is defined in contrast to the more positive (and masculine-coded) values of "'production,' 'authenticity,' 'individuality,' 'rationality'" (126). But she also refers to the work of Rachel Bowlby, who discusses two very different consumer models. Quoting Bowlby, Thornham explains: "One . . . is 'the consumer as dupe or victim or hedonist . . . infinitely manipulable and manipulated by the onslaughts of advertising.' The other is 'the consumer as rational subject, calculating and efficient and aware of his aims and wants'" (141). Thornham demonstrates how these two consumer types are gendered, the first as a "feminized" consumer and the second, "resistant or rational," as a masculine figure who "occupies a very different relationship to the commodity from that of his 'feminized' counterpart" (141). She continues:

> What we are being offered, in fact, is two quite different models of the consumer, models that are mapped on to ideological assumptions about masculinity and femininity. One is the possessor of an individualized subjectivity and capacity for agency; he actively pursues and takes possessions, as he actively pursues rational arguments. He may use these possessions to signal his identity, but his identity is not submerged in them. The other is passive and manipulated, linked emotionally rather than rationally to consumption; there is no clear distinction between her identity as subject and her position as object. . . . Her identity is constructed from and by the commodities with which she is identified. (142)

It is clear that *Images of Women* is reacting to gendered portraits of consumption that tend to relegate women to this passive, manipulated type.

In calling for the representation of women as experts and as sellers, it is essentially advocating a more active (and perhaps masculinized) model of consumption for women.

The Shopping Bags constructs an interesting image of consumption that draws on both these types. On the one hand, Matisic and Wallner operate as advocates of a "resistant and rational" approach to consumption. As hosts, they enable the viewer to adopt a position of agency by providing information, drawing on the perspectives of various experts, and putting the products to their own tests. They refigure women's relationship to these products by encouraging a more informed approach to their purchases that is based on the evidence they provide and informed by the scientific perspectives offered by their guests. At the same time, they are constructed as enthusiastic consumers themselves, frequently acknowledging the fun of shopping and validating the emotional pleasures that consumption can offer. The portrait of consumption that is presented on The Shopping Bags thus blurs the gendered lines that define these two consumer types and allows viewers to take up a variety of positions in relation to consumer culture.

Moreover, Matisic and Wallner encourage a critical and skeptical attitude toward television, especially in relation to the way women are traditionally addressed as consumers. This is particularly evident in their "As Seen on TV" segments. As Alison Clarke has argued, the "As Seen on TV" products, which originally arrived in the 1950s with the domestication of television, were directed toward women at home as "newly skilled televisual consumers in the late twentieth century" (160). On The Shopping Bags the hosts take the position usually occupied by the salespeople who demonstrate these products in commercials and infomercials. Adopting the promotional tactics deployed in these advertisements and using them to their own ends (that is, duplicating the demonstrations with often different results), the women encourage an active reconsideration of the claims of advertising and effectively complicate these performances of "proof" that are used to support them. The Shopping Bags models a mode of consumption that is skeptical, critical, distanced, and informed—and far from that of the "manipulable and manipulated" consumer. At the same time, shopping is also presented as leisure, enjoyment, and something that provides an emotional pleasure as well.

It should be noted however, that the program does tend to reinforce an image of middle-class consumerism. Matisic and Wallner are themselves middle-class professional women: likewise, the families and others featured on the program tend to evoke middle-class notions of a thrifty yet comfortable consumerism. The women's own homes (often the sites of their product tests) are tastefully decorated and upscale. Similarly, most of the other domestic spaces portrayed on the program evoke a middle-class milieu. Rather than simply being extensions of commercials, as Doyle suggests, *The Shopping Bags* constructs a different image of consumption that complicates the passive-active, manipulated-resistant, emotional-rational polarities that underlie gendered portraits of consumers. The program, however, asserts a clearly classed image that tends to naturalize and validate middle-class modes of consumption.

My Vice Is Slice!

Slice Network represents a different take on television for women. Its history has not been framed as a struggle to find a place for feminism on commercial television. Instead, since its inception as Life Network, its schedule has always primarily consisted of home improvement, cooking, and similar lifestyle-oriented programming that targets a broad audience. Like WTN, Life was launched in 1995 as one of seven newly licensed cable channels. In the popular press, the channel's programming mandate was described as "a lifestyle network that would arrange its programming around five different themes (one for each weekday): habitat; bodywork; explorations and travel; relationships; and Food Plus" (Riches). It was described as do-it-yourself programming, suggesting the idea of how-to television, or (as it was promoted) "Television You Can Use." Life's revamping and reinvention as Slice in 2007 involved an explicit shift toward marketing to an exclusively female audience, as it offered "the juicy channel women have been waiting for" (Slice Network, "About Us"). Slice now promotes itself as "guilty pleasure viewing" for women. In explaining the channel's address to women, Gail Rivett, vice president of marketing and publicity, says in an interview, "In developing Slice we spoke to women about what they want from a TV channel and heard loud and clear that they are craving irreverent programming that allows them to escape after a day filled with everyone else's needs." Their research, Rivett explains, "identified 'makeover' programming as the most enjoyable type of 'guilty pleasure' TV" (quoted in Doyle, "It's a Slice!"). Slice therefore makes no pretense toward feminism, nor does it purport to offer programming that resists traditional or conventional representations of women and women's issues. Its reframing of lifestyle programming, moving as it has from the concept of useful television to "vice" television (announced in its new tag line, "My Vice Is Slice!"), suggests a shift from notions of productivity to images of consumption. But it also constructs lifestyle television in a very different way: it acknowledges the questionable quality of much of what it offers (television we love but are secretly ashamed of admitting we watch), and effectively gives women permission to indulge.

The channel now offers a host of American reality shows (*Extreme Makeover, Rocker Moms, The Real Housewives of Orange Country, Nanny 911, Tori and Dean: Inn Love, Paradise Hotel*) as well as international versions of popular reality formats (*Britain's Next Top Model, The Biggest Loser Australia*). These appear alongside Canadian-made reality shows focused on family, makeovers, and romance (*Crash Test Mommy, Outlaw In-laws, Newlywed, Nearly Dead, Wedding S.O.S., Plastic Makes Perfect*). Like his critique of W, John Doyle's review of Slice was harsh, describing it as a "dumbing down of Life Network," in which women are addressed as "air-heads" whose interests include "chocolate, bubble baths, gossip, romance novels and shoes" ("It's a Slice!"). His review highlights *Real Housewives of Orange County* as an example of the trashy programming to be found on Slice. It is clear that this critique is framed as a matter of taste, expressing contempt not just for reality television generally (and its questionable cultural value) but also for the ways it has become intertwined with negative or stereotypical representations of women and their interests.

Plastic Makes Perfect: *Reframing the Makeover Narrative*

The tone of Slice and its marketing strategies highlights the kind of popular pleasure its programming may offer. And it does so through a traditional address to women that is used by mainstream women's magazines (such as *Cosmopolitan*). It also adopts a playful, ironic posturing as well, however, self-consciously reveling in the excessive pleasures it presents. Evoking the association between women's television and the pleasure derived from the "low" or "vulgar" is a familiar way that mass culture (as a number of critics have argued) has been coded as an inferior and "feminized" culture.[4] But a number of feminist critics have demonstrated the importance of pleasure and fantasy in women's genres, attempting to examine how women engage with these forms in different ways.[5] Slice's program *Plastic Makes Perfect* is a good example of a text that takes up a conventional makeover narrative yet introduces a variety of discourses that disrupt and reframe these familiar narratives. It is an interesting response to this genre, which, I argue, incorporates an ironic, skeptical reading into its representational strategies, in a sense translating a playful, resistant engagement into its address to women (perhaps drawing on the way many women may already be reading these types of programs). In the context of Canadian television, it also enacts a reframing of a particularly American narrative of transformation.

Plastic Makes Perfect focuses on cosmetic surgery and the issues it involves. Each episode follows an individual (male or female) who decides to undergo a procedure to improve his or her physical appearance. As is typical of most plastic surgery programs, this physical transformation is linked to a larger personal transformation (an increase in self-esteem, which allows participants greater success in their lives and careers). The main narrative follows the consultations with surgeons, explores the reasons for getting the surgery, depicts the surgery and its results (maintaining the before-and-after structure), and inevitably ends with an expression of personal satisfaction with the new appearance. The show's opening credits are constructed like a cover from a women's magazine, with article titles like "Bigger Breasts, Better Breasts?" and "How to Get a Better Body." Each episode poses a similar structuring question that is pursued throughout the program. For example, one episode dealing with breast augmentation examines the question "Is an Hour-Glass Figure the Only 10?" *Plastic Makes Perfect* therefore situates itself in the wider women's popular culture, referencing the way cosmetic surgery discourses circulate across different forms of media, and adopts a familiar way of representing these issues. Episodes convey statistics and information and include discussion of possible complications. The show also includes "hidden-camera" stunts that explore questions surrounding appearance. For example, a woman compares how she is treated differently when she has curves from when she doesn't by donning different body suits and asking for directions at a local café. Inevitably, the tests show that people are treated better when they conform to traditional beauty standards.

Many feminist critics have discussed the ways cosmetic surgery feeds anxieties about the aging body and reinforces culturally specific, homogenous, and oppressive standards of beauty.[6] Discussing the ideology underpinning the makeover genre, Dana Heller argues, "What American makeover shows often tell us is that self-realization and conformity to cultural ideals are twin virtues founded on one's unrealized desire for belonging: in this sense, makeover shows promise to make subjects more truly themselves by making them look, dress, decorate, and desire as others ostensibly do" (1).

The main narrative in *Plastic Makes Perfect* appears to support this contention, as it maintains a focus on a familiar pattern that emphasizes the success and desirability of cosmetic surgery as part of a journey of self-improvement. This narrative is disrupted in a number of ways, however, most notably in its introduction of comedy. The female comedians Debra DiGiovanni and Sabrina Jalees appear throughout the episodes, offering sarcastic commentary on the issues at hand. Both women represent challenges to traditional beauty standards ethnically and physically. Jalees is of Pakistani and Swiss descent, and DiGiovanni is a large woman who, while known for her self-deprecating style, seems comfortable with her size and uses it to her advantage. As performers outside this program, these women have used these attributes as integral aspects of their stand-up routines, and these also inform their personae on *Plastic Makes Perfect*. In an interview Jalees was asked how her background influenced her comedy. She responded, "I think that that has a lot to do with why I'm a comic. I think that oftentimes, comedy comes from these fish-out-of-water experiences, like, being a part of the masses but being outside the masses, so you can say 'Masses, why you do things like that?'" (Henderson). She describes a sense of exclusion that contributed to her humor. This seems also to influence her performances on *Plastic Makes Perfect*. Both women offer information and statistics on plastic surgery, which are then punctuated with jokes that mock the seriousness with which these topics are usually treated. For example, in the breast augmentation episode, Jalees provides information about why women's breasts sag and adds, "The next expected trend is that women will be competing on how high they can raise their breasts. We'll have ninety-year-old women gluing their breasts to their foreheads." These comedic (and perhaps carnivalesque) moments disturb the narrative, introducing moments of disorder in which their personae as "unruly women" complicate discourses surrounding plastic surgery, suggesting the ridiculousness of the current vogue of practices such as breast lifts and implants and opening up questions about their rationality.[7] In effect, these moments seem to approximate a resistant and skeptical viewing position from which these issues (and their corresponding ideologies) are cast in a humorous light.

The program also includes a variety of other voices and perspectives, such as the resident pop psychotherapist Rebecca Rosenblat, whose garish clothing and demeanor (in the breast augmentation episode she is shown reclined on a bar, sipping a martini) undercut her authority as expert. Other figures include Dr. Paul Rappaport from the Federation of Canadian Naturalists, who always appears naked and inevitably declares the virtues of the natural body, and various "real" psychiatrists, media critics, and professors who comment from more academic perspectives about body issues and pressures to conform. The medical, psychiatric, and academic discourses surrounding plastic surgery are also subject to a kind of carnivalesque treatment: different kinds of authority are presented and contrasted (some funny, some serious, some representing institutional knowledge, others popular knowledge) but also mocked, as the idea of "expert" itself is subjected to humorous treatment as well.

Overall, *Plastic Makes Perfect* is a very conflicted representation of cosmetic surgery. It maintains much of the conventional narrative found within typical makeover programs, offering some of the same, familiar pleasures of the transformations offered in programs like *Extreme Makeover* and *The Swan*. It also recasts this narrative through comedy, however, which opens up moments of contradiction. It treats cosmetic surgery in an irreverent, comedic way that offers the possibility of a resistant or oppositional reading of this central narrative.

It is important to note that the show is but one program in the entire Slice schedule, which features other surgery makeover programs. Heller describes the makeover narrative as invoking a specifically American mythology: "The complex cultural origins of makeover narrative can be broadly traced to myths of American expansionism, evangelicalism, and immigration" (2). Likewise, June Deery argues, "The makeover clearly invokes the self-consciously entitled and undoubtedly hegemonic 'American Dream'" (161). If we think of the makeover narrative as part of an American myth of success and reinvention, *Plastic Makes Perfect* takes on an added significance. This recasting of the central makeover narrative may also be examined as a potentially resistant reading from a national perspective as well. Canadians have always consumed American television programming with enthusiasm, a fact that has provoked anxieties about cultural imperialism and possible threats to cultural sovereignty (which the debates about reality television in Canada have replayed). Here we might read *Plastic Makes Perfect* as a rebellious and carnivalesque response to American narratives about beauty and bodies, as it maintains some of the pleasures associated with those narratives, and yet it adopts an ambivalent and sometimes contrary attitude toward them.

The two series I've chosen for analysis prompt a reconsideration of the easy association of reality and lifestyle programming with the decline in Canada of quality television programming for women. They appear on networks that address women viewers in very different ways. As I've attempted to demonstrate, these channels can be productively viewed as ambivalent spaces where a range of ideas (at times contrary) about women and women's issues is presented. As I've argued, *The Shopping Bags* and *Plastic Make Perfect* present interesting case studies through which to examine popular discourses on gender, consumerism, beauty, and nation. Though they may not fulfill the feminist agenda many had hoped for when WTN was originally launched, and though they are not without their problems, they nonetheless provoke a rethinking of how the story of the rise and fall of women's television in Canada has been told.

Notes

1. Derek Foster provides an in-depth analysis of this controversy and the debates about reality television on the CBC in his article "Chasing the Public: The CBC and the Debate over Factual Entertainment on Canadian Airwaves," *Canadian Journal of Communication* 34.1 (2009): 61–77. Interestingly, Foster's analysis highlights how these debates often figure reality TV (and its supposed questionable social and cultural value) as a form seemingly in conflict with the public service mandate of Canada's national public broadcaster.

2. This equity clause states, "It is hereby declared as the broadcasting policy for Canada that . . . the Canadian broadcasting system should . . . through its programming and the employment opportunities arising out of its operations, serve the needs and interests, and reflect the circumstances and aspirations, of Canadian men, women, and children, including equal rights, the linguistic duality and multicultural and multiracial nature of Canadian society and the special place of aboriginal peoples within that society" (quoted in Off 111).

3. See, for example, Mary Ellen Brown, *Soap Opera and Women's Talk: The Pleasure of Resistance* (Thousand Oaks, CA: Sage, 1994); Ien Ang, *Watch-*

ing Dallas: Soap Opera and Melodramatic Imagination (London: Methuen, 1985); and Laura Stempel Mumford, *Love and Ideology in the Afternoon* (Bloomington: Indiana University Press, 1994).

4. See, for example, Andreas Huyssen, *After the Great Divide: Modernism, Mass Culture, Postmodernism* (Bloomington: Indiana University Press, 1986).

5. Two key examples are Ien Ang, "Melodramatic Identifications: Television Fiction and Women's Fantasy," and Tania Modeleski, "The Search for Tomorrow in Today's Soap Operas," both in *Feminist Television Criticism: A Reader,* ed. Charlotte Brunsdon, Julie D'Acci and Lynn Spigel (Oxford: Oxford University Press, 1997).

6. Some examples mentioned by Sue Tait include Naomi Wolf, *The Beauty Myth* (London: Vintage, 1991); Sheila Jeffreys, *Beauty and Misogyny: Harmful Cultural Practices in the West* (New York: Routledge, 2005); Kathryn Pauly Morgan, "Women and the Knife: Cosmetic Surgery and the Colonization of Women's Bodies," *Hypatia* 6.4 (1991): 25–53.

7. Situating female comedy in the context of theories of the carnivalesque, Kathleen Rowe's analysis of Roseanne Barr as an "unruly woman" demonstrates how (through both her body and her behavior) her performances "provide a space to act out the dilemmas of femininity, to *make visible* and *laughable* what Mary Ann Doane describes as the 'tropes of femininity.'" (Rowe 77). The inclusion of performances by Jalees and DiGiovanni may operate to similarly expose and render comic the conventional discourses surrounding beauty that typically circulate within representations of cosmetic surgery and corresponding makeover narratives.

Works Cited

Andrews, Maggie, and Mary M. Talbot. "Introduction: Women in Consumer Culture." *All the World and Her Husband: Women in Twentieth-century Consumer Culture.* Ed. Maggie Andres and Mary M. Talbot. New York: Cassell, 2000. 1–9.

Atherton, Tony. "Women's Channel to Be More Entertaining as W." *Ottawa Citizen,* April 15, 2002, B5.

Blakey, Bob. "Shop till They Drop." *Calgary Herald,* June 22, 2002, ES07.

Canadian Radio-television and Telecommunications Commission. *Images of Women: Report of the Task Force on Sex-Role Stereotyping in the Broadcast Media.* Hull, QC: Canadian Government Publishing Centre, 1982.

Chidley, Joe. "Can the Seven New Channels Survive?" *Maclean's* 108.6 (February 6, 1995): 70.

Clarke, Allison J. "'As Seen on TV': Design and Domestic Economy." *All the World and Her Husband: Women in Twentieth-century Consumer Culture.* Ed. Maggie Andrews and Mary M. Talbot. New York: Cassell, 2000. 146–161.

D'Acci, Julie. "Television, Representation and Gender." *The Television Studies Reader*. Ed. Robert C. Allen and Annette Hill. London: Routledge, 2004. 373–388.

Deery, June. "Interior Design: Commodifying Self and Place in *Extreme Makeover, Extreme Makeover: Home Edition*, and *The Swan*." *The Great American Makeover: Television, History, Nation*. Ed. Dana Heller. New York: Palgrave Macmillan, 2006. 159–174.

Doyle, John. "CRTC Finally Does Something for Viewers." *Globe and Mail*, March 1, 2006, R3.

———. "It's a Slice! Female Viewers Are Airheads!" *Globe and Mail*, March 5, 2007, R3.

Dranoff, Linda Silver. "Strategy for Change." *Changing Focus: The Future for Women in the Canadian Film and Television Industry*. Toronto: Toronto Women in Film and Television, 1991. 59–72.

Fiske, John. *Television Culture*. London: Routledge, 1990.

Foster, Derek. "Chasing the Public: The CBC and the Debate over Factual Entertainment on Canadian Airwaves." *Canadian Journal of Communication* 34.1 (2009): 61–77.

Heller, Dana. "Before: 'Things Just Keep Getting Better . . .' " *The Great American Makeover: Television, History, Nation*. Ed. Dana Heller. New York: Palgrave Macmillan, 2006, 1–7.

Henderson, Peter, "The Young, Talented, and Funny: Sabrina Jalees." *University of Ottawa's Fulcrum* 68.8 (February 14, 2008), www.thefulcrum.ca/arts/young,-talented,-and-funny:-sabrina-jalees.

MacDonald, Gayle, and Simon Tuck. "CBC Execs Try Damage Control." *Globe and Mail*, June 22, 2006, R1.

McRobbie, Angela. "Post-Feminism and Popular Culture." *Feminist Media Studies* 4.4 (2004): 255–264.

Off, Shirley Anne. "The Women's Television Network: By, for and about Women . . . or Was That Ratings?" *PopCan: Popular Culture in Canada*. Ed. Lynne Van Luven and Priscilla L. Walton. Scarborough, ON: Prentice Hall Allyn and Bacon Canada, 1999. 106–112.

Pearce, Deborah. *Victoria (BC) Times-Colonist*, December 10, 1993, 1.

"Proposed TV Channel to Reflect Women's Reality." *Herizons* 8.1 (1994): 16.

Public Notice CRTC 1986-351, December 22, 1986, www.crtc.gc.ca/eng/archive/1986/pb86-351.htm.

Public Notice CRTC 1992-58, Ottawa, September 1, 1992, www.crtc.gc.ca/eng/archive/1992/pb92-58.htm.

"Real Women Won't Watch the Women's Network." *Alberta Report/Newsmagazine* 22.7 (January 30, 1995): 35.

Riches, Hester. "The Play for Pay: Or How to Get a Specialty TV Channel and View Happily Ever After: Channels: A Seven-Step Program to Understanding." *Vancouver Sun*, January 14, 1995, B5.

Rowe, Kathleen K. "Roseanne: Unruly Woman as Domestic Goddess." *Feminist Television Criticism: A Reader.* Ed. Charlotte Brundson, Julie D'Acci, and Lynn Spigel. Oxford: Oxford University Press, 1997. 74–83.

Slice Network, www.slice.ca.

Spears, George, and Kasia Seydegart. *The Portrayal of Sex Roles in Canadian Television Programming* (Commissioned by the Canadian Radio-television and Telecommunications Commission). Erin, ON: Erin Research, 1985.

Tait, Sue. "Television and the Domestication of Cosmetic Surgery." *Feminist Media Studies* 7.2 (2007): 119–135.

Thornham, Sue. *Feminist Theory and Cultural Studies: Stories of Unsettled Relations.* New York: Oxford University Press, 2000.

Urlocker, Michael. "WTN's Search for an Audience." *Financial Post*, July 20, 1995, 1:5.

Van Den Broek, Astrid. "Has WTN Gone Too Soft?" *Herizons* 11.2 (Spring 1997): 20.

Zerbisias, Antonia. "CRTC's Unpopular Job Is to Protect the Public Interest." *Toronto Star,* May 29, 2006, D02.

DEBBIE CLARE OLSON

Babes in BonanzaLand

Kid Nation, *Commodification, and the Death of Play*

On the Web site for the CBS reality show *Kid Nation* (2007) the tagline reads: "40 kids have 40 days to build a brave new world without adults to help or hinder their efforts." The show takes place in a New Mexico ghost town called Bonanza City, where one can just imagine Lorne Green or Michael Landon lurking somewhere offscreen. The children are charged with creating this new world on their own, a heavy responsibility for a cast ranging in age from eight to fifteen. Aside from the obvious biblical reference to Noah and the Flood, the show offers visual nostalgia for the grand ol' days of a shoot-'em-up Wild West that must be tamed (minus, of course, outlaws or hostile Native Americans). According to Jyotsna Kapur, "Children are invoked as mediums through which the past [glory and power] can be restored" (87), and *Kid Nation* functions as a modern fusion of such ideological themes as civilization versus nature, individual strength against great odds, the glory of the Western frontier, and the innocence of childhood. The series alludes to such cultural artifacts as William Goldings's *Lord of the Flies* and John Ford westerns. The tagline on the Web site continues, "Will they come together as a cohesive unit or will they succumb to the childhood temptations that lead to chaos?" This question challenges broad cultural fantasies of an imagined Victorian-style childhood innocence. In our postmodern society, childhood is increasingly conceived of in nostalgic terms that infuse it with a desire for a "perfect" past that has not yet been created. In reality, the postmodern child's material and geographic condition is an increasingly multitextual space: urban, wired, materialist, graphic, and more adultlike; here nostalgia for a "lost" childhood works alongside a youth's desire for adult autonomy. Reinforcing that quest for an idealized childhood are the growing communities of "cyber-real" space (computer and video games, online communities, text messaging, Facebook, YouTube, and so on), which offer the promise of multiple satisfactions. The image of childhood, as commonly conceived, is being transformed as a result of the constant infusion of technology into daily life. Childhood has become "staged for public consumption" (Postman 82–83) to fit a nostalgic ideal of what childhood should be. *Kid Nation* is one, perhaps inevitable, move toward uniting the reality show with the adult quest for youth in this era of an increasing loss of "childness." As Postman argues, broad access to the information superhighway has allowed for a certain level of knowledge now available to children that, in an earlier time, would have been exclusive to adults (85). The line between adult and child in *Kid Nation* is blurred; it is situated between children's desire to be adult (adultifying) and adult desire to recapture youth. The series attempts to offer a fantasy to both groups.

The reality show experience changes the discourse of childhood as a socially negotiated space by authenticating existing social structures in the series' myth of creating a brave new world. The series sets up the typical conflict dynamic between participants expected from a reality show within the coming-of-age frame. This site of mediation between childhood and adulthood in *Kid Nation,* as a display, requires a reexamination of common assumptions about what it means to be a child in the digital age. The sociopolitical structures implemented in *Kid Nation* severely restrict the children's ability to actually create the new society that the series promises; instead, childhood is displayed as a condition that must be overcome in the quest for increased productivity in Bonanza City. *Kid Nation* commodifies childhood and then systematically destroys it. In a paradoxical move, the rhetoric of recaptured youth (free from adults) instead offers the visual and emotional destruction of childhood while the viewer commiserates with the young people trapped within adult social matrices, much like rats in a maze: how will the children negotiate the assigned challenges of money, class, race, religion, prejudice—and their own state of childhood?

Reality Shows

Television, unlike film, creates a sense of immediacy, of the "now" and the "real," what Jane Feuer calls "liveness." In contrast to the highly scripted formats and star personalities of classic television of the 1950s, modern reality-style television has changed the way ordinary people are presented, blurring the line between star and everyday individual. Formerly, regular people were "taken in themselves as signs of the real" (Biressi and Nunn 4), but in the reality TV of the twenty-first century, the real has encompassed both ordinary and star to such an extent that the line between real and the imaginary has become fuzzy. Expectations for a "realist representation" have become the frame through which reality shows compete with each other—who is the most "real"? And those real people now include blue-collar workers, professionals, educators, and a broad range of participants from a wide variety of social and economic conditions. Even marginal groups (the very poor, Goths, punks), normally invisible to the mainstream, are represented in reality shows such as the MTV documentary-reality series *True Life,* which follows the lives of people living in different sub-cultures, such as welfare moms, homeless families, and people living in "the projects." Reality TV has taken the shine off the mystique of celebrity, and many has-been celebrities have become more "real" and revamped their careers through their "authentic" appearances on such reality shows as *The Salt-N-Peppa Show* (2007–2008), *Scott Baio Is 45 . . . and Single* (2007), and *Hogan Knows Best* (2005–2007). Biressi and Nunn argue that the new "scopic technologies," those technological products that "watch" (i.e., cell-phone cameras, mini–digital video cameras, and particularly Web cams), transmit a "sense of immediacy and intimacy and 'unscripted' ma-terial featuring 'real' people" that have helped reality TV "claim to reveal social, psychological, political and historical truths" (3). Seeing people in their private homes gives an illusion of historical and social truth. Accord-ing to Mark Andrejevic, "The penchant for voyeurism associated with the explosion of reality programming . . . [is] symptomatic of a waning sense of reality in the postmodern era and a symptom of the merging of news and entertainment" (8). The 1980s Reagan era of expanding capitalism spawned a new social and political atmosphere that privileged social mo-bility and media visibility as the "touchstone of individual achievement," which has been intensified through the rise of the Internet, series such as Donald Trump's *The Apprentice* (2004–), and the wide participation in the reality phenomenon today through an explosion of public postings of amateur digital videos on sites such as YouTube and MySpace (4), and even into television "news" with the iReports segment on CNN (video news and opinions sent in by viewers—"real" people). The space of the real today is intertwined with media technologies and exhibition.

According to Matthew J. Smith and Andrew F. Wood, the actual reality shows' locations or premises may vary, but all reality shows follow the same basic plot: "introduce a diverse group of people, put them into situations bound to induce conflict, and watch them squirm" (1). The popular reality game show *Survivor* (2001–) provides the model for *Kid Nation*. In *Survivor*, a group of adults is dropped on a deserted island—in later episodes an exotic but extreme locale—and charged with living off the land for a predetermined length of time. They are to construct shelter and forage for their food. The entire experience is devoid of any modern conveniences or accoutrements. The participants divide themselves into tribes and create primitive signifier rituals as part of their new social space. Each week, however, the contestants compete for prizes and vote one of their members off the island, which creates multiple layers of deceit, disingenuousness, and competition within and between the tribes. The tribes have "no fixed, central State apparatus and no global power mechanisms or specialized political institutions," which Deleuze and Guattari argue creates "social segments that [have] a certain leeway between the two extreme poles of fusion and scission" (209). The participants organize themselves in opposition: they compete against each other yet must help each other. This oscillation between two positions creates a social "segmentarity" that allows for the two tribes to produce for the viewer a fluid, ever-changing overlap of loyalty, competition, and survival. *Survivor* is a TV phenomenon that sparked a multilayered convergence of media-based fan activity as viewers clamored to be a part of the *Survivor* experience through fan sites, discussion boards, mediated videos posted on YouTube, and a host of other online participatory activities. *Survivor* and its interplay among contestants, extreme material conditions, and the negotiations between loyalty, competition, and endurance became the baseline model for the myriad popular reality shows that followed in its wake, including *Kid Nation*.

Kid Nation adheres to a similar trajectory of contestant negotiations of temporal, social, and geographic space, though no one is actually voted out of the town. Instead, each week the council awards one child a gold star worth $20,000. The series does, however, divide the children into labor "classes" and attaches an economic value to each class and its assigned duties. The participants are given a supply of basic foodstuffs such as pasta, potatoes, flour, and a small flock of chickens, but they do not have any canned items. The second episode features the council's decision to butcher a couple of chickens, which elicited much criticism from animal rights organizations; Last Chance for Animals condemned

A town hall meeting on *Kid Nation* (CBS, 2007) shows children participating as adult citizens. Courtesy of CBS/PhotoFest.

the chicken "murder" as "staged purely for entertainment." The LCA also criticized CBS's position on the incident: the network argued that the only way for the kids to get any protein was to kill and eat an animal ("LCA Condemns"). During episode 11 the council again decides to kill some chickens, but this time young Taylor (eight years old) declares that only the "ugly" chickens should be killed and that the "pretty" brown chickens deserved to live: only "ugly animals should die, but not the pretty ones . . . they don't matter as much as the beautiful ones." The episode briefly highlights only two children who criticize Taylor's segregation of the chickens—a disturbing commentary on and evidence of how some children learn that only aesthetically pleasing life has value.

Class Time

Rather than allow the children to create a society completely on their own, *Kid Nation* replicates Western social apparatuses—power divisions by color [race] and labor class—capitalism and consumption being the forces that drive the children to cooperate. Each week the series' moderator, John, and the "Journal" (a conveniently placed, conceptually biblical book that serves as a visible script for the participants to follow) insert into the society a new condition: first, the division into groups by color (red, yellow, green, blue), then the introduction of four social "classes" (Upper Class, Merchants, Cooks, Workers) with corresponding pay rates (a dollar, a half dollar, a quarter, a dime, respectively). Ellen Goodman charges the show with promoting the "three C's" of our culture: "cutthroat consumerism, class divisions, [and] unrelenting consumerism." Only the four council members are allowed to read the Journal, and they interpret it for the rest of the group, an arrangement that seems to advocate a hierarchical power structure in which the populace's access to knowledge is only through the filter of the political elite, which in turn validates the social structures the children must negotiate. If any participant questioned the pay, class, or power arrangement, such doubt was edited out of the series. Each week the Journal gives a suggestion to the council—such as instituting law and order, religion, education—that will help their new society flourish. At the end of each episode there is a competition, called a showdown (another reference to the Wild West), to decide which group will inhabit which class. These showdowns—which rely on physical prowess, aggressive competition, and group cooperation—are the only condition that allow for movement between the classes.

Despite CBS's claim that the children are free to create their own society, they are explicitly directed to add specific sociopolitical conditions to the community during both the Journal readings and strictly scripted town hall meetings. The producers do not allow the children to create their own social matrices as a natural consequence of their environmental, geopolitical, or sociopolitical groupings. Aside from the ability of the four council members to choose whom they wanted in their groups (and the children they chose had no say in the matter), none of the social conditions evolving in *Kid Nation* was devised, decided, or even voted on by the children. Those with special skills or knowledge, such as cooking, are restricted to doing the work of their assigned class, rather than the labor they are most suited for or desire to do; for instance, in episode 1, Sophia takes on cooking for the town, as she enjoys it and knows how. But when the council divides the kids into groups, and those groups then compete in the first showdown for their class designations, Sophia ends up with the Workers, not the Cooks. Though she has the cooking skill, she is not allowed to do the cooking because she does not belong to that class. Such constraints on social mobility reflect many real-life restrictions on individual mobility that are based on economic limitations or social myths about those who belong to the labor or worker classes. The class segregation continued through the series until the final episode, which opens with the job board on fire. The town pulls together to put the fire out, but then the moderator appears and tells them there are no more assigned jobs or classes. Sophia immediately shoulders the cooking, as she had done during the first episode.

Another example is the yellow group, which has the youngest children, most of who are female; yet they land in the Cook class numerous times throughout the series. They were unqualified and unskilled in the art of cooking, particularly for that many mouths. The second time they "earn" that spot through their performance during the showdown, they go on strike and refuse to cook. What follows the yellow group's strike declaration is a brief montage of sound bites by some participants about the girls' laziness and lack of work ethic. When they finally fold under pressure and cook, the meal they prepare—fried potatoes—is not enough to feed the whole town. The yellow group's apathy toward a responsibility they are physically and mentally unsuited for in turn leads to a naturalized belief by the other participants in the younger children's laziness, instead of compassion for their very real condition of immaturity and inexperience. Rather than encouraging or helping these participants to perform their assigned work better, the peer-group criticism gives the younger girls (and it is always the youngest girls who are perceived as lazy, never the youngest boys) license to wallow in a fantasy of perpetual "victimhood," an attitude the younger girls assume throughout the series.

The series' rhetorical framework appears to encourage the ideals of "the good of the many"; in practice, however, the grouping of labor functions by class division (which are signified by color) creates discord and apathy among those who are stuck in a class for which they are mentally or physically unsuited or unqualified. The Upper Class is exempt from doing any work (unless they choose to), and their patrician position garners the most gain (one dollar per episode for producing the least, while the Workers do the most for the least money (ten cents). Money itself is conveniently introduced into *Kid Nation* by the moderator (episode 1), who decides the amount each group will be paid. The children are not allowed to vote for or decide on any other pay scale and must adhere to conditions that emanate from the omniscient producers, who dictate (through the Journal and the moderator) the "natural" division of wealth and labor. The Upper

Class's monetary gain for producing the least gives the impression that just being in the Upper Class is equivalent to deserving wealth, and any real-world labor behind that gain is conspicuously absent, which validates the "natural" power of the elite. The series' construction of the Upper Class also functions to reinforce social stereotypes of the lazy affluent, who do nothing for their wealth, a cliché that removes all hints of the real social, political, and economic conditions that make it possible to accumulate such wealth, particularly from the exploited labor of the Workers. What the series rarely makes evident are those in the Upper Class who do work and do help out. Most of the shots of those in the Upper Class consist of their brief comments about how they do not *have* to work like the others. Conversely, rarely do the producers highlight the drudgery of the Workers' chores, other than to emphasize someone's refusal to do those duties—and in this case the series consistently makes Taylor the brunt of such criticism. The actual labor itself is not worthy of screen time as much as the *refusal* to labor is. The low pay and heavy responsibilities of the Worker class also make evident the real-world social exploitation of those who do the majority of the work to maintain a high standard of living for the rest; yet the Worker class reaps the least profit or appreciation for its efforts.

The same type of division of labor and class, and the emphasis on adult material gain, is most evident in *Kid Nation*'s lack of normal child-like behaviors, particularly its lack of images of play.

The End of Play as We Know It

There are no toys in Bonanza City but for a few stuffed animals that the younger girls have brought with them. During episode 1, the girls create a "stuffed animal day care," but the episode's framing of their play implies that it is a silent rebellion against the girls' assigned work, rather than the natural behavior of young children. The accompanying music is slightly ominous, rather than lighthearted, and there is a montage of the exasperated expressions of the others as they criticize the girls' lack of participation in their assigned tasks. None of the children is ever shown creating toys or playing with available materials. In fact, throughout the series the complaint that gets the most camera time is that someone is lazy (play = laziness) and not working. The majority of the gold stars are awarded on the basis of how hard a participant has worked. Furthermore, most of the workload and other activities shown in each episode

Children experience firsthand the frontier experience on *Kid Nation* (CBS, 2007). Courtesy of CBS/PhotoFest.

are traditionally gender-determined. The series highlights the "natural" gendered division of labor, which functions as a reaffirmation of the status quo and allows the *Kid Nation* childhood fantasy adventure to "endow reality with fictional coherence and stability, which seem to guarantee that such reality, the social world in which we take our place," is legitimized within adult desire (Edelman 34). The girls are always shown doing traditional "woman's work"—such as cleaning and cooking—while the boys do most of the physical labor—carrying water and fixing things. During the first episode Greg (fifteen years old), who desperately wants to earn a gold star, rarely helps out and functions as the show's juvenile delinquent. After his group (blue) wins Upper-Class status, Greg and Eric (fourteen) write "blue" in chalk all over the others' bunkhouses. Greg consistently and aggressively confronts the younger children and uses foul language (to which the series immediately responds with a reaction-shot montage of the younger children's shock). With the gold star as a lure, Greg goes out of his way to help out, though that help is mixed with his frequent bouts of anger, abusive language, and occasional physical threats. During episode 2, Greg and the Upper-Class boys do the dishes, but that action is contrasted with his violent outburst earlier in the episode. It takes until episode 5 for Greg to win the gold star.

Aside from the gendered division of labor, the series also genders what little play does exist. In fact, when images of play do appear, as in episode 11—the council chooses a free arcade as the showdown prize—the series frames the play as dangerous to the town. Rather, it is labor that is the defining characteristic of being adult and mature. When play is shown, it is disturbingly masculine and, in the case of the party at the Saloon in episode 3, behavior that promotes substance abuse. The first single all-community playtime occurs at the opening of episode 3, when there is a rip-roaring party at the Saloon. But this "play" is disturbingly adultlike, as the children mimic drinking liquor—chugging and binge-drinking while they cheer each other on. As Lindsey Ward describes:

> Unless there's something I'm missing, kids probably shouldn't know how to mix boilermakers. . . . But on Wednesday, there the young pioneers of Kid Nation were, feet planted firmly on the tables of the town saloon, chuggin' 'em back like they were Frank the Tank. Of course, all work and no play makes for dull girls and boys. And their concoctions were made of root beer. But it's the way they consumed it—in assuming mugs, bottles, lowballs and shotglasses—that was unsettling. That and the fact that the kids who had taken part in the particularly rowdy bash were very "tired" the next day.

The "play" that the series espouses is the play of adults' fantasy, not children's. The Wild West framing of the series' experience creates a reliving of the glorious American frontier past that is a stand-in for childhood play.

Though the girls in the series are rarely shown playing, Kid Nation offers a much different vision of the boys. The series frequently closes episodes with shots of boys going off on "manly" treks of discovery or challenging nature; in episode 3, for example, Colton (eleven) displays his budding manhood by challenging a longhorn cow. In the same episode, two of the younger boys are in the kitchen throwing flour at each other, giggling and tussling and running around the room. In the next shot, Mallory, an eight-year-old girl, is struggling to clean it all up, the boys conspicuously absent. The girls are rarely shown exploring their surroundings, and they never go off on adventures. The younger girls are often shown in the early morning giggling or goofing off in their beds, usually bundled up in coats and tucked into their sleeping bags (a confined space, yet the only "free" place to play), evidence of their immaturity, but the play is framed as negative, as a resistance to their assigned duties, their lack of labor, their *laziness*.

Rather than exhibit normal childhood behavior and desires, the children are conditioned by their enforced material conditions and the lack of technology to desire adult things. When the children arrive, the town consists of one outhouse for all forty of them (which hints at a Freudian producer control over bodily functions). After the first showdown, the council has to choose between two community prizes—seven more toilets, or a television. The council (not the town) is forced to choose necessity—the toilets—over pleasure—the TV—which only intensifies the desire for the TV. All the showdowns end with a choice between an object of necessity and one more pleasurable and suited to children. In episode 3 the choice is between a microwave oven and forty heavily topped pizzas, which elicits a near riot from the half-starved children. The group loudly demands the pizzas, but Taylor, speaking for the council, chooses the very unpopular microwave, which draws heavy criticism from the other participants. Until the final episodes, the council consistently chooses the necessary items.

In episode 11 the council chooses play over necessity for the first time: a fully stocked arcade. Pandemonium ensues, and soon the entire town spends hours in the arcade. There are numerous shots of dishes piling up, of garbage left unburied, of chores abandoned, all juxtaposed with shots of children zoning out on video games or intently shooting pool. Most of the shots of the arcade play are close-up or medium shots that tend to emphasize the loose abandon of the arcade play; the participants finally get to be children. The council meets in secret to figure out what to do, as no one is working. The Journal tells them they must have "law and order"; they therefore elect Sophia as the sheriff. The episode then dissolves into a power struggle between the council and the others for access to play. The arcade is padlocked, and playtime within it depends entirely on the amount of work that gets done. Play here is emphasized as bad, negative, a disruption of social responsibility, and something that must be doled out—in timed increments and by a representative of authority—only to those who deserve it.

The town's lack of traditional childhood trappings and the series' heavy emphasis on choices that force the children constantly to confront, and then deny, their childish impulses lend support to the notion that in a capitalist reality childhood is only ancillary to the real condition of becoming a consuming adult. It is perhaps an unintended sociopolitical marketing strategy that works to sell youth to adults while at the same time selling adulthood to youth; this creates a desire for the accessories of one condition and a constant yearning for the other. This space between childhood and adulthood is constantly filled with conflicting desires—for the innocence of youth, but also for the maturity and freedom from authority adulthood brings. On *Kid Nation,* however, that desire for adulthood is coterminous with the desire for wealth and material gain. According to Sharon Stevens, "The domain of childhood . . . is increasingly shot through with the values of the marketplace and the discursive politics of postmodern global culture" (24), which is increasingly materialistic. The material conditions on *Kid Nation* are contrived by its producers to place the participants in a situation of constant lack and then taunt them with choices that highlight that lack. The material conditions of Bonanza City reinforce for the young participants the denial of childish pleasure in favor of necessity. Perhaps for CBS's advertising support, which increased after the first episode aired,[1] "children's imagination, when not turned into a source for generating profit, becomes a terribly fearful thing that threatens to overturn the economic . . . and social status quo" (Kapur 164), a status quo that *Kid Nation* seeks to render natural, validated by images of children that emphasize labor, material wealth, and purchasing rather than imagination and play.

In episode 1 the General Store and the Saloon are magically stocked to the brim—rendering certain manufacture and distribution invisible—with a myriad of products, from jars of penny candy to a bicycle that becomes the object of desire for Sophia. As a Worker, Sophia does not make enough money to buy it, so she resorts to dancing and begging in the street for donations so she can buy the coveted bike, which she does by the end of the episode. The children's daily survival becomes the vehicle through which consumerism is possible, rather than a social networking of equals working for the good of the community. There is a constant struggle by the Upper and Merchant classes, for instance, to get the Workers and Cooks to wash the dishes, which pile up until in one episode they have to hold their dinner in one bare hand and eat it with the other. But the participants do work together to help Sophia purchase something by giving some of their hard-earned money (as charity) to her. As Jyotsna Kapur argues, "Capitalism . . . consumes the young by withdrawing the social protections from them and consequently turn[s] them into labor, subjecting children to the same exploitation as adults" (113). The *Kid Nation* participants learn to do this through the trajectory of the series' capitalist agenda. The episode does not linger long on Sophia's imaginative attempts to raise the money or on her ability to save money, but only on the end result—the *purchase*. Though the closing scene shows Sophia riding her new bike (riding off into the sunset?), it is her ability to buy it that the series privileges, rather than the pleasure and fun the bike gives her. (The series never divulges whether Sophia shared her bicycle with those who so generously contributed to its acquisition. The bicycle is never seen in the series again.)

The *Kid Nation* participants are manipulated into exploiting each other and their labor through the series' preestablished class divisions; "the social order exists to preserve . . . a notional freedom more highly valued than the actuality of freedom itself" (Edelman 11) is an idea that parallels the myth of childhood innocence, the return to which has become an American cultural obsession. Giroux argues that "innocence in this instance makes children invisible except as projections of adult fantasies—fantasies that allow adults to believe that children do not suffer from their greed, recklessness, perversions of will and spirit and that adults are, in the final analysis, unaccountable for their actions" (40). By placing children in the adult structures and conventions of the "reality show," adult viewers can satisfy their nostalgic desire for childhood innocence within the discourse of childhood itself as conceptually more "real," while enjoying the destruction of that very myth that is denied them. The series constructs conditions that demand "that social welfare be abolished and individuals, including children, provide for themselves through their own effort and labor" (Kapur 164), yet that effort and labor must fall within a predetermined pro-capitalist space. Any notion of the common good is secondary to the need for establishing class position or escaping the labor required to benefit the entire group. By instituting socioeconomic conditions that re-create today's social apparatus, the series conveniently nullifies any chance for the children to truly create their own society.

The Death of (the Real?) Childhood

The quest for the real in the postmodern fractured truths has led to a new "economy of realism" that requires "confession, exhibitionism and emotional revelation" as the marks of authenticity or of truth (Biressi and Nunn 7). Children within such a cultural frame are perhaps perceived as more authentic and closer to the real than adults, yet they carry a mystique, a myth, of an innocence that for adults is idealized in much the same way as the myths of Hollywood stardom. It would seem that there would have to be a very careful consideration of the conditions under which children would be placed on a reality show—they could not be as harsh as conditions for adult participants—and the conflicts would have to be less contentious than the ones adult reality show contestants experience. This particular reality TV premise challenges the very nature of childhood as a protected space by placing children in the very conditions adults are to protect them from: "Critics of reality TV have described these conditions as that of a 'human zoo' or a container under pressure which forces inmates 'inwards,' making them deal with one another continually and under highly constrained conditions" (Biressi and Nunn 15). These difficult circumstances provide pleasure for the adult viewing audience, a pleasure that is heightened by the perverse notion of watching the destruction of the very thing many adults desire: a return to childhood innocence.

In reality shows like *Kid Nation* several elements intersect—"the fetishization of the ordinary, the elevation of the personal and the interpersonal to the level of grand narrative, and the exploitation of the real subjects who consent to appear in the shows" (Brenton and Cohen 9). In *Kid Nation*, fetishizing the "ordinary" (i.e., the child) refers to an adult who assigns an overabundance of meaning to both the child body as desired youth and the idea of innocence that body symbolizes. Henry Giroux argues that "within the myth of innocence, children are often portrayed as inhabiting a world that is untainted, magical, and utterly protected from the harshness of adult life. In this scenario, innocence not only erases the complexities of childhood and the range of experiences different children encounter, but it also offers an excuse for adults to evade responsibility for how children are firmly connected to and shaped by the social and cultural institutions run largely by adults" (Giroux 39–40). The participants in *Kid Nation* are first directed to negotiate adult social matrices and harsh material conditions, and then framed for reality TV as symbols of the innocent youth "myth-in-crisis," a condition the children are set up to survive and negotiate without adult protections.

In *Tarrying with the Negative*, Slavoj Žižek argues that perversion (of which fetishism is one specific type) always bears the structure of a "closed loop": "It is quite normal to say to the beloved woman, 'I would love you even if you were wrinkled and mutilated!'; a perverse person is the one who intentionally mutilates the woman, distorts her beautiful face, so that he can continue to love her, thereby proving the sublime nature of his love" (194). This kind of perversion of human emotion is demonstrated in our society every time a man or woman kills a spouse or partner because he or she "loves" that person. If "child" is substituted for "woman" in Žižek's argument, the distortion of the "beautiful face" becomes a distortion of "childhood," a way instead for adults to prove a kind of love for childhood itself by rendering it even more out of reach by its very destruction. For the myth of childhood innocence to be visually reinforced, onscreen children must act like children—make irrational or immature decisions and use their heightened imaginations to pretend and play, to be silly, and to revel in a perceived natural freedom from worry or adult pressures. *Kid Nation* offers very little in the way of childlike images and instead lingers, almost malevolently, on the youthful appearance of the children, but then takes the greatest pleasure in watching the faces of those same children in distress or conflict, particularly in their constant emotional and physical struggle to become more adultlike. The American frontier theme that frames the children's struggle functions in a similar way: like childhood, it is much romanticized, and it cannot be returned to in its original form.

In every episode of *Kid Nation,* the participants must confront some aspect of their material condition that adults normally protect them from, and in each confrontation the children are pressured both from peers and from the dictates of the Journal to make the most grown-up decision. Some of the participants are overwhelmed by the emotional struggle between their actual childness and the expectation of adult maturity. The children's struggle with choices about food or daily survival is visually fixed by a camera that lingers on the girls' woefully large, weepy eyes or a young boy's struggle to suppress welling tears as he wrestles against his youth to maintain his burgeoning manliness. In episode 3, little Taylor (ten years old) handles the pressures of being a council member by resorting to the phrase "deal with it" as she imperiously makes unpopular decisions while struggling to be more adult and yet acting the most childlike. During the town hall meeting (shot in a long take), the group verbally attacks her for not working and for her arrogance and "queen-like" manner; Taylor thereupon bursts into tears (zoom to close-up), a much sought-after commodity on *Kid Nation*. The camera lingers, lovingly, expectantly, using extreme close-ups of the children who cry, particularly the boys, as they struggle with homesickness, peer pressure and abuse, hunger, cold, overwork, and, for the boys, the constant push for heterosexual, masculine behavior. There are numerous shots of Greg hugging the smaller girls who suffer from homesickness and tears. There are shots of the older girls—Sophia or Migle—comforting a sobbing younger girl. But there are no scenes of the same type of physical comforting between the older and younger boys. There are many pats on the back and, in episode 12, a quick arm-around-the-shoulders between two boys who are "like brothers" (DK and Guylan) as they struggle with their emotional stress.

The very setting of *Kid Nation* in the Wild West seems an added pressure on the boys to aspire to a traditional "John Wayne–style" masculinity—mental toughness, maturity, determination, qualities that are beneficial and not exclusively masculine. Yet the series positions the attainment of those qualities as directly the result of labor alone, rather than being achieved through imagination or interpersonal struggle. The image of the historic Wild West cowboy, not to mention the vast conventions of the western film genre, functions in *Kid Nation* as an unspoken yet constantly hovering shadow over the boys. The series framework follows that of the traditional western: a hero's quest into the unknown and an emphasis on open spaces, rugged individualism, trials of individual participants, loners, and the righteousness of the settlers. The children are continually reminded that their purpose is to create a new world, a new Eden. Brought together, the conventions of the Western frontier as the geographic setting and the discourse of creating this paradise create an Edenic geopolitical agenda that affirms both the innocence of childhood (though lost) and the colonizing of the American West. The series effectively creates nostalgia for both. But the condition of innocent childhood is continually denied on *Kid Nation,* particularly for boys.

Rather than fostering sympathy for the boys who cry on *Kid Nation,* the series' visuals tend to criticize the boys who cry as weak. In episode 4 Cody (age nine), who had been one of the most "masculine-framed" of the boys for his exploits chasing cows with Colton, gets a letter from his girlfriend that sends him into deep homesickness. He is frequently framed in close-up, tears streaming down his face, as he tries to explain his pain. The series at first appears to sympathize with him through tight shots of his swollen, tear-stained face, but it then mocks him by following those shots with a montage of comments by the others about Cody's lack of toughness. His homesickness is presented as pathetic through the frequent emphasis on his lapses into tears and, in the end, his decision to leave the show. Each time the moderator asks at the town hall meeting if anyone wants to go home, the question is positioned as a challenge by both the moderator's tone and by the dynamic tension-building, game show–style music that usually prefaces a particularly significant answer from a contestant. There are quick shots of the children's faces all looking around to discover who is going to quit. When Cody raises his hand, there is a quick zoom on his tearing eyes and trembling chin as he stands, turns, apologizes for being weak, and says that he "can't stand it anymore."

Beyond Bonanza

For young fans of *Kid Nation,* the transmedia experiences that extend beyond the actual broadcast of the show offer only one example of the changing cultural landscape of childhood. As Edelman explains, it is the "image of the Child, not to be confused with the lived experiences of any historical children, [that] serves to regulate political discourse" (11), and that discourse is solidly consumerist in nature. *Kid Nation* juxtaposes childhood and adulthood in an artificially constructed landscape that marketers hope will create what Jenkins calls a "consumption community" (85), where viewers can interact with the children of *Kid Nation* through blogs, fan sites, discussion boards, spin-off stories and fan-based fictions, and a cornucopia of products. (Shop.seenon.com and the CBS store offer *Kid Nation* T-shirts in all four group colors that sport the Bonanza City logo, correspondingly colored bandanas, and water bottles. There are *Kid Nation* ring tones available, and the official *Kid Nation* site advertises iPod songs for download.) The seduction of the online imaginative spaces where kids believe they can participate in the "reality" of Bonanza City underscores the participants' position as spectacle to be consumed, a condition that becomes just a part of their everyday lived experiences—the "scopic technologies" that constantly observe and watch. At the series' end, numerous blogs and reality TV Web sites were calling for a reunion of the *Kid Nation* participants; not surprisingly, the majority of those comments were from adult viewers of the series. For example, Brian Stelter's article on the *New York Times*'s Web site, "Kid Nation Makes Little Racket, after All," elicited ninety-one responses—all from adult viewers.

In the pre-Internet era, a show with a premise like *Kid Nation*'s would have perhaps sparked imaginative neighborhood children to re-create Bonanza City in their backyards or local parks, possibly with a tree house serving as the town hall. The predigital child had the same real-world negotiations of political and material conditions, but within different space and time frames. With whom a child negotiated space depended on such limiting factors as transportation availability or actual physical proximity to other children. Today, however, heterogeneous participation by many children across cyberspace social networks like YouTube, MySpace, and Facebook, and the numerous *Kid Nation* fan sites (Junior Celebs, BuddyTV, Technorati, Yahoo, and Mahalo, to name a few) have changed the way children perceive the real world by encouraging the transference of their actual physical play into such digital media as Web sites, iPods, blogs, cell phones, and instant messaging. To network with each other through virtual space has in some ways become a replacement for live, local, real-world interactions between children. Before the series ended, seven children were so eager to become a part of the next *Kid Nation* experience that they'd videoed their auditions for *Kid Nation 2* and posted them (along with a handful of *Kid Nation* parodies) on YouTube. Although the future of *Kid Nation 2* is undecided, "the network admitted that 'there has been casting and other preproduction activity so the show would be ready in the event of a pick-up'" ("Officials Drop").

The brave new world that *Kid Nation* advertised does not take place on the series or through watching the forty children negotiate adult social matrices. Rather, the growing digitalization of childhood through the series' inspired virtual networks is, according to Manuel Castells, the "social morphology of our time" within the "growing enclosure of communication" (419) in niche-market Web sites and blogs. Through these children can engage in virtual discourse about the series, an activity that is encouraged as a form of play, which in turn may foster consumption of related products. Children in the digital age, much like the adults they seek to emulate, can be seduced by the illusion of real participation in the experience of Bonanza City, or in the case of the YouTube auditions, commodify themselves in the hopes of becoming a participant (417).

The *Kid Nation* Web site interface is very kid-friendly; it has links to Facebook, Google, and Diggs, where children or adults can participate in the digital cybersphere created by fellow Nationites. The site encourages viewers to spend time reading each of the children's biographies: "We challenged the Kids to create their own pages with artwork, pictures, colors and even YouTube video links! Enjoy each Kid's own page as designed by them, each with their own unique look, feel and voice. There aren't any grown up rules here. The Kids have taken the reins and made their very own pages for everyone to read and explore. Listen to the Kids sing or play piano, read their poems or check out their pictures from home. It's all about the Kids. Check it out now" (CBS).

For younger children, the personalized Web pages of each *Kid Nation* participant offer virtual friendship. For the network and producers of *Kid Nation,* the economic possibilities of forty characters' stories extending beyond the television broadcast to Web communities and spawning an infinite amount of intertextual and self-referential discourses are a function of "new models of marketing [that] seek to expand consumers' emotional, social, and intellectual investments with the goal of shaping consumption patterns" (Jenkins 63). As marketers continually seek to command early brand loyalties and shape children's future consumption patterns, *Kid Nation* offers a broad communal reception experience that crosses racial, gender, and generational lines. The site's message board contains hundreds of kids' remarks about the show, such as "OMG Greg was so mean to those little kids!" (posted by glossygal90) and Hopeful777's ruminations about the possibility of a romance (or sex) between Greg and Sophia. The message board discourse ranges from analyzing the characters, the show-downs, and the economic, social, and political conditions in the town to criticisms of individual participants, as well as of the series itself. A great many of the children who post comments on the message boards gleefully speculate about season 2.

The series suffered a bit from pre-air controversy about casting children in a *Survivor*-type reality show. The state of New Mexico, where Bonanza City is located, charged the production with violating child labor laws (McNary). But CBS and Tom Forman, the executive producer, defended the show: "CBS has detailed the precautions and procedures put in place to ensure that adults were ready to step in should real danger arise during the shoot"; these precautions included "on-site paramedics, a pediatrician, an animal safety expert and a child psychologist, not to mention a roster of producers assigned to monitor the kids' behavior" (Littleton 3). Parents of the *Kid Nation* participants were required to sign a twenty-two-page contract that left "little room for parents to argue that they did not know what their children might encounter. . . . The parents and children agreed not to hold the producers and CBS responsible if their children died or were injured" (Wyatt). Eventually, New Mexico's attorney general announced the state was dropping its investigation owing to the lack of complaints by the participants' parents ("Officials Drop"). But the legal scare made it difficult for CBS to find a location for *Kid Nation 2*. It should be noted that the agreements between CBS and the participants' parents also includes a gag clause (under threat of a multimillion dollar liability) that forbids the parents from speaking about *Kid Nation* without first obtaining permission from CBS. All the early controversy, however, kept *Kid Nation* in the spotlight. Though ratings were strong at first, they had leveled off by the time of the series finale, which had a "fourth-place finish in the 18–49 demographic" (Stelter). The controversy surrounding *Kid Nation* before it even aired perhaps helped to fuel the vibrant digital participation and media convergence that is a part of the new cultural landscape of childhood.

The "cult of the child" in the case of *Kid Nation* does not signify a new, innocent, "better society, brighter tomorrow," but instead offers a fantasy that functions to "reproduce the past, through displacement, in the form of the future" (Edelman 31). The geographic space of the series is a signifier of the reaffirmation of the power of the American Wild West past within the present, while at the same time the geographic space on *Kid Nation* is infused with objects of modernity in the shape of portable toilets, a microwave oven, pizza, a TV, washing machines, hot-air balloons, dune buggies (which the kids were unable to win), and other techno-objects— including the video arcade that the children won in episode 11. According to the series' producers, it appears that the "new social order" is a land filled with modern appliances and the desire for techno-toys (products), restricted freedom, and adherence to classism and domination by an elite group. The child participant in *Kid Nation* is infused with adult longing for a better world that is not based on any actual comparison to a real lived past (since they are only children). Rather, that longing for a romantic past functions as a constant flux in the interstitial space between desiring child and adult, what Andrejevic calls "moving forward into the past" (199). To achieve a "better world" the *Kid Nation* participant must deny her childness in favor of the more "real" pleasures of being like an adult consumer. The child's denial of her own natural state of being in favor of the more satisfying and autonomous condition of consuming adult suggests a cultural Fordist (i.e., ready-made, assembly-line production) approach to the reimagining of childhood in the postmodern age. Under such conditions of commodification, childhood today is in the process of becoming what Jean Baudrillard calls the "idea of the object": we no longer take pleasure in the object itself but in its fantasy ideal (92). Childhood becomes merely a "sign of [its own] absence" (93), experiencing and desiring its own end, in this case within the reality show format, "as an aesthetic pleasure of the highest order" (184); its absence is privileged in favor of the more fulfilling space of adulthood, a space that continually desires to return to its roots in childhood.

The "cult of the child" is not just misplaced; it is missing in *Kid Nation*. Instead, the series structures a replica of an adult world: a cult of consumerism that inserts desirable products (and the children are encouraged to desire them) and infects their budding society with adult prejudices (groupings by color and class), intolerances (religion), social Darwinism (showdowns), and capitalist exploitation (wage hierarchies and labor exploitation). What *Kid Nation* does not give the viewer is the vision of play, make-believe, creativity, imagination, and the general joy of experiencing the world through a child's eyes, the very things that are idealized by those adults who search for a return to youth. The question of whether children, if truly left on their own, can create a better society (or a worse one) is never answered on *Kid Nation*. During the finale, when the job board has burned and is left a smoldering pile of ash, and the children are finally free from the dictates of the Journal, they succumb to their newfound freedom and their forty days of deprivation and raid the general store in what one blogger calls the "Great Candy Riot of 2007 . . . liberated from the powerful fear of reprisal that kept them from indulging their every antisocial desire, [they] descended upon Bonanza City's confectionary, swallowing every gobstopper, licorice whip, and Sour Patch Kid their rapidly distending bellies could handle" ("The 'Kid Nation' Ends in Ruins"). Finally, the series allows a brief glimpse of true, unfettered childhood behavior.

The series ends with a bang, however, in the form of three extra gold stars worth $50,000 each that the council has to award to the participants whom they believe have captured the spirit of Bonanza City: one final commodification. The children's parents arrive, running as an invading horde down the dirt road into town. The final episode highlights the many tears and the parents' shocked reactions to the children's lack of clean living conditions, another form of visual reinforcement of the inadequacy of childhood and the rightness of being adult. The parents are allowed to sit in on the final town hall meeting and witness the three lucky recipients winning their gold stars (Sophia, Migle, and Morgan). The series ends with a final shot of the kids singing around the piano, an unusual glimpse of simple play.

What is apparent in the series, however, is the resilience and adaptability of *real* childhood, demonstrated by the forty participants as they gracefully, and with as much dignity as their young years allow, throughout the series negotiate difficult socioeconomic intricacies for the enjoyment of a voyeuristic adult world. It is ironic that children, the most defenseless and marginalized of us all, are insidiously manipulated into creating the illusion of a paradise that, in reality, is a glorification of their own childhood's demise. As Jyotsna Kapur so insightfully explains:

> Here we see once again that the growing up of the young, an extension of their power made possible by technology and to a limited extent by their status as consumers, is perceived as a threat not only to the hierarchy of children and adults but also ultimately to the status quo of society more generally. After all, if children separate from their parents, they stand to invent a new society in which the older norms of class, gender, race, and sexuality may no longer operate. Choosing to focus only on technology, the spread of consumer culture of the relationship between children and adults to the exclusion of the overarching domination of capital and the specific ways in which the bourgeois home is under transformation leads to a reactionary call for the old-fashioned family with the old-fashioned child at the center. (Kapur 126)

And *Kid Nation* offers up the old-fashioned child placed in the heart of that nostalgic American Eden—the Wild West. Perhaps that is the real fear of the adult producers of *Kid Nation*—that if left to their own devices, the children of *Kid Nation* would create a society that establishes as natural more equitable material distributions and denies the seduction of consumerism and the state of constant nostalgia for a lost innocence that is, like the idea itself, a fiction.

Note

1. According to *Advertising Age,* after the first episode aired CBS picked up advertising from "Capitol One, Red Bull, and a handful of pharmaceuticals, including Pfizer's Chantix." General Motors also ran an ad for its OnStar service (Steinberg).

Works Cited

Andrejevic, Mark. *Reality TV: The Work of Being Watched.* Lanham, MD: Rowman and Littlefield, 2004.
Baudrillard, Jean. *The Conspiracy of Art.* Trans. Ames Hodges. New York: Semiotext(e), 2005.
Biressi, Anita, and Heather Nunn. *Reality TV: Realism and Revelation.* New York: Wallflower Press, 2005.
Brenton, Sam, and Reuben Cohen. *Shooting People: Adventures in Reality TV.* New York: Verso, 2003.
Castells, Manuel. "Materials for an Exploratory Theory of a Networked Society." *American Cultural Studies: A Reader.* Ed. John Hartley and Roberta E. Pearson. London: Oxford University Press, 2000. 414–426.
CBS. *Kid Nation,* www.cbs.com/primetime/kid_nation/bio.shtml.
Deleuze, Gilles, and Felix Guattari. *A Thousand Plateaus: Capitalism and Schizophrenia.* Minneapolis: University of Minnesota Press, 1987.
Edelman, Lee. *No Future: Queer Theory and the Death Drive.* Durham, NC: Duke University Press, 2004.
Feuer, Jane. "The Concept of Live Television." *Regarding Television.* Ed. E. Kaplan. Los Angeles: American Film Institute, 1983.
Giroux, Henry. *Stealing Innocence: Corporate Culture's War on Children.* New York: Palgrave, 2000.
Goodman, Ellen. " 'Kid Nation' Sure Isn't a Bonanza!" *Tulsa World,* September 28, 2007, A15.
Holloway, Sarah L., and Gill Valentine. *Cyberkids: Children in the Information Age.* London: Routledge Falmer, 2003.
Jenkins, Henry. *Convergence Culture: Where Old and New Media Collide.* New York: New York University Press, 2006.
Johnny, Leanne. "Reconceptualizing Childhood: Children's Rights and Youth Participation in Schools." *International Education Journal* 7.1 (2006): 17–25.
Kapur, Jyotsna. *Coining for Capital: Movies, Marketing, and the Transformation of Childhood.* New Brunswick: Rutgers University Press, 2005.
Keveney, Bill. "Future of 'Kid Nation' Undecided." *USA Today,* December 13, 2007.
Kid Nation. CBS. Episodes 1–13. September 1–December 12, 2007.
"The 'Kid Nation' Ends in Ruin," http://defamer.gawker.com/333850/the-kid-nation-ends-in-ruin.

"LCA Condemns CBS for Chicken Killing on 'Kid Nation,' " www.marketwire
.com/press-release/Last-Chance-For-Animals-774710.html.

Littleton, Cynthia. " 'Kid Nation' Producer Answers the $64,000 Question."
Variety, August 24, 2007.

McNary, Dave. "SAG Blasts 'Kid Nation' Again." *Variety,* September 20,
2007.

"Officials Drop 'Kid Nation' Investigation," www.buddytv.com/articles/kid-
nation/officals-drop-kid-nation-inve-14499.aspx, December 8, 2007.

Postman, Neil. *The Disappearance of Childhood.* New York: Vintage,
1994.

Schnoop, Jackie. "Kid Nation: I Just Like the Recess Part," www.tvsquad
.com/2007/11/28/kid-nation-i-just-like-the-recess-part/.

Smith, Matthew J., and Andrew F. Wood. *Survivor Lessons: Essays on Communication and Reality Television.* Jefferson, NC: McFarland, 2003.

Steinberg, Brian. "A Few More Advertisers Tiptoe into 'Kid Nation.' "
Advertising Age, September 27, 2007, www.adage.com/results.php?en
deca=1&return=endeca&D=01%2F14%2F2009&Nty=1&Ne=28&N
=4294958308.

Stelter, Brian. " 'Kid Nation' Makes Little Racket, After All." *New York Times,*
September 28, 2007, http://tvdecoder.blogs.nytimes.com/2007/12/14/kid-
nation-makes-little-racket-after-all/.

Stevens, Sharon. "Children and the Politics of Culture in 'Late Capitalism.' "
Children and the Politics of Culture. Ed. Sharon Stevens. Princeton:
Princeton University Press, 1995. 3–48.

Ward, Lindsey. "Booze and Kids Should Never Mix." *Edmonton Sun,*
October 6, 2007, www.edmontonsun.com/Entertainment/Television
/2007/10/06/4555419-sun.html.

Wyatt, Edward. " 'Kid Nation' Parents Gave Show Free Rein." *New York
Times,* August 23, 2007, www.nytimes.com/2007/08/23/arts/television/
23kids.html.

Žižek, Slavoj. *Tarrying with the Negative.* Durham, NC: Duke University
Press, 1993.

PART III

Reality TV and the Living History Experiment

JULIE ANNE TADDEO AND KEN DVORAK

"A Storybook Every Day"

Fiction and History in the Channel 4/PBS House Series

> In the world of television, if "The Bachelor" or "Fear Fac-
> tor" isn't your cup of tea, we recommend several alterna-
> tives to "reality TV." Have you ever wished you could step
> back in time and experience the way people lived in your
> favorite era of history? Do you long for a slower pace of
> life where your family could live together on your own
> homestead and farm your own plot of land? Do you envi-
> sion the sparkle of a magnificent chandelier in a Regency
> ballroom where Mr. Darcy might have first laid eyes on
> Elizabeth Bennet? (www.erasofelegance.com/entertainment/
> television2.html)

When the first of the British-themed and -produced historical House
series, *1900 House,* aired in the United States on PBS in June 2000, the
network described the project as "classy voyeurism" and the place where
"the sci-fi drama of time travel meets true-life drama."[1] The success of
1900 House has since led to other Anglo-American productions, including *1940s House* (2000), *Frontier House* (2001), *Manor House* (2002),
Colonial House (2003), *Texas Ranch House* (2006), and even PBS's own
version of reality dating (albeit in corsets and tights), *Regency House Party*
(2004). Determined to distinguish the House series from other reality TV
programs aired on commercial networks, PBS's producer Beth Hoppe
insists that this is the only one "with something to offer. We're exploring
history. No one else is doing that."[2]

It is true that the producers consult historians and provide rule books
and period-appropriate clothing, but it is not always history that drives
the series' ensuing drama. As the above quote suggests, participants and
viewers of these shows prefer a Fantasy Island version of the past: family togetherness, chandelier-lit drawing rooms, and heroic endeavors.
As the Texas ranchers or Edwardian aristocrats try to live through their

particular moment in the past, they perform their assigned roles, and the exploration of history, the so-called goal of the series, becomes a game (de Groot 403). Indeed, the professional historian is rarely visible in the series. When a military historian is invited to the final dinner of *Regency House Party* to lecture on the Battle of Waterloo, his words are drowned out by music; he is obviously too dull for viewers who prefer to see the developing romances among the guests.

The social historian Tristram Hunt takes issue with reality TV programming that uses history for purposes of "edutainment" and self-discovery. In his essay "Reality, Identity and Empathy: The Changing Face of Social History Television," Hunt observes that the recent media craze for history suggests a cultural and psychological search for "nourishment" by a secular society. Though more history is certainly being consumed, he adds, "it is far from clear how much is nurturing a deep and abiding sense of the past" (843). Indeed, historical accuracy takes a backseat to the time traveler's need to understand the self, as the programs' personality clashes and emotional breakdowns move front and center. The past, meanwhile, is reconstructed as a decorative backdrop and the "life lessons" gleaned from the video confessionals all tell a similar tale. The teenaged Tracy Clune of *Frontier House,* for example, predicts that when she returns to her twenty-first-century life, she will be less materialistic, and hence a "better" person: "I'm not the same person, and I'm happy about that" (www.pbs.org/wnet/frontierhouse/families/profile_tracy.html).

As the participants in these experiments typically conclude, the point of all their "suffering" (e.g., doing without shampoo or processed foods) is to understand and question their current lives and values, while realizing that the past and present are not so different after all. The penniless singer in *Regency House Party,* Mr. Carrington, explains how the experience "opened my eyes to a world I knew little about, which changes your perspective on the modern world we live in." Not surprisingly, historians criticize such a superficial approach to learning history, in which issues of class, race, and gender inequality, which clearly mark the past as different and distinct, are glossed over. But even Hunt acknowledges that the same analytical rigor that is demanded of the published historical text does not always make for a "lucrative media commodity" (843). Furthermore, to call reality history TV "bogus history" or "trash" misses the point of these programs and of the volunteer's and viewer's personal relationship to history (Nelson 143). In her study of the mythology of the American

West, Liza Nicholas observes that "what people believe to be true about their pasts is usually more important in determining their behavior and responses than truth itself" (xvii). It is through these myths, she adds, that we make sense of ourselves and explore our identity. Even Hoppe admits that her childhood memories of the *Little House* books and TV series based on them prompted her desire to revisit the pioneering experience in *Frontier House* and to see if twenty-first-century citizens could measure up to the Ingalls family.

As soon as the viewers meet the volunteers on the House programs, it becomes clear that the "living history" experience is dependent less on the advice of historical consultants and more on fictional depictions (and collective memories of such depictions) of the various pasts that the House programs aim to faithfully re-create. Since the "total" experience cannot possibly be re-created (no one dies from TB, dropped bombs, or malnutrition in these shows), we are ultimately left with more fiction than fact, and the myths that Hoppe says the series aim to "bust" often remain intact. Watching an episode of *Regency House Party* or *Texas Ranch House* cannot help calling to mind certain familiar novels, films, and earlier TV programs that tried to capture these same eras. And the performances of those who take part in these time-traveling experiments are shaped (both unconsciously and at times deliberately) by such fictions, such as the housewife coping with rations in *1940s House* who imagines herself in "my Mrs. Miniver mode," *Manor House*'s tutor and his Jane Eyre fantasy, and the girls on the frontier who clearly want to emulate the gumption of the Ingalls daughters. Even as the volunteers gain a general familiarity with a particular era and its hardships, they remain reluctant to let go of certain notions about the past. In the words of *Regency House Party*'s Captain Glover, what they really want is "a romantic experience as well as a historical one."

Creating a Winning Formula

Media critics, quick to distinguish the House series from the "worthless trash" of other reality TV fare, typically refer to it as the "Masterpiece Theatre" of the genre, further collapsing the boundary between history and fiction.[3] Each series follows a set formula in which the applicants are introduced and begin their preparation for their impending ordeal; volunteers who generate the most drama (whether in the form of a love

The Bowler family of *The 1900 House* (PBS, 2000) pose in their Sunday best. Courtesy of PBS/PhotoFest.

story, a feud, or a revolt against the rules) stand out, and video camera "confessionals" and postseries interviews highlight the conflict between the volunteers' historical role-playing and their twenty-first-century lives. There are no prizes for enduring a harsh winter or emptying chamber pots, although the American productions grade the volunteers. This grading system at first seems to undermine the community spirit so essential to the volunteers' survival but also forces them to question their own modern notions of individualism, competition, and self-interest.

The total immersion process and length of time the volunteers are required to spend in their historical contexts, ranging from three to five months, make for grueling, and ratings-savvy, "hands-on history." In these televised experiments, the volunteers have to struggle for their subsistence, submit to authority, rely on outdated medical remedies, and abandon their modern dress for uncomfortable, often dirty period costuming. Despite these inconveniences, the volunteers are surprised by the ease with which they take up their assigned roles—the submissive lady's maid, the class-conscious butler, the domineering husband, the lowly ranch hand. Yet the volunteers never fully *become* their roles; they adapt their historical identities to their twenty-first-century mentalities and experiences when, for example, the servants of *Manor House* mouth off to their master or the colonists in *Colonial House* refuse to cheat their Native American trading partners. Much to the producers' dismay (or perhaps glee), the volunteers rewrite the past as they wish it had been, sans socioeconomic hierarchies and prejudice.

Although the producers claim that they do not generate the story lines or prompt the participants to react in particular ways to various situations, they do predict that the experiments will challenge the volunteers' preexisting assumptions about the past.[4] But just what are those assumptions and where do they originate? Ian Roberts in his audition video for *Texas Ranch House* declares he had been prepared to play a cowboy since childhood, having "watched a lot of *Bonanza* growing up." Many years later, he now longs to lie out "under the stars by the fire and ride a horse in the rain. . . . This is a chance to show America that we lost values, we lost beliefs, we lost integrity." Like many of the House volunteers, he idealizes the past, but his main source of knowledge is reruns of a 1960s TV series. Audition videos typically show applicants expressing a fascination with the time period under investigation, but the selected few usually

202 / Julie Anne Taddeo and Ken Dvorak

arrive on the set with very little background knowledge other than what they are given by the producers. In an interview Lady Olliff-Cooper of *Manor House* reveals that the producers "discouraged us from reading up about it. . . . The rule book was very slender and only gave you the barest outline of where you were supposed to be."[5] Mr. Edgar, the butler, adds, "Although I'd read a lot about servants and the role of the butler, I said I could do with some training from a real butler. I was extremely lucky and had training for four days from the adviser to *Gosford Park*, and that was wonderful because lots of little details I may have overlooked, he made me aware. Apart from that, we weren't encouraged to know very much."[6] Their responses to their new environment, therefore, are dictated not only by their twenty-first-century attitudes and values but also by how they imagine characters from film and TV would behave in similar situations. "But at the end of the day," as Mr. Edgar shrewdly observes, "the producers must have been jolly glad."[7]

"Jane Austen It Ain't!": British Time Travelers and Regency House Party

Britain's Channel 4 clearly found a winning formula with its 1999 production of *1900 House*. The House series that have followed have become much more sophisticated and interactive, and thousands of applicants have vied to relive suburban life during World War II or serve as a butler for an aristocratic Edwardian family. With *1900 House* the producers seemed determined to convince the media and viewers of the project's seriousness—advertising the program as a documentary and offering lesson plans for teachers on its Web site. By 2002 *Manor House* was being promoted as "a gripping new series that brings class to reality television." Even its accompanying Web site had abandoned pretensions to historical seriousness, offering viewers a "Snob-o-meter" to test "just how snobbish you are," and applicants who admitted to fantasies of "shagging the scullery maid" received the most airtime. Surprisingly, more than 80 percent of the applicants to *Manor House* wanted to work as servants, and those quoted were motivated by the popular television series *Upstairs, Downstairs* (1971). Promotional advertising for the series even referred to *Manor House* as "in the tradition of *Upstairs, Downstairs* and Robert Altman's *Gosford Park*," stressing its similarity to other popular, fictional fare rather than its putative resemblance to history.

Nevertheless, *Manor House* works hard at challenging the volunteers' romanticized views of life on a country estate, as the camera focuses on the backbreaking labor performed below stairs and the shocking reminders to the servants that they must "know their place." Yet when certain volunteers stay *too* true to their historical roles, it becomes difficult for modern viewers to empathize with them. For example, when Sir Olliff-Cooper defends the class structure and the empire, or exercises authority over his wife and spinster sister-in-law (who at one point abandons the house to avoid a real-life breakdown), he seems, by twenty-first-century standards, boorish and arrogant; in short, he has become his historical alter ego. In the final episode of *Manor House,* as the aristocrats upstairs dance and celebrate the British Empire, the staff below stairs read about such events as militant suffrage and trade union marches and the *Titanic* disaster—all of which hint at the impending death knell of the Edwardian age and its hierarchies. But the servants have already written their own ending to this age, since they have repeatedly refused to accept their lower position in the household; they have burned the master in effigy, romped in his sheets, swapped jobs, and become drunk while on duty. They simply refuse to "live history," and their pride in their ability to endure three months of hard work and poor hygiene suggests how they have reduced history to a version of "today" minus its twenty-first-century amenities.

Since the Edwardian time-traveling experiment, set in a country house, proved a great success (reaching an audience of more than 3 million), Channel 4 used another rural venue two years later to re-create the early nineteenth century. The architectural historian Adrian Tinniswood points out the enduring significance of the country house for even twenty-first-century tourists and TV viewers—a part of the past "with as much to say about contemporary society as it has about what has gone before" (quoted in Troost 478). Evoking a nostalgia for the alleged simplicity of the preindustrial past, the country house conveys a physical and emotional space in which the stresses of modernity can be abandoned. But whereas *Manor House* made some effort to re-create a less romantic version of *Upstairs, Downstairs* and used the class and gender inequality of the Edwardian era to generate dramatic tension among its volunteers, *Regency House Party* shed any pretension to historical accuracy when it used as its leading historical consultant the novelist Jane Austen (1775–1817). In 2004 Channel 4 announced that it was offering a "marriage of reality dating programs with history by giving five aspiring Mr. Darcys and five

Miss Bennets the chance to go back to the England of the early 1800s and live at the height of the age of romance." When the show later aired on PBS, the theme song from the 1970s program *The Dating Game* played in the background, as American audiences (likely more familiar with this piece of TV history than with the British Regency era) were promised "the ultimate dating game."

Again, the producers chose volunteers with self-admitted low history IQs. Guy Gorell Barnes, the master of the house, and a "Mr. Darcy look-alike," was "excited about living in history," but he noted, "We were given very little information about what to expect." Likewise, Mr. Foxsmith, the amateur scientist in both his twenty-first- and nineteenth-century lives, admitted, "I had very little idea about the period. I've never read a Jane Austen book." Even the London stage manager–turned–Regency gentle-man, Mr. Everett, was "frustrated by my lack of knowledge. . . . I knew nothing about the period before I started the project." Perhaps two of the better-prepared volunteers were one of the chaperones, Mrs. Hammond, who admitted to watching "a lot of Jane Austen videos," and Miss Braund, who "had read all of Jane Austen's works and was very interested to find out how the reality matched my own romantic views."

On the *Regency House Party* Web site, the producer Caroline Ross Pirie explains that when looking over 30,000 applicants, she was search-ing for "the modern day equivalents of the people who feature in Jane Austen's popular novels." The selected guests are too good to be true—a retired female army officer turned romance novelist now in the role of chaperone; a former model and society debutante playing hostess of the party; an actual Russian countess (and waitress) in the role of a secretly impoverished noblewoman in pursuit of the host; a dot-com millionaire; and a disenchanted speed dater; the only one to quit the experiment in its early stages is the hairdresser, who expected his character, Captain Robin-son, to be like Austen's militiaman Mr. Wickham—"gambling, womanising and drinking." Instead, he realizes that lessons in walking and gentlemanly etiquette are not for him: "I don't want to be posh." The experience, however, does make him "proud of my (working class) roots."

Without a script, the only guidance the volunteers have is an individu-alized pocket book outlining the behavior expected of them. According to the narrator, it is up to the "guests" to decide "the extent to which they would conform to Regency protocol and etiquette." Though historical consultants were used "on everything from Regency sanitary arrangements to popular card games," the real go-to source remained fiction. Many of the episodes' titles come from Austen's novels—"Pride & Prejudice," "Sense & Sensibility," and "Persuasion"—and the volunteers eagerly take to their new roles. There is a self-professed Fanny Price character—the penniless lady's companion Miss Martin (also referred to as the Cinderella of the party)—and a meddling Emma (Miss Hopkins, an "industrial heiress" who plays matchmaker but then steals her friend's chosen mate for herself). Abandoned by Mr. Everett in favor of the heiress, the impoverished Miss Braund resembles *Sense and Sensibility*'s Marianne Dashwood; after losing the attentions of young, handsome Mr. Everett, she is rescued in the final episode from spinsterhood by an engagement to her older friend, Captain Glover. Among the male volunteers, the tension between the youthful Wickhams and the older, steadier Captain Wentworths leads to comical displays of physical strength and even the padding of tights. The interactive Web site encourages further Austen fantasy role-playing for those who wish to "find out if you've got what it takes" to be a Mr. Darcy–like catch or one of the Bennet sisters.

The other literary reference that influences the party guests' behavior is Lord Byron (1788–1824), and the episodes titled "She Walks in Beauty" and "Mad, Bad, Dangerous Liaisons" offer up the raciest (and most uncomfortable) moments of the series. For example, to capture the attention of Mr. Gorell Barnes, the countess "serves herself up" as the dinner's centerpiece. Covered only by strategically placed fruits and peacock feathers, she says she is paying homage to Byron's lover, Lady Caroline Lamb, and in the end does indeed win her man. (Interestingly, like Mr. Darcy, who initially found Elizabeth Bennet's face only "tolerable," Gorell Barnes first remarks that the countess would be attractive "without her glasses.") This particular moment, though it spices up the diner party, represents a missed opportunity to comment on the position of women in early nineteenth-century society. The female volunteers complain endlessly about having to rub their underarms with lemons (a Regency-style deodorant) or their inability to drink with "the guys," but they never fully grasp how even upper-class women were disenfranchised in Regency England. Lamb's act was not only scandalous but earned her the reputation of being mentally unstable and almost ruined her husband's political career, and Byron shunned her for another woman. Byron, not Austen, is used whenever the volunteers want to break not only the dull routine of the day but the rigid gender conventions, but it is mainly the men who reap the benefits.

Conveniently discovering that his cellar once housed a meeting place of Byron's Hell Fire Club, Barnes invites his male guests and several exotic female dancers to an after-hours party, which prompts Captain Glover to exclaim, "Jane Austen, it ain't!"

Aside from these moments that scandalize the elderly hostess of the party, most of the romantic intrigue remains tame—daisy chains, serenades, and love mazes. In addition to dating rituals, the volunteers learn about dueling, boxing, and dining etiquette; there are a few passing references to the slave trade and the class hierarchy that divides the servants and guests and allows the latter to be so pampered at the expense of others. An outsider is invited into the house to stir up controversy and expose some of the realities of the past that period novels often ignored. None of the House series can resist this type of moralizing, but such moments of historical accuracy are regarded as a nuisance by the volunteers, who want to sustain their fantasy of the past. According to the narrator, with the arrival of a West Indian heiress in episode 3, "the guests must confront the truth behind their lavish lifestyle." Unfortunately, this plot device goes nowhere, and no romantic partner is provided for Miss Taylor, despite her millions and beauty (which the chaperones initially resent and the other young ladies envy). Miss Taylor, does, however, get a chance to lecture the group about the wealth of landowners reaped from the slave trade of the preceding two hundred years. Still, an attempt to stage a boycott of sugar for just one day is met with resistance—as the underprivileged lady's companion Miss Martin says, "I just can't feel guilt or shame for something I've never done. . . . I can't feel guilty for history." Miss Martin's response is a rare example of being "true" to the historical era under examination, but she is shushed and Barnes mandates the daylong sugar boycott.

After this brief lecture on slavery, the series returns to its main theme: romance. The houseguests cannot seem to stop themselves from straying from their nineteenth-century roles, as an unchaperoned Miss Martin repeatedly visits the estate hermit, and the chaperone Mrs. Davenport, rather than promoting her female charge, falls in love with the younger Mr. Foxsmith. Whenever they are shown together, sepia tones are used—comparing this "indiscreet" relationship to Byron's penchant for older women. Alas, aside from a midnight meeting in the stables, their love is not meant to be, as she finally reverts to her historical identity and insists that he be free to marry a younger woman of fortune. Mr. Foxsmith finds solace in his scientific experiments, and part of episode 3 pays homage to

Mary Shelley's *Frankenstein* (1818) as the guests discover electricity and meet an anatomist.

The gothic, yet another literary creation of the Regency era, dominates the second episode, as the guests write and perform their own ghost story, and lovers hunt for phantom spirits at midnight. The often forced nature of the drama is most evident when a "violent row" between Miss Braund and her chaperone erupts (physical blows allegedly were exchanged off camera). The camera flashes to a full moon and a bat flying across the window, and a beating drum and shouting voices signal that "the house party is in crisis." Any pretension to a history lesson is abandoned for this costumed and carefully edited catfight.

Watching such drama unfold and listening to the narrator, TV audiences might reasonably assume that the Regency era really was nothing more than romance, poets, and ghost chasing. (To be fair, the Channel 4 Web site does offer a brief history for "those still a bit in the dark about the Regency period.") Politics can no longer be ignored, however, and in the final episode, a discussion of the Napoleonic Wars (1803–1815) occurs. The guests receive a history lesson on the Battle of Waterloo of 1815 (though, as previously noted, the guest historian's words are drowned out by music), and Captain Glover, who would have served in the navy, receives a fortune and a title as a reward for his heroism. Though the oldest of the male guests, and previously trying, and failing, to catch the ladies' attention with his workouts and padded tights, he now has become the most attractive man in the household, richer even than the host. Though he should court the countess, he chooses instead the middle-class Miss Braund, who decides "there's something to marrying a best friend."

The final episode asks, "Will this storybook tale of mating and dating have a happy ending?" The wedding, by convention the culmination of the Regency novel, certainly would signify the success of this living-history experiment, and the impending nuptials of Miss Braund and Captain Glover follow this formula. Some of the houseguests, however, have written their own preferred ending. The lady's companion has run off with the hermit, and one of the guests, dismayed by her marital options, decides she will become a courtesan, with her own salon—two very un-Regency-like decisions. Furthermore, the countess and the host, after a drunken one-night stand, are declared by the narrator to be engaged, superimposing modern dating practices on Regency courtship rituals. So though the houseguests have had, in the words of Captain Glover, "a romantic experience," did

208 / Julie Anne Taddeo and Ken Dvorak

they have a "historical" one? Was the show's intention to learn about the period? To appeal to and create more Austen fans? As the historian Hunt notes, it is really about the volunteers getting to know themselves—not history—better. During a church service, an actual twenty-first-century clergyman explains to the cast that they are enduring the inconveniences of primitive hygiene and rigid etiquette "out of a desire to find a new way of looking at relationships." Yet again, the study of history—the supposed aim of these "hands-on history" projects—becomes secondary to exploring contemporary individual identity. Captain Glover honestly addresses the serious omissions of history when he wonders, "Would I have been suited to the Regency House War? The Regency House Amputation? The Regency House Wife Death in Childbirth? . . . I would need a real time machine to answer the question truthfully."

Texas Ranch House: *American Time Travelers Head West, Again*

The urge to treat history as a story, with plot lines easily rewritten to suit the time traveler's own contemporary code of ethics and sensibilities, can also be seen in such American versions of historical reality TV as *Frontier House, Colonial House*,[8] and, most recently, *Texas Ranch House,* all on PBS. As the *Texas Ranch House* Web site promises, this "latest and most ambitious experiment in living history" explores "what the saddle-sore, rope-burned, and sun-blistered ranch life was really like." But, though the producers promise to "bust some myths," they carefully edit the several weeks' worth of collective experiences, showcasing the confrontations as the volunteers rebel against the strict rules and hierarchies of the ranch; swaggering in their chaps and boots, they cling to their own fantasy of the cowboy life.

Myths about the Old West have captivated generations of Americans, who, according to the historian Frederick Jackson Turner, view the frontier as the site where American democratic ideals were fulfilled.[9] In less than one hundred years the American West was settled, native tribes were vanquished, and railroads stretched across the prairies and mountains; cattle drives romanticized the cowboy, and telegraph and telephone lines linked the Eastern Seaboard with California and tales of golden sunsets. Popular culture has enshrined the frontier through literature, paintings,

Wild West shows, radio and television, and Hollywood films from *The Great Train Robbery* (1903) to the most recent "old-fashioned modern western," *3:10 to Yuma* (2007).[10] Clearly, the American West continues to exert a powerful attraction for twenty-first-century audiences still rooting for heroes with "true grit."

Hollywood westerns, on film and TV, according to the film historian Peter C. Rollins, have created "an American culture . . . almost unimaginable without the West as a touchstone of national identity" (2). Even the environment plays a part, as western landscapes have helped shape this mythology; as Deborah Carmichael has observed: "The importance of the landscape itself, the idyllic or treacherous environment negotiated in these films, often receives supporting-role status, yet without the land, American national mythmaking would not exist" (1). Jared Ficklin, a native of Austin, a *Texas Ranch House* cowboy, and a descendant of Benjamin Ficklin, cofounder of the Pony Express, agrees, wanting only to become a "true Texan" worthy of his famous ancestor.[11]

Unlike the Hollywood westerns by directors Howard Hawks and John Ford, reality TV works with little scripting (though much postproduction editing), and as one TV critic notes of *Texas Ranch House,* "what seems familiar from movies and TV takes on fresh significance when there are real people—not pampered actors—trying to scratch out an existence on the frontier 24/7, with no plot to guide them."[12] Though the producers of PBS's *Texas Ranch House* adhere to this no-script approach to their living-history experiment, the Hollywood myth of the Wild West nevertheless shapes the participants' actions. In fact, many of the interactions between the *Texas Ranch House* volunteers seem lifted from classic westerns, in particular Hawks's *Red River* (1948). *Red River* is a tightly woven story about a hardened cattle baron, Tom Dunston (John Wayne), and the younger, gentler Matt Garth (Montgomery Clift), who, despite their own personal animosities, succeed in building a cattle empire in post–Civil War Texas. The film's familiar themes of an epic quest, male bonding, and strong-willed women are all found in *Texas Ranch House.* Still, the volunteers manage to challenge not only the advice of historical consultants but also certain aspects of the Hollywood myth to produce their own version of a western, modified by a collision with modern values.

Among the 10,000 applicants to the show, the few selected include two Californians, Bill and Lisa Cooke, as the ranch owners (along with their three daughters—all *Little House on the Prairie* buffs); a self-proclaimed feminist, Maura Finkelstein, in the role of "girl of all work"; and a motley group of ten male cowboys, including a gruff, short-tempered ranch foreman, the Colonel, and a temperamental ranch cook, Nacho. After a two-week "cowboy skills camp" conducted by historians of the period, the volunteers find themselves settled on a private cattle ranch in the rugged Chihuahuan Desert located thirty miles south of Alpine, Texas, re-creating ranching life circa 1867.[13] The daunting task for these time travelers is to round up two hundred longhorn cattle and sell them in order to save the Cookes' ranch from financial disaster. In post–Civil War Texas, hundreds of thousands of longhorn cattle roamed the Texas prairie, abandoned by their previous owners, who had left to serve in the Confederate Army. This challenge clearly falls within the scope of the historical record, and it also parallels the story of John Wayne's character, Tom Dunston, in *Red River*. The shadow of Wayne, Hollywood's iconic cowboy, looms over the entire TV production, setting a standard of Western masculinity for the volunteers and audience, who are urged on the program's accompanying interactive Web site to "Test Your True Grit" and "Speak Cowboy."

According to series producer, Jody Sheff, "*Texas Ranch House* may be the most challenging hands-on history series we've done. The ranchers and cowboys are constantly working with temperamental horses, riding a harsh terrain riddled with ravines and rattlesnakes, not to mention the 100-plus-degree heat. The physical demands on our participants and the distances they must cover make the House experience unique."[14] But as one of the cowboys remarked in a WashingtonPost.com interview, "the drama aspect of it drained me more than the actual ranch work."[15] The paucity of historical knowledge that the volunteers are given before their adventure begins contributes to the feuds that later ensue, as most of them refuse to stay in character when their modern values (and notions of comfort) are challenged. The volunteers may have learned how to rustle cattle, but the camera seems more interested in capturing the clash of personalities. In fact, as the ranch owner's wife, Lisa Cooke, notes in a postseries interview, the producers clearly had their own agenda, which was at odds with the goal of "living history": "As participants we were told very clearly that we were to be 21st century people living in an 1867 environment."[16] This certainly explains the cowboys' lack of deference and the outright acrimony and distrust between them and the Cookes. In the opening montage the cowboys view the arrival of their employer and his family with disdain, as one proudly declares that "first to be a cowboy, you need a set of balls!" The men will use said balls not only to endure the hard work that awaits them but to defy repeatedly the ranch owner for whom they already have little respect. (Cooke did admit in his audition video, after all, that he likes to pick berries for his wife's jams.)

But the challenge to Cooke's patriarchal authority will come not just from his cowboys but from those in his own home. Just as Dunston's fiancée in *Red River* warns him, "You'll need me for what you've got to do," the female volunteers in *Texas Ranch House* refuse to let the experiment be what one Cooke daughter calls a "sexist ranch house." Maura Finkelstein, the "girl of all work," adds that she should be rounding up cattle instead of playing the Cookes' domestic servant. Posing a "Calamity Jane" threat to a historically masculine enterprise, she cannot help being disappointed, noting: "I was very angry. I actually thought that I might have the possibility of starting out as a cowboy and not necessarily the maid, so it was a disappointment at first. . . . As a woman, I felt very conflicted. I had no problem doing the work, but through the labor I performed I was treated differently. I balked when I found an organic sexism growing out from the division of labor."[17] The series' producers jump at such opportunities to create a divisive atmosphere, which quickly places the time travelers into oppositional groups.

Indeed, most of the drama of *Texas Ranch House* derives from the "gender battles" (this phrase streams across the series' Web site) as the female volunteers try to re-landscape the Wild West into an egalitarian terrain. Though women's role in the Hollywood western has always been that of being a civilizing influence, the female volunteers on the show do not seem to understand that "civilized" in 1867 actually meant maintaining separate and gendered spheres and creating a "home, sweet home." Several of the young cowboys start the experiment "dreaming about . . . young ladies" with whom they might flirt, but instead encounter a "middle-aged . . . wife and a couple of kids" and a defiant servant. As the men resist the women's efforts to invade a traditionally hypermasculine world, Finkelstein shakes her head in disgust, remarking: "What's so interesting is that all of the guys come from different places and different experiences and they all, inherently, are sexist bastards, every single one of them. And they all love it. And they embrace it. And it took them five minutes to put on that jacket."[18] But veering from the role of "sexist bastard" would violate history as well as the script of the western and would not earn respect for the man who does so, especially when that man is the ranch owner.

Lisa and Bill Cooke modify their assigned historical roles as Lisa demands to be her husband's partner in the ranching enterprise, just as she claims she is his equal in their twenty-first-century home. Refusing to act the part of a submissive wife, she declares: "You men don't comprehend how much you hurt women on this ranch. And you hurt them in a way that as 21st century men you would never do in your regular lives. I'm raising three daughters. I'm not raising them to feel pathetic about themselves." Clearly miscast in the role of ranch owner, Bill Cooke loses any semblance of authority when he attends to domestic chores and puts family harmony before the success of the ranch and the cattle drive.

Curiously, though Lisa Cooke demands equal treatment for her daughters and herself, she has no qualms about denigrating the foreman's top hand, Robby Cabezuela, a modern day *vaquero* of Mexican and Spanish ancestry who seems much better equipped for the role of ranch owner than Bill Cooke. Lisa's treatment of Cabezuela, bordering on racist, is at least true to the historical moment under examination, but it makes for uncomfortable viewing nonetheless. Unlike the peacemaker in *Red River*, Tess Millay, who urges the warring men to love each other, Lisa exaggerates every slight toward her husband and family, accusing Cabezuela of being "disrespectful from the beginning."

As a respite from the "gender battles" that crowd the action, the producers introduce another classic feature of the western, the "cowboy versus Indian" plot line. Looking for cattle, Jared Ficklin and Robby Cabezuela "unexpectedly" (i.e., they are not forewarned by the producers) encounter a Comanche raiding party, led by a Native American, Michael Burgess, in the role of Chief. Tense talk ensues as they debate the Comanches' need for cattle and the ranch's need for fresh horses. The Comanches decide to hold Jared overnight so that he can be used as leverage, and they advise the men that in different times they would have been killed on sight. The next morning the Comanche's Chief rides into the Cooke compound to discuss the trade with an agitated Bill Cooke. When the Chief demands forty head of cattle in exchange for four horses and the hostage, Cooke initially refuses, stating that "he doesn't deal with terrorists," until he is gently reminded that the Cooke ranch is on Comanche land and exists only at their whim. A humorous and truly twenty-first-century moment follows when the Chief thanks the Cooke women for the meal they have prepared and asks if he may take some of the food in a to-go bag. At the conclusion of this episode, Jared Ficklin is seen playing an Indian flute, seemingly at ease with his captors after just an overnight stay.

This episode is an interesting reversal of the typical captivity narrative, in which the hostage is usually a female who, in such Hollywood versions as *The Searchers* (1956), resists rescue. This entire episode points out the dilemma for these time travelers who want to relive the Old West but not repeat its racist practices, using anachronistic words like "terrorists" to describe the Native Americans rather than that classic slur used by Hollywood heroes: "dirty Injuns." That the Chief is the most rational and gracious—putting Cooke in an even worse light—also undermines the western's dichotomy of civilized-savage. Since this is not a Hollywood western, or a truly faithful reliving of history, there are no violent confrontations between the two groups of men. Jody Sheff suggests that guns were not allowed on the set because of "insurance reasons," but it is also possible that no twenty-first-century man, regardless of his John Wayne fantasy, wants to be cast in the unsympathetic role of "Indian killer" as millions of PBS viewers watch.

Fraught with tensions (albeit mainly harmless ones) between the men and women, and between the cowboys and Indians, *Texas Ranch House*, like all westerns, is ultimately a battle of man versus man. The climactic moment occurs during the cattle drive and Bill Cooke's final showdown with his cowboys. Emboldened by his success in selling his cattle and encouraged by Lisa, Bill is now ready to redress the outrages he believes the cowboys have inflicted on his family. Bill's desire for revenge brings to mind *Red River* and the ongoing conflict between Dunston and Matt. When he refuses to honor Jared's purchase of a horse before the cattle drive, accusing him of cheating him during his stay with the Comanches, Jared rises to this challenge, announcing his intention of riding out with "his" horse. With Lisa, the Cooke girls, and Maura Finkelstein all intently listening from the safety of the ranch house, Bill Cooke shouts that he will "kick the shit" out of Jared if he leaves with Cooke's horse. This threat notwithstanding, Jared rides away, followed by the other cowboys, heading off into the sunset. Asserting their independence (and defying the ultimate authority of the ranch owner), the cowboys have written their own twenty-first-century ending to the western. The historians' final pronouncement, that the Cooke ranch, by nineteenth-century standards, would surely have failed in the face of such poor management and rebellion by the cowboys, does not seem to daunt any of the volunteers. The postproduction confessionals all attest to the volunteers' "giving it their best"—blaming each other for the ranch's failure—which for modern audiences, but not historians, is good enough.

The English manor's drawing room of *Regency House Party* and the fly-infested dwellings of *Texas Ranch House* seem worlds apart, but viewed together, the two House series highlight the strengths and weaknesses of the genre of historical reality TV. PBS's producer Jody Sheff insists, "While of course we'd like to have as many people watch the show as possible, our only priority is making a great educational show that is also entertaining—but the historical element is always the primary focus."[19] Audiences watching the volunteers struggle with their unfamiliar environments and with each other get a glimpse of how challenging it is to make the past come alive and remain "authentic." Tristram Hunt is undoubtedly correct, however, in questioning the latter part of Sheff's claim, noting that reality TV reduces the study of history to issues of individual identity and what moderns learn they can or cannot endure as they reenact the past.

The presentism of the nonhistorian producers and the participants undoubtedly shapes the outcome of the living-history experiment and leads to more melodrama than history. The volunteers, often and deliberately kept by producers in the dark about the period they are about to relive, cannot help being shocked when they realize they must passively submit to another's authority, empty someone else's chamber pot, or uphold the slave trade. That they measure their performances against those they have seen on TV, like the Cartwright brothers, or have read about in their favorite Austen and Ingalls Wilder novels, reveals just how difficult it is for the volunteers to distinguish fiction from history. When they break the rules, as they inevitably do, the volunteers imagine they will be rewarded, like Austen's outspoken heroines whose impoverished status never seems to deny them a favorable love match, or John Wayne's macho heroes who refuse to take orders from weak-willed men. Even though an occasional historian is shown shaking his or her head over the historical inaccuracies of the House series, the producers still allow the volunteers the freedom to write their own script. Meanwhile, the postproduction editing team transforms their three months of interactions into a miniseries with love triangles, feuds, and background music, furthering the fiction behind the stated objectives of the living-history project itself. Perhaps a more accurate description of the appeal and the limits of historical reality TV is expressed by *Regency House Party*'s countess, who concludes that such programs keep alive the fiction that history was simply "a storybook every day."

Notes

1. Description of *1900 House,* "About the Series," www.pbs.org/wnet/1900house/about-series/index.html.

2. Beth Hoppe quoted in Dan Odenwald, "Back to These Old Houses," *Current,* April 21, 2003, www.current.org/hi/hi0308house.html.

3. Mark D. Johnson, "The 'Masterpiece Theatre' of Reality TV" (review of *Manor House*), www.partialobserver.com/article.cfm?id=718.

4. Hoppe in Odenwald.

5. See http://discuss.washingtonpost.com/wp-srv/zforum/03/sp_tv_manor042903.htm.

6. Ibid.

7. Ibid.

8. For a discussion of *Colonial House* and *Frontier House,* see Julie Taddeo and Ken Dvorak, "The Historical House Series: Where Historical Reality Meets Reel Reality," *Film & History* 37.1 (December 2007): 18–28.

9. Frederick Jackson Turner, *The Frontier in American History* (New York: Dover), 1996 [1920].

10. See www.filmsite.org/grea.html and www.imdb.com/title/tt03881849/.

11. "Texas Ranch House," online interviews of cast members conducted by WashingtonPost.com, May 1, 2006. No longer available on the *Washington Post*'s Web site; hard copy in authors' possession.

12. Nancy DeWolf Smith, "The West That Never Was," *Wall Street Journal Online,* April 28, 2006, http://online.wsj.com/public/article_print/SB114618251554138180.html.

13. *Texas Ranch House* press release, www.thirteen.org/pressroom/pdf/texas/TexasRanchOnline.pdf.

14. Ibid.

15. Ibid.

16. "Texas Ranch House," online interviews, WashingtonPost.com.

17. WashingtonPost.com, April 4, 2006. No longer available on the *Washington Post*'s Web site; hard copy in authors' possession.

18. *Texas Ranch House* press release.

19. See http://pbs.org/texasranchhouse.

Works Cited

Carmichael, Deborah. *The Landscape of Hollywood Westerns: Ecocriticism in an American Film Genre.* Salt Lake City: University of Utah Press, 2006.

De Groot, Jerome. "Empathy and Enfranchisement: Popular Histories." *Rethinking History* 10.3 (September 2006): 391–413.

Hunt, Tristram. "Reality, Identity and Empathy: The Changing Face of Social History Television." *Journal of Social History* 39.3 (Spring 2006): 843–858.

Nelson, Michael. "It May Be History, but Is It True? The Imperial War Museum Conference." *Historical Journal of Film, Radio, and Television* 25.1 (March 2005): 141–146.

Nicholas, Liza J. *Becoming Western: Stories of Culture and Identity in the Cowboy State*. Lincoln: University of Nebraska Press, 2006.

Rollins, Peter C., and John E. O'Connor, eds. *Hollywood's West: The American Frontier in Film, Television, and History*. Lexington: University Press of Kentucky, 2005.

Troost, Linda V. "Filming Tourism, Portraying Pemberley." *Eighteenth-Century Fiction* 18.4 (Summer 2006): 477–498.

MICHELLE ARROW

"What about giving us a real version of Australian history?"

Identity, Ethics, and Historical Understanding in Reality History TV

> Where are the Aboriginals? Why are the men, as they look for their selection, walking across cleared land? What about giving us a real version of Australian history? This whitewashed reality TV version is just another copout. ("Richhosk")

In the last few years, Australia's colonial history has become bitterly contested terrain, picked over in public in a series of debates known as the "history wars."[1] These debates have centered on conflicting interpretations of indigenous-European history and the violence of colonization and have been fought not just between academics, but also among politicians and neoconservative newspaper commentators. Such furious debate framed the production and reception of Australia's first forays into reality history TV in 2005: *The Colony*, which screened on the Special Broadcasting Service (SBS) in January,[2] and *Outback House*, produced by the Australian Broadcasting Corporation (ABC) in midyear. All reality history TV series reflect and shape popular ideas about the meaning of the past, and they gain added resonance when that past is a deeply contested one. Reality history TV dramatizes (even exaggerates) an essential historical problem—namely, the impossibility of ever re-creating the past in the present, to know what "really" happened. Reality history can only show us what twenty-first-century citizens choose to make of the past. For this reason, reality history offers a limited means of learning about the past: it focuses on the material conditions of the past at the expense of politics; it gazes at the past through the prism of personal relationships and conflict, and it reproduces, rather than challenges, popular social memory of the past. Yet reality history can offer interesting possibilities for understanding the significance of the past. It confronts the ways ordinary people in the present make sense of the past—indeed, how they understand their past—in more explicit ways than other kinds of television history and even some written histories. Both *The Colony* and *Outback House* promised that participants and viewers would "step back in time" to different periods of Australia's colonial history. Did these programs offer a "real version of Australian history"? Or did they merely present a "whitewashed version," as the angry viewer quoted above alleged? This essay will explore the possibilities and limitations of reality TV as a form of history, with particular attention to issues of national and personal identity, empathy, and ethics.

Australian History

Australian history has recently been one of the most contentious areas of cultural, political, and media debate. Successive Australian prime ministers have used history as a tool to define their particular vision of national identity. While Australia was secure in its identity as a nation united by British race patriotism up until the 1960s, this was a relatively simple proposition. Yet by the 1970s Australia's cultural and ethnic unity came under challenge from new social movements, and diversity was nurtured by a new nondiscriminatory immigration policy and the anti-assimilation ethos of multiculturalism. This meant that telling a story of national unity through the country's history became more difficult to sustain (Curran). The bicentenary of white settlement (or invasion) in 1988, marked by extensive official celebrations, became the focal point of Aboriginal protest and its slogan, "White Australia has a black history." The bicentenary emphasized the division between those who wanted to celebrate Australia's white pioneers and those who insisted that such a celebration ignored the dispossession and oppression of Aboriginal people that had accompanied the achievements of those pioneers (Macintyre and Clark 93–118).

In the early 1990s Australian Labor Party Prime Minister Paul Keating attempted to retell the story of Australia centered on republicanism, radical nationalism, and reconciliation with Australia's indigenous peoples, a story most famously summed up in a speech that acknowledged the role of white Australians in the dispossession and attempted destruction of Aboriginal Australia: "We took the traditional lands and smashed the traditional way of life. We brought the diseases. The alcohol. We committed the murders. We took the children from their mothers. We practiced discrimination and exclusion. It was our ignorance and our prejudice" (quoted in Curran 232). The speech sparked a barrage of claims that Keating was perpetuating a "black armband" view of history designed to induce guilt and shame (Blainey). The black-armband view also prompted vehement denials from Keating's successor, the conservative Liberal Party Prime Minister John Howard, who stated upon his election in 1996 that to teach children "that we're part of a sort of racist and bigoted history is something that Australians reject" (quoted in Macintyre and Clark 137). Prime Minister Howard was keen to promote a new pride in Australian history.

These political responses were in reaction to the rise of a new kind of Aboriginal history, which told the story of Australia's past through a different lens. Violence on Australia's colonial frontier was central to this historical narrative, and a large body of scholarship was produced that detailed the extent and nature of this violence, based both on European accounts and on Aboriginal oral testimonies. This scholarship was widely accepted among academic historians, yet it came under challenge in public conflicts in the media and in schools, in debates that became known as the history wars. The wars kicked off when an independent historian, Keith Windschuttle, released his deeply contentious book, *The Fabrication of Aboriginal History,* in 2002. In it he claimed that Australian history had fallen prey to an academic orthodoxy that had deliberately falsified and distorted Australia's frontier history to tell an exaggerated story of white violence that was designed to provoke guilt and that would in turn bolster indigenous claims to land and self-determination. Most notoriously, Windschuttle alleged that, by his calculations (which included only indigenous deaths recorded by white witnesses) "only" 118 Aboriginal people had died on the Tasmanian frontier. "To his mind," John Hirst noted, "with this low figure, he has rescued the reputation of the British empire and its successor settler nation from their detractors" ("How Sorry" 80). Windschuttle managed to find evidentiary and citation mistakes in the works of some historians, and one could argue that the debate as a whole aired important historiographical issues (the trustworthiness of evidence, for example) in a public context. Yet for the most part the debate was conducted in a dichotomous way through the mass media, which reduced complex issues to sound bites and created a charged backdrop for the reception of *Outback House* and *The Colony.* Beyond these debates, however, we need to consider further questions about the ways Australians conceive of their past: is Australia, as Graeme Davison argued, a society with "a strong sense of the past, but with only a weak sense of history"? (28).

A "Weak Sense of History"?

Many Australian historians and critics have drawn attention to the trope of victimology in Australians' sense of their past. Australia's origins as a penal settlement were, until recently, the subject of an ashamed silence, although by the bicentenary in 1988 genealogists were eagerly seeking out their convict ancestors (Griffiths 115–118). In popular presentations of history, convicts remain victims of a brutal system. Yet Australia's pioneering past—the explorers, pastoralists, and farmers who pushed the frontier of settlement inward throughout the nineteenth century—has long been the source of both nationalist and victim mythologies. John Hirst dubbed this nationalist celebration of those white pastoralists and farmers the "pioneer legend," a discourse that "celebrates courage, enterprise, hard work, and perseverance." He adds that this legend "can scarcely help being conservative in its political implications. It encourages reverence for the past" ("Pioneer Legend" 174–175). Long-standing popular notions of pioneering are about sacrifice and struggle, but this struggle is with the land, not the land's indigenous inhabitants. In these imaginings the Australian landscape is a malevolent unknown, unpredictable and predatory, and this, according to Peter Otto, "offers a colonial society a way of displacing the conflict between settlers and indigenous peoples onto a more acceptable narrative of a direct conflict between the settler and the land itself. The land and the indigenous people become merged, the former foregrounded, the latter denied a place in history at all" (quoted in Curthoys 13).

Andrew Lattas writes that conservative political discourse celebrates these pioneers, and their suffering in particular, because their suffering "becomes white settler society's right of ownership to the land" (235). This discourse emphasizes not white pioneers' achievements but victimhood, robbing them of agency in a struggle with Aboriginal people. Ann Curthoys argues that the prevalence and emphasis on suffering is central to Australia's history wars: "How *good* non-Aboriginal Australians are at memorialising their own sufferings. Looked at more closely, the contest over the past is perhaps not between positive and negative versions, but between those which place white Australians as victims, struggling heroically against adversity, and those which place them as aggressors, bringing adversity upon others" (Curthoys 3). Curthoys identifies these two conflicting impulses at work in the history wars, and those who oppose the latter view see those who perpetuate it as defaming the national past.

John Hirst has detected an additional impulse at work in popular responses to the history wars. He recounts attending a public debate about the history wars where the two panelists were debating the number of Aboriginal dead. A woman in the audience stood up and declared that she was sick of the debate about numbers. Hirst continues the story: "Even one death, she said, was too many. This remark was met with spontaneous applause, which though not universal was nevertheless revealing. The woman and those who applauded believed it was possible to dispossess the Aborigines without bloodshed. The woman did not speak of dispossession but she . . . was located in [a] theatre which stands on land that formerly belonged to Wurundjeri. Let us label this the liberal fantasy of our origins. It avers that conquest could have been done nicely" ("How Sorry" 82).

Hirst's argument is provocative but useful because it emphasizes, as he notes, that "we are all a long way from 1788," that it is impossible to think oneself back to the mindsets of the period. While I do not believe that this fantasy applies to historians, I do think traces of it can be found in popular responses to the history wars. Many white Australians are horrified at the violence perpetrated in the process of invasion and dispossession and, as Hirst notes, want to wish it away in an ethical reenvisioning of the past. Of course, this desire by some to atone for the wrongs of the past has been positive—it has been the wellspring of the reconciliation movement between indigenous and nonindigenous Australians, for example. But such an impulse can also lay the foundations for a rose-colored reworking of our past, one that disavows present-day Australians' investment in—indeed, reliance on—colonial dispossession and the violence in our past. I would suggest that Australians' desires for their history as identified by Curthoys and Hirst—to see themselves as victims, not agents of suffering and mistreatment, to see themselves in struggle with the land, rather than with indigenous people, and finally, to wish that the white settlement of Australia could have been enacted without violence—can be found in the presentation and enactment of Australian history in *The Colony* and *Outback House*. I will explore these ideas through considering how "the past" is constructed in these programs in three ways: through emphasizing technology and material culture, a focus on personal relationships and conflict, and a reliance on nostalgic understandings of the past.

Constructing the Past in Reality History TV

At first glance, reality history programs seem to offer some kind of access to the past in that they reproduce, reasonably faithfully, the material conditions of the past. In reality history, technology is the dominant signifier of "pastness," rendering the past accessible, allowing audiences to understand the past in these programs through technological change. This becomes particularly clear when we see the work involved in cooking and cleaning. On the one hand, this emphasis on technology allows audiences and participants to comprehend something of the strangeness of the past. Yet on the other hand, as John Hughes argued, it reproduces a myth of modernity as progress. Technology, Hughes argued, stands in for the radical cultural difference that is the actuality of the past, and all historical elements are submerged as plot, if they are dealt with at all. Robert Rosenstone dubbed this obsession with objects in historical films "false historicity": in short, history is no more than a period "look," and "things themselves *are* history, rather than *become* history because of what they mean to people at a particular time and place" (60). This goes for clothing as well as technology: both programs focus on the strangeness of the women's clothing (multiple layers, hoop petticoats, hats, and numerous impracticalities) without providing any insights into the cultural conditions that created it. As Gardiner comments: "To fetishise the 'authentic' object does not necessarily foster empathy with or understanding of those who lived with it, nor does it automatically raise questions about how the object was made [and] under what conditions" (19). We retain the objects of the past in these programs, but we lose their context and their ideological moorings. The absence of politics leaves the way open for a conservative, personalized view of the past (a point to which I will return).

The "past" of reality history programs is viewed through the tightly focused lens of interpersonal relationships, and especially through conflict, rather than through politics. The past is personalized, as conflicts are caused by personalities, not, for example, by class or racial differences. Beth Seaton argues that this emphasis on the subjective or personal is characteristic of reality TV: "Reality programming expresses social or moral dilemmas in emotional terms; and it is the emotional affectivity of the programme which acts as the key support for its 'truthfulness' or credibility." Reality history works as television when it keeps the facts of history submerged and emotional immediacy uppermost in the drama. This produces a personalized past, where, Tristram Hunt argues, issues of "class, social structure and inequality" are generally "pursued through the prism of identity—'how would our forefathers and mothers have lived,' not why, or how did it change over time" (856). Hunt sees this as symptomatic of a general shift in television history away from explanation and toward experience, identity, and empathy, a "'living history' which invites few questions about the nature of the past" (845, 857). Indeed, this may reflect the ways that audiences use history: American and Australian surveys of people's uses of the past revealed that most tend to make "'intimate' uses of the past; they turn to the past to live their lives in the present" (Rosenzweig 861, Ashton and Hamilton). The personal focus of reality history, then, is a major source of its appeal to audiences, yet this can expand historical understanding as well as truncate it.

Closely related to this focus on the personal is the genre's reliance on popular or social memory, rather than on knowledgeable participants, for its sense of the past. Participants in the programs generally rely on their own (often limited, often nostalgic) knowledge of the past, a knowledge that tends to be drawn from popular sources such as the media—and popular history, as Chris Healy argues, forms part of social memory (5). We can share a memory of a past that we have never experienced directly by drawing from sources like film, television, radio, and the press (Burns 68); in Australia social memory is a product of colonialism, and its most powerful narratives date from that period, beyond the range of lived experience (Healy 5). Graeme Davison argues that these histories specialize in presenting the veneer of the past, "leaving its human meaning to be filled in by inference or juxtaposition. Often its underlying social message is one of uncritical nostalgia" (Davison 28–29). Reality history programs speak to Australia's social memory of its colonial past—"histories of discovering, exploring, pioneering . . . struggling in a new land" (Healy 6) and, I would argue, at least partly reproduce it—in a new forum. Reality history participants are generally given minimal historical training about the period they are "entering" beforehand (Bignell 81), which means that they tend to revert to popular conceptions—or misconceptions—about what the past was like. The participants on *Outback House* were given historical training, yet they were not compelled to adhere to it (Hardy and Corones). Thus, they tended to rely on a social memory of the past. Claire, the cheerful maid on *Outback House,* remarked on the online forum for the program, "We were real people trying to make the best of a new way of life that was completely foreign to us. If there were any historical inaccuracies it was because we were not experts and so tried our best with the knowledge we had" ("toothpowder").

Stepping into the Colonial Past

In the opening episode of *Outback House,* viewers are told that the participants on the program are going to "test themselves against the mythology of the outback": instead of struggling against the indigenous inhabitants, or even against the land, the people on the program are going to be testing themselves against the myths of history. This was clearly a popular desire—*Outback House* had around five thousand eager applicants, and *The Colony* attracted two thousand (Lynam 38, Gibbon 348). Those chosen made clear their yearning to experience historical conditions and to prove themselves against history. Paul and Juli Allcorn, the squatter and his wife from *Outback House,* said they applied "to see if we could do it. We'd just had that trip around Australia and . . . we'd also taken the kids to various museums . . . so we had an increased awareness of the history of settlement, of how people survived then. How did they do it? . . . As a family we'd always had an interest in history, but that trip brought it all to a head" (Lynam 45). The Allcorns saw the program as a chance to exercise their interest in history, but the Hohnkes, a family from Tasmania who were cast as ex-convicts in *The Colony,* offered a more directly nostalgic reason for their participation. Tracy Hohnke said, "Kerry and I are always saying we wish we lived in the olden days. Life now . . . well, everything seems so false" (Gibbon 28–29). Glen Sheluchin, the original overseer on *Outback House,* offered a similar motivation: "I have an affinity with olden times—I often feel more at home back then than now." His wife added, "We always said that we were born in the wrong era" (Lynam 188–189). Though these participants expressed nostalgia for a time they had never directly experienced, others felt less rosy about the past they were preparing to enter. Trish Hurley, a feisty Irish settler on *The Colony,* declared that she would be "your traditional women's libber here in that everyone has to do their share regardless. But I grew up in a situation where the girls did the work in the house and I wasn't too happy about it. . . . My daughters might find it difficult. They grew up with equality in everything." She added that she was keen to take the show on because "women don't figure too much in history. You mostly get it from a male point of view" (Gibbon 24). Others saw participating as a personal challenge. Declan Hurley, another Irish settler on *The Colony,* said he was expecting the show would be "a psychological challenge more than [a] physical one" (Gibbon 23), whereas Dan Hatch, a young man from Perth who was initially employed to work as a shepherd on *Outback House,* said that "the idea of going back to basics has some appeal. . . . I am a complete city boy, so this is a challenge to see if I could manage to go back" (Lynam 193). The obvious question, however, is: go back to what? How do these programs represent the relationship between the present and the past, especially as the participants negotiate it?

Australian History in Reality TV

I have argued that reality history programs tend to present a picture of the past that necessarily relies on social memory, generally nostalgic and personalized, and that substitutes technology for a deeper understanding of the complexities of life in the past. I would now like to examine the ways the programs represented the contentious histories I outlined earlier: Do the representations of pioneers and convicts perpetuate both pioneering and victim mythologies of white Australians? Do representations of the indigenous participants and their interactions with others on the programs offer visions of reconciliation—an ethical reenvisioning of the past—or do they enact a (mythical) peaceful settlement of Australia? Or might the genre offer new ways of raising questions about historical understanding on our television screens?

The opening credits of *Outback House,* set to swelling violins, depict wide open bush spaces, the participants at work on the land and in the house, and a lone man on horseback, while the voiceover tells us that the participants on the program are about to "take on the challenge of life in 1861." By 1861, according to the narration, the property of Oxley Downs would have been a prime candidate for carving up into small farms. The squatter and his team must successfully harvest a good wool clip to ensure the survival of Oxley Downs. Of course, though this is the driving force for all the participants on Oxley Downs, in effect it means different things to the men and the women, as the women are largely reduced to support-ing roles. Women are praised for their "pioneer spirit": for example, Juli Allcorn takes over the kitchen "in true pioneer spirit" when the cook is sacked (episode 2). Women are represented as guardians of culture in the program, just as white women were seen as essential to frontier civilization in Australia's history. The arrival of the women on the farm in episode 2 is described as bringing "a new order on Oxley Downs," and the arrival of the prim-looking governess in episode 3 is described as a "civilizing influence." This representation of women recycles historical views of white women on the frontier to bolster myths of pioneering.

Yet though the female participants are still confined by the gender ideologies of the pioneering era, male participants are judged by the way they measure up to the "pioneer spirit." Dan Hatch, a young gay man from the city, fears toward the end of the first episode that he cannot meet the imagined standards of 1861. Left alone for a few hours with a large group of lambing ewes, he delivers a tearful piece to the camera as the sun sets: "I've had enough. . . . I can't do this. I'm filthy, I reek, the flies won't leave me alone, my feet are killing me . . . and I can't see things getting any better. This is reality, this is what it would have been like. I'm not tough enough to handle three months out here." Dan is reassigned to tend the farm's vegetable garden, described as a "houseboy" in episode 3, and by episode 4 is planning the wedding of Peter, the overseer, which takes place on the program. Dan might have what he describes as a "dif-ferent skill set" from the other men on the farm, but the voiceover text leaves the audience in some doubt about his pioneering mettle (and, by implication, his masculinity): "While Dan makes his decorating decisions, Russell takes on Baldy, the biggest, strongest, and most cunning horse on the station" (episode 4). The men on Oxley Downs manage to measure up to their pioneering forebears by washing, shearing, and delivering their wool. In the final episode, when the wool must be loaded onto a bullock dray (a cart drawn by young bulls), a laborious task they complete over many hours, Dan comments, "It all comes down to teamwork—we all have to work together . . . in order that we can function as a group, as a squattocracy, as a community." The program affirms the pioneer spirit of the men, who have been able to complete this difficult task together. The voiceover builds the tension as the moment of judgment approaches: "So would our twenty-first-century pioneers have survived in 1861? How will they stack up beside their original forebears of the mid-nineteenth century?" When they discover that, in nineteenth-century financial terms, they have succeeded in their task to sell the wool for a high price, we are told that "the volunteers have not only survived the nineteenth century, they've done a lot better than many of the original pioneers" (episode 8). So in *Outback House,* the modern "pioneers" test themselves against the pioneer legend and emerge triumphant.

Pioneering on *The Colony* was somewhat different and arguably more difficult. Reenacting the first years of European settlement in tents and basic wooden huts in demanding weather must have been challenging for the participants, especially those from Ireland and the United Kingdom. The stakes were high, and they were established by the expository voiceover that opens the program: "Two centuries ago the British Empire pulled off a deed of mythic stature: it planted the seed of a new civilization on the edge of a fantastic land. Home to an ancient Aboriginal culture for some 50,000 years, to Europeans Australia remained a vast, untouched unknown until the British seized the entire continent. It was to be a massive prison for the criminal underclasses of Great Britain, and only the bravest and most desperate would join them there."

This opening text establishes that the early history of Australia was potentially riven with conflict: between black and white, between convicts and their masters. Yet in the program itself, the tensions are not between convicts and their masters, but among the three settler families; again, a focus on interpersonal conflict comes at the expense of a richer social history. This is possibly because the convicts controlled by each family cannot be punished in the ways they would have been punished in the early colony. (That is, there is no threat of violence for those who misbehave.) Thus, social tensions along class lines are muted, while the participants are at pains to minimize tensions between indigenous people and invaders (a point I will return to shortly). If the three male heads of household are not fighting with each other, they are struggling against history itself: as the voiceover warns in episode 1, in three months "we will know whether each of our modern-day families are tough enough to cut it on the frontier." Again, white families must test themselves against a mythic set of pioneering values and thereby affirm conservative understandings of the nation's past.

The representation of indigenous peoples, and the fraught history between indigenous Australians and Europeans, is critical to representing history in Australian reality history programs. As I outlined earlier, the question of how Australia writes, understands, and reconciles its often violent and disturbing history of colonization and dispossession is central to Australian national identity in the twenty-first century. It is also a history that seems furthest from our grasp in terms of representation. It would be ethically impossible to accurately re-create such a history—to reenact colonial violence, dispossession, and indigenous resistance—in a reality TV program. So how do these programs deal with this issue: Do they implicate contemporary Australians in this history and present an ethically and morally complex past? Do they present a colonization without victims? Or do they offer viewers new ways of thinking about the relationships between the present and the past and exploring the ways people today construct notions of their national past?

Both programs situate violence between Aboriginal and European Australians as "in the past"—it is literally in the past for the twenty-first-century participants, but it is also in the past in the periods being reenacted—dispossession has *already happened*. In *Outback House* there were two indigenous participants: the teenager Danielle, playing a maid, and Mal, a farmhand. In the scenario of *Outback House*, armed resistance to colonization is in the past; the story that predominates is one of Aboriginal assistance to Europeans in the process of colonization. For example, Mal and Tom, a visiting elder, comment that the first settlers would have perished without help from indigenous people (episode 3). This highlights the interconnected nature of indigenous and white history, but it has the effect of presenting the story of colonization as peaceful and cooperative, rather than offering an equally plausible narrative of violence and resistance. Yet could such a history be presented onscreen? It would be ethically impossible to represent the violence and dispossession of colonization in reality history, but the absence of this violence distorts history.

Other aspects of indigenous depiction in *Outback House* hint at a different, more subversive representation. Danielle, the maid, is just seventeen, and early in the series she complains of her role: "I hate it that I have to wait on people and wash their dishes but I'm gonna try and do what people would have done in this day—just ignore it" (episode 2). The producers arranged a visit for Danielle, who was ready to quit the program, from her mother, who tells her, "This place is so significant to us and our heritage because our family and our ancestors worked on this same property" (episode 3). Danielle excitedly tells her mother, "I've had so much déjà vu it's not funny, and I swear it's because I know that . . . people who are related to me have been here already." A sense of earlier occupation, of an Aboriginal history connected to this place, is quietly established. Crucially, Danielle is working as a servant, the occupation for which most mixed-race indigenous girls were trained when they were removed from their families in the late nineteenth and twentieth centuries as part of a large-scale policy of assimilation of Aboriginal people in Australia. (Boys were similarly removed and largely trained to be rural workers.) Her resentment at her heavy workload and desire to quit the program take on a new historical resonance in this context, as does the powerful moment between her and her departing mother. Saying good-bye, Danielle's mother tells her, "You just stay strong, stay strong, and whatever they want you to do, you do it, do it with happiness, because you'll be through this so much better and happier, it's only for a short while." Danielle in parting from her mother stands in for the thousands of indigenous children who were never able to say good-bye to their parents when they were removed to institutions. The scene resonates strongly in an environment where the issue of the "stolen generations" (as these children who were removed from their families are now known) has only recently come to public attention and has been the subject of bitter political debate (Haebich, Manne).

When the producers of *The Colony* first called for indigenous participants, they drew a blank: no Aboriginal families wanted to be involved, partly because there was concern among the Aboriginal community about "appearing on a show that focused on a tragic time for Indigenous people" (Tedmanson). The producers eventually found families willing to participate, who were told that they would be "living back in time" but not naked, having exchanged clothes with the British settlers. The families (the Costelloes and the Donovans) lived outside the white settlement and were given no preexisting shelter, unlike the white families. An early voiceover summed up the potential for violence in the early colony: "The frontier saw many skirmishes between black and white, a conflict which some historians have called an undeclared war. Settlers feared attacks from the spears of Aboriginal people, and they feared the muskets issued to each settler. But there were also places where indigenous and settler relations were good. How will modern race relations unfold in our colony?" (episode 2).

Yet even if we, the audience, believe violence is possible or even justified, we know it won't eventuate—to allow violence would be unethical on the part of the producers. So colonial violence is displaced in favor of disputes over history. For example, though the voiceover emphasizes the potential for both violence and harmony, the indigenous historian John Maynard, who visits the indigenous clan in episode 3, tells them that it is important to note that all race relations weren't pleasant—that there was constant conflict and outright warfare in the region in which the program was set. Hearing Maynard's account of colonial violence, Anto Donovan reflects: "I know that history part really gets to me. Even today some of us, where we grew up, we can't even walk back onto that land, and I don't think that's right. But that history should not have even been how it was" (episode 3). Here Donovan expresses both a sense of anger at the past and a desire to rewrite it in an ethical way. His anger at dispossession and loss of place is emphasized by the earlier arrival of Richard Greene, one of only a tiny handful of fluent speakers of the local indigenous language, Dharug. Greene tells the Aboriginal families that it has been one hundred years since the language has been heard in the area—and, of course, no one can understand the language. The fact that the indigenous families need guidance in finding local bush food, or in the local indigenous language, shows the importance of place and locality in indigenous culture, what the loss of place could mean for cultural traditions and food supplies, and the effect of land loss for all aspects of indigenous life. So though we see some of the consequences of colonial dispossession for Aboriginal people, the reenactment of the beginnings of settlement by the white participants evades this, settling instead for a focus on whites' hardships as the settlers struggle to make their land fertile and build a community.

Outback House limited some of the female participants to being little more than "civilizing influences," but this was not the case for all the women on the program. Indeed, one of the most interesting possibilities of reality history is that it has the potential to present aspects of the lives of women in the past, especially working-class women, and invite an empathetic identification with them. Anecdotal evidence (and my own experience working in history television) suggests that Australian history television is largely produced and consumed by older men, which often means that programs are commissioned with men's interests in mind. Stories about women's historical experiences are more difficult to shepherd through the development process (Arrow 46–3). In its focus on "ordinary people" and everyday life in the past, reality history differs from much conventional history television, which still tends to examine the great, the good, or the notorious (Hunt 848). Catharine Lumby has noted that some critics argue that reality television is degrading because it invades the privacy of its participants. She claims, however, that opening up the private realm (traditionally associated with women) to public surveillance is not necessarily degrading, and that relegating certain issues and behaviors to the private sphere has not served all social groups equally well. By exposing so-called private behaviors—such as the expression of emotions—to the public gaze through television, Lumby argues, "reality television might be understood as a forum in which so-called 'ordinary' people are able to participate, if only partially, in the process of quite literally representing themselves" (Lumby 23). Liesbet van Zoonen concurs, noting that through reality television, "we rediscover on television what has become ever more invisible in the world around us, the private life of ordinary people" (van Zoonen 672). Jerome de Groot argues that reality history programs "emphasise a dynamic, interrogative history of lived experience and of everyday normality—the otherness of history is enacted through the lack of shampoo, rather than the temporal distance of events," which produces a vision of "history from below" rather than the neat narratives of television historians (402–403).

Although this can lead to an overwhelming focus on experience rather than explanation, as Tristram Hunt bemoans, one of the things reality history does best is help us imagine how difficult women's lives in the past were. The press for the programs expressed astonishment at the lives of Edwardian-era scullery maids, for example: "Required to work between 16 and 18 hours a day, and not permitted to talk during meal breaks, a scullery maid in 1905 earned less than a dollar a week" (Oliver 3), and the voiceover on *Outback House* emphasized that women's "daily work was laborious, repetitive, and unrelenting" (episode 2). Throughout the series the men are shown working together on different tasks—building a sheep run to wash the wool, or baling the wool to prepare it for market—whereas the women's work—washing, cooking, and cleaning—remains monotonous and demanding. The women are looking for respite from their endless labors; the cook Brigid says she'll do anything to get out of the kitchen (episode 8). Danielle, the maid, complains, "Everyone said it's going to be great fun . . . it's not fun at all. You have half an hour of fun each week. It sucks!" (episode 3). In representing the difficulties of a nineteenth-century working woman's life (as experienced by a twenty-first-century woman, of course), reality history can portray in empathetic ways historical experiences and ways of being that would otherwise remain elusive to history television.

Further, reality history can represent the past in such a way as to raise "complex questions about the nature of historical understanding" (Gardiner 19). Reality history participants are shown engaging with the past in the present to extract modern meaning from it, and the disjunction between the past and present often becomes a structuring device in these programs (Cook 493). For example, in episode 3 of *The Colony,* the women from all the families spend time together, making flags that represent their various clans. (It seems that the producers supplied the women with materials to make these flags.) While the Irishwomen make a historically accurate green flag with a harp on it (which dates, according to the voiceover, to 1798), the Aboriginal women make an Aboriginal flag (a striking red, black, and yellow design that dates to the modern land rights struggle of 1971 [see Ausflag, "Aboriginal Flag"]), and the Hohnkes make a Eureka flag, which was created during a radical political struggle on the Victorian goldfields in 1854 and is a symbol of radicalism used by both the political left and right in Australia (Ausflag, "Eureka Flag"). Thus, notions of historical accuracy are jettisoned in favor of creating symbols that carry modern resonance for the participants; Tracy Hohnke comments, "What we want to do is to represent what we believe in. Makin' the flag made us Aussies feel like we were having our say, that we wouldn't be dictated to in any way" (episode 3). This sets the scene for a confrontation with the historian Michael McKernan, who acted as an onscreen mediator between the participants and the producers. McKernan reads a proclamation that declares that the Aboriginal families must not visit white homes; the white families will lose their rations if they disobey. This sparks the Hohnkes' anger: Tracy vows to defy the order, saying, "I don't give a shit what the history man says." The men, led by Tracy's husband, Kerry, carry out a protest in which all the participants raise the Aboriginal and Eureka flags. The situation is resolved when the Aboriginal families, not wanting to jeopardize the food supply of the white families, leave the camp—and the series. The flag raising is partly a gesture of solidarity with the Aboriginal families, partly an act of defiance, yet it is also an attempt to find the moral meaning of the past in a present-day context. Australian historians writing the history of Aboriginal dispossession, and the dark history of the history wars, are, in many ways, attempting to do just that, and it is the struggle over the moral meaning of the past that gives the history wars their energy and controversy. This roaming across time in reality history can reveal the ways that people make sense of the past far more concisely than the occasionally laborious debates of academic historians.

As I have outlined here, depicting Australia's controversial, checkered past of colonization and dispossession in reality history TV has produced decidedly mixed results. The programs emphasize the impossibility of ever re-creating or reproducing the past in the present—all we can know is what we twenty-first-century citizens choose to make of the past. For this reason, reality history offers a very limited means of learning about the past, for all the reasons I have discussed: it focuses on the material conditions of the past at the expense of politics; it gazes at the past through the prism of personal relationships and conflict; and it reproduces popular social memory of the past. Yet this is not the only function of reality history, and, as I have shown, reality history TV offers interesting possibilities for understanding the ethical significance of the past. The standard criticism of reality history is that it is neither reality nor history (Stearn 27)—de Groot has speculated that many historians dislike the genre because it displaces them from their traditional televisual role as "gatekeeper to the past" (399). Reality history is important precisely because it confronts the ways present-day people make sense of the past—in more explicit ways than other kinds of television history. Though they are not unproblematic, for all the reasons I have outlined, reality history programs and the discourses they engender demonstrate, perhaps more effectively than written history, the ways in which, as Patrick Wolfe writes, "we remain the legatees and beneficiaries of [our] continuing past" (30), and in an era in which history remains more popular and more contested than ever, this is a worthy and timely project.

Notes

1. See Macintyre and Clark. Macintyre adopted the American term *history wars* to describe Australia's debates over its history.

2. *The Colony* was produced by Hilton Cordell Productions for SBS Independent, Radio Telefís Eireann, and the History Channel U.K. with the assistance of the New South Wales Film and Television Office.

Works Cited

Arrow, Michelle. " 'Television Program Yes, History No': Australian History according to *Rewind*." *History Australia* 2.2 (2005): 46-1–6.

Ashton, Paul, and Paula Hamilton. "At Home with the Past: Initial Findings from the National Survey." *ACH: Australian Cultural History* 22 (2005): 5–30.

Ausflag. "Aboriginal Flag." 1995, www.ausflag.com.au/flags/ab.html (accessed July 11, 2006).

———. "Eureka Flag." 2005, www.ausflag.com.au/flags/eureka.html (accessed July 11, 2006).

Bignell, Jonathon. *Big Brother: Reality TV in the Twenty-first Century.* New York: Palgrave Macmillan, 2006.

Blainey, Geoffrey. "Drawing Up a Balance Sheet of Our History." *Quadrant* 37.1–8 (1993): 10–15.

Burns, Maureen. "Nostalgia for the Future: Nation, Memory and Technology at ABC Online." *Southern Review* 35.1 (2002): 63–73.

Cook, Alexander. "The Use and Abuse of Historical Reenactment: Thoughts on Recent Trends in Public History." *Criticism* 46.3 (2004): 487–496.

Curran, James. *The Power of Speech: Australian Prime Ministers Defining National Identity.* Melbourne: Melbourne University Press, 2004.

Curthoys, Ann. "Expulsion, Exodus and Exile in White Australian Historical Mythology." *Journal of Australian Studies* 61 (1999): 1–18, 215–218.

Davison, Graeme. "A Sense of Place." *Boundaries of the Past.* Ed. Bain Attwood. Melbourne: History Institute, 1990. 28–35.

De Groot, Jerome. "Empathy and Enfranchisement: Popular Histories." *Re-thinking History* 10.3 (2006): 391–413.

Gardiner, Juliet. "The Edwardian Country House." *History Today* 52.7 (July 2002): 18–20.

Gibbon, Belinda. *The Colony: The Book from the Popular SBS Living History Series.* Sydney: Random House, 2005.

Griffiths, Tom. *Hunters and Collectors: The Antiquarian Imagination in Australia.* Cambridge: Cambridge University Press, 1996.

Haebich, Anna. *Broken Circles: Fragmenting Indigenous Families, 1800–2000.* Fremantle: Fremantle Arts Centre Press, 2000.

Hardy, Susan, and Anthony Corones. "Colonising the Past? History, Medicine, and Reality Television." *Health and History* 8.2 (2006), www.historyco operative.org/journals/hah/8.2/hardy/html (accessed May 1, 2009).

Healy, Chris. *From the Ruins of Colonialism: History as Social Memory.* Cambridge: Cambridge University Press, 1997.

Hirst, John. "How Sorry Can We Be?" *Sense and Nonsense in Australian History.* Melbourne: Black Inc, 2005. 80–103.

———. "The Pioneer Legend." *Historical Studies* 18.71 (1978). Reprinted in his *Sense and Nonsense in Australian History.* Melbourne: Black Inc, 2005. 174–196.

Hughes, John. Participation in OzDox forum, "Making Australian Histories: How Are Documentary Filmmakers Working with Ideas of 'Nation' and Storytelling," September 8, 2005, www.ozdox.org/x_2005/v080905.html (accessed March 23, 2006).

Hunt, Tristram. "Reality, Identity and Empathy: The Changing Face of Social History Television." *Journal of Social History* 39.3 (2006): 843–858.

Lattas, Andrew. "Aborigines and Contemporary Australian Nationalism: Primordiality and the Cultural Politics of Otherness." *Race Matters: Indigenous Australians and "Our" Society.* Ed. Gillian Cowlishaw and Barry Morris. Canberra: Aboriginal Studies Press, 1997. 223–283.

Lumby, Catharine. "Real Appeal: The Ethics of Reality TV." *Remote Control: New Media, New Ethics.* Ed. Catharine Lumby and Elspeth Probyn. Melbourne: Cambridge University Press, 2003. 11–24.

Lynam, Bernard. *Outback House: Behind the Scenes of the ABC Television Series.* Sydney: ABC Books, 2005.

Macintyre, Stuart, and Anna Clark. *The History Wars.* Melbourne: Melbourne University Press, 2003.

Manne, Robert. *In Denial: The Stolen Generations and the Right.* Melbourne: Schwartz Publishing, 2001.

Oliver, Robin. "Maid in England." *The Guide, Sydney Morning Herald,* August 12, 2002, 3.

"Richhosk." *Outback House* message board. "Authenticity?" in "Historical Authenticity." June 12, 2005, www2b.abc.net.au/tmb/Client/Message.as px?b=8&m=57&ps=20&dm=1&pd=3 (accessed November 29, 2005).

Rosenstone, Robert A. *Visions of the Past: The Challenge of Film to Our Idea of History.* Cambridge: Harvard University Press, 1995.

Rosenzweig, Roy. "Historians and Audiences: Comment on Tristram Hunt and Geoffrey Timmins." *Journal of Social History* 39.3 (2006): 859–864.

Seaton, Beth. "Reality Programming." *Encyclopedia of Television.* Ed. Horace Newcomb. Chicago: Fitzroy Dearborn, 1997.

Stearn, Tom. "What's Wrong with Television History." *History Today* 52.12 (2002): 26–27.

Tedmanson, Sophie. "TV Show Digs Up Old Wounds." *Australian,* August 30, 2004, www.eniar.org/news/colony.html (accessed November 29, 2005).

"toothpowder." *Outback House* message board. "Chummy behaviour in 1861, I don't think so!" in "Historical Authenticity," June 20, 2005, www2b. abc.net.au/tmb/Client/Message.aspx?b=8&m=389&ps=20&dm=1&pd=3 (accessed November 29, 2005).

van Zoonen, Liesbet. "Desire and Resistance: *Big Brother* and the Recognition of Everyday Life." *Media, Culture and Society* 23.5 (2001): 669–677.

Wolfe, Patrick. "Operation Sandy Track." *Overland* 183 (2006): 26–31.

Living History in Documentary Practice

The Making of The Colony

> The documentary horizon is a virtual terra incognita,
> studded with promise and peril for the resourceful analyst.
> And the stakes have never been higher. (Michael Renov, in
> Gaines and Renov 324)

In a television environment where potential audience ratings remain integral to any program's success (whether news or entertainment, commercial or public broadcaster), the boundaries of the documentary's form and practice have been undergoing significant shifts. Ten years since Renov made this statement, and ten years since the reality TV format really took hold of television schedules, the documentary's stake remain high. This essay discusses the "edutainment" format of historical reality TV from a production perspective, looking at one Australian case, the living-history series *The Colony* (2005).

In offering to provide not only entertainment but information and history education, some makers of historical reality TV claim the mark of *documentary* practice. According to the director of Australia's first living-history series, *The Colony,* the genre is "pure observational documentary *with constructs*" (Scheelings, rushes, emphasis added). The series producer of *The Colony,* asserts: "The living history method doesn't just tell history; it also records the experiences of those who relive it" (quoted in Gibbon 342). From the claims made by the makers of historical reality TV, in the series publicity and through the programs themselves, the audience is promised an interesting documentary-like investigation from which to better understand our past.

In considering this premise, it is relevant to ask questions about living-history production that are traditional to documentary film critique. How was the program made and by what principles did the professionals working within it operate? What has led me to take up the issue of production *process* over the more familiar analyses of program *content* is my practical involvement in *The Colony* series as a documentary filmmaker.

In 2004 I was employed by the Australian public broadcaster Special Broadcasting Service Independent (SBSi) Television to produce a behind-the-scenes documentary about the production of *The Colony*. During the six-month production period of *The Making of The Colony* documentary and *The Colony* living-history series, the anomaly presented by the different roles—"portraying a reality" and "creating the illusion of a reality"—came to a head. Complex ethical and philosophical issues confronted both endeavors, and the nature of these reflected a theme central to a long-standing debate surrounding documentary film: "How real is it?"

This essay tackles this fundamental documentary question of authenticity in relation to the Australian case of *The Colony* and *The Making of The Colony*. In offering an account of the production process of one historical reality TV series, I hope that some ray of light can be shed on the ever-hybridizing world of documentary and history program making as it is practiced in contemporary television.

Background of The Colony

Set in the period 1800–1813, *The Colony* was the result of three years of research and development by the Australian documentary production company Hilton Cordell Productions. Designed for public and educational broadcast, the six-part historical reality TV–style series was the first of its kind in Australia and an international coproduction financed by the Australian SBSi, the Irish Radio Telefis Eireann (RTE), and the United Kingdom History Channel. Hilton Cordell also received financing from state government through the New South Wales Film and Television Office and also, somewhat controversially, from the major supporting arm for national documentary production, the Film Finance Corporation (FFC). The support received from the FFC resulted in an outcry from within the Australian independent documentary sector (Meade), as eligibility for these funds specifically excluded reality TV projects. Despite *The Colony*'s obvious link to reality TV, Hilton Cordell was able to maintain its claim that because of the educational merit of the living-history format, it rightly belonged to the *documentary* genre and it was consequently financed as such by the various supporting bodies. I refer to this FFC funding in more detail later in the essay.

During *The Colony*'s 2005 premiere on Australian television, an online chat forum was posted on the SBS Web site to facilitate daily discussion and promotion of the series. After the broadcast, a DVD set of the series and a companion book were marketed for educational use in the history classroom. In the foreword to the book, an academic historian involved in the series, Michael McKernan, sanctioned the series as a worthy exploration into what one could imagine the past to have been like (quoted in Gibbon 8).

Five volunteer families were chosen to participate in this historical social experiment: a family from England and another from Ireland to represent newly arrived 1800s free settlers; one white family from Australia to portray the first generation of established emancipated convicts; and two Aboriginal Australian families to exemplify the traditional owners of the area—the Koori Clan of New South Wales. In addition, single men and women from around Australia volunteered to take on the roles of convicts, providing the three white settler families with two indentured slave laborers each. From two thousand hopeful applicants, thirty-three participants were selected to take part. The contract the volunteers entered into with Hilton Cordell required them to join *The Colony* in the "spirit and intent" of the early settlement, to "relive" this period of Australian history for four months (Scheelings, film). This time was later reduced to three months, as it became obvious to Hilton Cordell that another month was unnecessary for the six-episode television series. After firsthand experience of living-history deprivation, the volunteers were happy to comply with the reduced sentence.

Background to The Making of The Colony

The idea for a documentary film showing the making of a living-history television series was initiated by Hilton Cordell, which had wanted the film to be a promotion of its series, known in the industry as an electronic press kit (EPK). The company pitched this documentary along with the series, intending to produce the film itself until budget limitations made it untenable. Keen for a behind-the-scenes film to go ahead, SBSi Television, in agreement with Hilton Cordell, took on the responsibility for *The Making of The Colony* by commissioning it as an in-house production.

This new contractual agreement between Hilton Cordell and the public broadcaster stated that the documentary's crew was to be granted full access to film all aspects of *The Colony*'s production, and SBSi was to be the final arbiter and copyright owner of the completed film.

The major difference that this revised agreement and consequent shift in ownership created for the behind-the-scenes film was the form that the documentary would take. Unlike Hilton Cordell, SBSi was not interested in an EPK for *The Colony;* rather, the broadcaster wanted a documentary in the truer sense of the word—a nonfiction film portraying what it was really like, the ups and the downs in making a living-history series. This was the behind-the-scenes documentary that SBSi commissioned, that I was employed to produce, and in which Hilton Cordell agreed to participate.

When I began work on the project, Hilton Cordell was already two months into preproduction for *The Colony.* My role was to document the remaining six months of the endeavor, which consisted of three more months of planning and preparation, operating out of Hilton Cordell's Sydney-based office, and three months in production on an isolated plot of land along the Colo River in the Hawkesbury region of New South Wales.

The documentary was to portray Hilton Cordell's production journey, based on observation and interviews; the direction of the film's narrative was decided in collaboration with the SBSi commissioning editor and executive producer, with whom I consulted regularly. SBSi agreed that Hilton Cordell was entitled to use footage from *The Making of The Colony* rushes as well as the completed film for its series, including postbroadcast use in its DVD release. The documentary could also use both footage and music from *The Colony* series. Hilton Cordell was permitted to sell *The Making of The Colony* documentary to other broadcasters (namely, RTE and the U.K. History Channel) as the seventh episode in its series and was able to retain any profit gained from such a sale.

The Colony premiered in Australia on Australia Day (January 26) 2005, and *The Making of the Colony* was to follow six weeks later, as the final episode of the series.

Theoretical Context

Although there is a strong behind-the-scenes documentary tradition revealing the machinations involved in fiction filmmaking,[1] no such established film subgenre exists following the process behind television production. This gap has been filled with fictional, often satirical portrayals of television practice.[2] Thus, when I was first asked to produce *The Making of The Colony,* I believed it was a project that would present substance and relevance through its potential to offer a documentary film account not just of television practice but of the most recent and all-encompassing phenomenon on television: reality TV.

Though historical reality TV has obviously sprouted from reality TV roots, many of its makers have tended to disassociate it from the controversially "no-brow" genre, epitomized by the likes of *Big Brother* and *Survivor.* For instance, on the Web site of an American Public Broadcasting Service (PBS) series, *Colonial House* (2004), the series producer invites the public to explore the online publicity to "find out why this is not 'reality' TV" (Colonial House).[3] Similarly distancing the reality TV format, the director of a British Broadcasting Corporation (BBC) "extreme history" series, *The Ship* (2002), stated the "deeper purpose" of the series, as recounted by the Australian historian involved in the program, Iain McCalman: "[The director informed me that] ours would be a hybrid genre, balancing serious historical inquiry with the contingent psychological and social dramas of an experiential retracing. . . . The words 'reality TV' were noticeably absent from his [the director's] enthusiastic blueprint" (McCalman 478). Other program makers have distanced themselves from reality TV by aligning their work more closely with that of documentary practice. The director and coproducer of *The Colony* claim it is "observational documentary" (Scheelings, film), whereas the series producer furthers the documentary assertions by referring to the educational merit of the format, saying: "[*The Colony*] aims to explode myths and illuminate the historical truth. . . . As factual filmmakers we are dedicated to illustrating the historical accuracy of the time" (Australian Television Archive).

As I mentioned earlier, loud protest arose from within the independent film community in Australia regarding the limited government funds allocated for documentary filmmaking being given to what was essentially viewed as a reality TV series. These complaints were met with the counterclaim by the producers of *The Colony* that "three years of research" with a "serious intent"[4] to "illuminate the historical truth of life in Australia's early colonial days" was proof enough that their series was a legitimate history documentary series (Hilton Cordell Productions quoted in Meade). Though few scholars would consider this a documentary in the traditional sense of the term, within the television industry a "serious intent" toward "historical truth" appears to have given rise to the new history documentary hybrid—"living history," "extreme history," "hands-on history." Call it what they will, the claims are the same and the aim is for the product to be accepted as both a legitimate historical inquiry and one aligned with the tradition and practice of the documentary. The historian McCalman recounts the confident guarantee made by *The Ship*'s director: "As participants in one of the most expensive BBC historical productions of recent times, we would, the director assured me, have an opportunity to revolutionize the practice and pedagogy of history" (477).

Without exception, from the assertions made by the makers of historical reality TV and from the claims made in the programs themselves, the format promises to be an interesting if not invigorating investigation into the past, while offering a better understanding of our condition in the present. As the series producer of *The Colony* stated, "We don't have much Australian history on television, especially of this period, so to bring Australian history to a wide audience was always the dream behind this thrilling project" (Scheelings, film). An alternative view to living history as pedagogy was expressed by one wearied television reviewer when *The Colony* was broadcast; she described the proliferation of reality TV as having "erupted, throwing up a cloud of dust so great no light can penetrate," inevitably having an effect on public broadcasting, where "the non-commercials aim to add class using history" (Cunningham).

Though it is a bold and, some argue, contentious move for government funding bodies and public broadcasters to commission reality-style shows such as *The Colony* as a documentary series, it is not altogether unprecedented. As public broadcasters look more and more to quantitative indicators to measure success, the content and quality of programs are increasingly judged according to their accessibility and potential for popularity with a mass audience (Hill, Kilborn and Izod, Nichols). What cannot be so quickly transformed by the desire for high ratings, however, is the documentary tradition.

Envisioned and defined as "the creative treatment of actuality" by the pioneer of the documentary film movement, John Grierson (13), this film form was to represent reality in the public service of edifying society. Within this premise the cause of the everyday person was taken up, as one early documentarist and cinematographer, John Grierson's sister Ruby Grierson, famously demonstrated in *Housing Problems* (1935) when she took the cumbersome film and sound equipment to the residence of her film subjects living in substandard housing conditions and instructed them to "tell the bastards what it's like living in slums!" This kind of consciousness applied to filmmaking brought to the screen a realization about real life, and along with it an ethical commitment to participants and audiences alike, that had not previously been accomplished through the cinema.

Individual personal purposes or motivations aside, most documentarists acknowledge that they are united by this undeniable and fundamental common heritage, founded in a strong social movement. So, whatever the forces dictating documentary production at any given time, it is according to the documentary tradition and not purely the demands of the day that the "community of practitioners" (Nichols 15) advances and negotiates the development of the genre. The members of this community do so in discussion with one another, both directly and indirectly, and through their own films (Kilborn and Izod 171–172; Nichols 15). This open forum of debate and discussion among practitioners is an integral component of the documentary film movement, and ongoing critical peer review is central to the healthy development of the form.

As the contemporary documentary movement evolves in a globally consumer-driven television environment, however, the founding idea and raison d'être of the documentary film is in peril of becoming sidelined by a perceived necessity to be a marketable commodity. In the desire to make a successful television product, or "great TV," what is increasingly becoming less essential among the "community of practitioners" is the integrity of the genre and the inherent professional protocols that come with that craft. As the Canadian filmmaker Geoff Bowie comments in the narration to his documentary on Peter Watkins,[5] "There was a time when the documentary was about seizing a reality and a commitment to social change." In detailing the integrity that characterizes Watkins's work, and the exclusion from television he experienced as a result, Bowie describes the current documentary movement as he sees it: "Filmmakers mutate as the suppliers of products and brands" as they strive to produce marketable documentary merchandise. With a new impetus to meet the needs of television executives, the traditional roles of the documentary to address the needs of society and to work in the public's service are in danger of being marginalized. As a result, the "community of practitioners" could be accused of losing a sense of the documentary purpose, where its members are uniting not over a shared social conscience, but over a shared desire to sell their commercially designed products; this is ultimately at the expense of documentary participants, whose personal experiences are, in essence, the commodity being sold. In adopting such an allegiance to commercial practices, documentarists inevitably will be inclined to forgo the original purpose of the form and in so doing change the practice and the nature of the genre itself. In discarding the traditional imperatives of the craft, as Bowie comments on this contemporary film movement, the fallout is that "rather than revealing reality, the documentary is covering it over."

Illusions of a Reality in The Colony

The priority for *The Colony* was to make history accessible and entertaining for a mass audience while maintaining the premise that it was *not* reality TV but a seriously intentioned history documentary series, as it had been pitched and commissioned. The priority for *The Making of The Colony* was not to promote the series, but rather to give an accurate behind-the-scenes account of living-history television in production. Despite these intentions, it became apparent early on that both productions faced significant obstacles that threatened the likelihood that they would achieve their respective objectives. Making a serious history program by following a reality TV format creates its own complications; and providing a genuine account of this production process for the behind-the-scenes documentary was not without its own particular challenges.

Any representation of history is going to be somewhat ironical, and it was inevitable that *The Making of The Colony* would end up being the ironical eye of living-history production, showing the distance between the history as it was created, which involved illusion, and the production as it was executed, which also involved illusion. The problem that my role presented for the series producer and director of *The Colony* was that they wanted the challenges inherent in living history to remain hidden from the audience. Although the documentarist assumes the presentation of reality to be the goal, this was not Hilton Cordell's aim for *The Colony*. And though other reality TV programs typically make known the construction and the artifice that exist as part of the television process, *The Colony's* series producer and director paradoxically believed that their higher-brow living-history, social experiment documentary (and "not *Big Brother* in historical costumes") series would be discredited if they were to be up-front about a lot of the illusions that existed (Scheelings, rushes).

The aim of the series, as stated by its series producer, was "to make history come alive" (Scheelings, film), and showing how this was done was not part of that intention. In fact, it was believed that revealing the process behind the production would be in direct opposition to what the series was trying to accomplish. The director felt that if *The Making of The Colony* portrayed a different version of events from those *The Colony* showed, the integrity of scenes portrayed in his living-history series would be undermined. "People don't want to know information, they just want the drama," the director informed me; this was his justification for censorship and for prohibiting filming of specific scenes for the documentary. It was important to Hilton Cordell, which wanted *The Colony* to be accepted as a documentary series, that *my* documentary account did not conflict with its own. This was obviously an impossible requirement, however; as our roles were very different, the depiction of events would also differ.

For example, *The Colony* begins energetically with dramatic, traditional Celtic-style music over magnificent aerial shots of a thirty-three-meter brigantine traversing the open seas. Closer shots present the time-traveling participants in period dress, and the iconic Australian actor Jack Thompson's voice-of-god narration begins: "Two centuries ago the British Empire pulled off a deed of mythic stature. It planted the seed of a new civilization on the edge of an invisible and fantastic land, Australia, eight months' hard sailing from home." The audience is then introduced to those who will "travel back in time to relive the birth of the Australian colony" (*The Colony*). Over sweeping aerial shots of the land they will inhabit, viewers are further informed: "Here in this isolated valley, they must plant crops, raise livestock and build houses. For four months, they'll face hardship, history and each other in the colony of 1800." This beginning of what promises to be a fascinating journey follows the participants as they row down the picturesque river in longboats to disembark finally on the land that will be their remote, historically reconstructed world. The narration continues, "Our colonists are to be given their stores and enter four months of total isolation. By the end, we'll know which of our families and their convicts are tough enough to have cut it on the new frontier." The participants are met by the historian McKernan, who has been appointed three roles in the production: onscreen historical authority, "riverboat trader," and supplier of the colonists' rations, or "government stores." In this opening scene he assigns the families their convict labor before departing, promising to return in ten days with more government stores. The participants then continue on their journey to "the past," walking the one-kilometer (two-thirds of a mile) stretch lined with native melaleuca trees, carrying their 1800s rations and belongings into the prepared valley that will be their settlement. Captivating images of the historically costumed group amid the native Australian bush are accompanied by light violin and harmonica playing in traditional Celtic style: a beautiful scene that is soothingly mythical, awe-inspiring, and picture-perfect.

In filming the behind-the-scenes activity for *The Making of The Colony*, I needed to document the actualities of that production day. This arrival scene was the biggest event on *The Colony*'s calendar, and the logistics were extensive, with helicopter shots, boat-to-boat shots, the transfer from sea to river, and the participants arriving on the land for the first time. Hilton Cordell's planning for the arrival scene had centered on the crucial two-day sea voyage and the river passage. Once these sequences had been filmed, the participants safely transported to the land, there was no plan in place for the filming of the next sequence: the newly arrived colonists entering their settlement for the first time. This was the first time on set for some of the freelance crew, and they had not been briefed on the best position for filming. While this was being negotiated, the colonists joined the production crew for a modern-day packed lunch of assorted sandwiches, chocolate biscuits, and fruit juice. The director felt that I should not film this, as he believed it would disappoint the audience's expectations of living history to know the participants were given a twenty-first-century meal upon their arrival.

After lunch the colonists were required to wait while the logistics for the film crew were organized. The director continued to express his reticence about my filming this next activity, this time because he thought that an audience would be upset to find out that there had been production delays before the participants could enter their historical settlement. Showing the production process, he felt, would "destroy the magic" for a television audience (Scheelings, film). The production designer was also showing signs of anxiety, but for very different reasons. As instructed by the director, he had prepared the chests full of period items for the families' four-month sojourn and, knowing the weight of the load, was concerned for the participants' safety during this arrival scene: "I just can't watch them carrying all this stuff. It's so heavy! They've got to carry it all the way up the valley, the poor buggers. It's distressing!" (Scheelings, film). Meanwhile, as the camera crews found their positions, some needing to climb up the valley's steep ridges with their heavy equipment, the director explained to the series producer how he viewed this next scene: "To me, it's just a beautiful mood sequence with music, you know, with great shots and introducing the convicts over the close-ups" (Scheelings, film). While the director conveyed his vision, he did not notice that the colonists had begun walking toward the valley. The first assistant director caught his attention: "Um, . . . should we, we're not ready for this yet are we?" The director, looking up from his imaginings, confirmed, "Umm . . . no." The first assistant director then ran toward the colonists, arms flailing above her head as one does when warning of imminent danger: "Everybody! Everybody! Just stop there for a minute, please! We're not quite ready for you yet! We want to catch this wonderful moment on camera!" (Scheelings, film).

In an interview later, the first assistant director described her role at that time: "We don't want to spoil the *illusion of a reality* for the participants, but we have to get cameras in place to be able to get the shots" (Scheelings, film; emphasis added). Once the first assistant director had caught up to the colonists, she gave them a crash course in the rules of making television, and she explained the route that they should take once the cameras were ready. In case they were confused about where to go, she reassured them, "I'll be in the bushes going, 'That way! That way!'" After some hours being instructed when to stop, when to start, what to carry and where, and the route that should be taken, the colonists finally made it to their historical microcosm settlement with all their 1800s belongings.

These weary travelers, after arriving on land at lunchtime, the English and Irish families having begun their living-history experience with a rough sea voyage two days earlier, had a couple of hours in which to orient themselves to their new environment before nightfall. The production crew needed to get the remaining shots required for the day while there was still light, so, a little bewildered and unsure of what was expected of them next, the participants tentatively explored their new surroundings as the director instructed them. With cameras at the ready to capture their every response, the participants were directed to inspect the "abandoned" slab hut, a replica of a settler dwelling, which the new arrivals obediently entered. Looking around, showing polite consideration as if in someone else's home, they admired without touching anything, frustrating the director, who began gesticulating with furious conductor-like movements for them to get more involved: "Pick things up!" "Look inside!" "Shake it!" "Open it!"

Unaware of the effect that fatigue and the production demands had had on the participants thus far—by this stage, it seemed as though they were taking care not to do anything wrong—the director perceived their reticence as a lack of initiative or gumption. With his vision for certain television scenes unfulfilled, he aired his exasperation: "They think that they have to ask permission before they can do anything! They have it in their heads that they have to be told what to do for some bizarre reason!" (Scheelings, rushes). Needless to say, in reality there was no violin or harmonica playing, and the atmosphere was somewhat less serene than that portrayed in *The Colony*. Some of these behind-the-scenes events from that day appear in *The Making of The Colony*. It is not damning of Hilton Cordell but rather offers an accurate account, showing the kind of stress that a production like this puts on those in charge and how this stress is managed. I suggest it would not be an unfamiliar scene to anyone who has worked in the television industry.

The Colony's director, however, expressed his conviction regarding what *The Making of The Colony* was documenting: "If an audience knows what goes on behind the scenes, they will hate me and they will hate SBS because they will feel gypped" (Scheelings, rushes). Interestingly, he was not referring to anything I had filmed that could rightly provoke criticism; rather, the impetus behind this statement was the repercussions he believed would result from revealing the little everyday artifices involved in television production and historical re-creation. It was already a highly contentious issue that *The Making of The Colony* would show some of the logistics behind television production, but what was regarded as almost insupportable was its potential revelation that the series incorporated other intrusions from modern life.

For example, cutthroat or straight razors were unanimously pronounced unsafe for the participants to shave with and, as the director wanted the men to remain clean-shaven, modern razors were distributed. The director felt it would "destroy the magic" for an audience to know of the participants' historical infidelities. In a similar vein, one of the women's long skirts had been set ablaze by an open-flame oil lantern, which led to a request for battery-operated torches, a request agreed to by the production company. Again, not seeing this as part of the investigation being made into living history, the director felt it would anger the audience to know of the twenty-first-century exchanges, and he felt strongly that neither *The Colony* nor *The Making of The Colony* should reveal the switch. I was also not permitted to film the Koori Clan being given fish by the production company because Hilton Cordell wanted to portray the Kooris as having been fishing at the river. If I showed something different, the company felt the integrity of its series would be threatened. Because of the frozen appearance of the fish, the SBSi commissioning editor advised Hilton Cordell during editing to be up-front about such constructions in *The Colony,* advice that the makers chose not to take.

Another twenty-first-century intrusion into the historical reenactment was a modern-day renovation that, though gratefully received by the colonists, was a feature queried by the SBSi commissioning editor on his visit to the set during *The Colony*'s preproduction:

> SBS [*laughing, looking over at director*]: What's the story with the dunnies?
>
> DIRECTOR: The dunnies?
>
> SBSi COMMISSIONING EDITOR: In particular the throne!
>
> DIRECTOR: We have a contract with the owner that we weren't allowed to dig long drops because supposedly there's a high water table and he's done all the calculations on how much thirty people would shit in four months and has insisted on organic toilets which has cost us $15,000. And there they are!
>
> SBSi C.E.: And what about the throne itself [*laughter*]—the twenty-first-century throne [*laughter*]?
>
> DIRECTOR: I don't know. That's just what they came with and we haven't thought further to replacing that.
>
> SBSi C.E.: I would have thought you'd have the old wooden seat or you know the old bench with the slat. . . . They're going to have this massive culture shock when they come out of the slab hut and walk into the dunny [*laughter*]! (Scheelings, rushes)

Censorship of The Making of The Colony

My role in revealing the everyday realities involved in the historical illusion that was being created in *The Colony* was perceived as an ongoing and contentious problem for Hilton Cordell. Requests to turn my camera off and attempts to stop the filming process were so frequent during the course of making the documentary that the footage captured of such access denials could fill a television program in and of itself. Hilton Cordell's fears that the documentary would "destroy the magic" being created by revealing the illusions that were inevitably present was ultimately an intractable concern. While *The Making of The Colony* condemns neither the living-history production nor the production company Hilton Cordell, it does show a balanced view of the obstacles that such a venture presents, and it raises some pertinent ethical and philosophical questions inherent in both reality TV and documentary practice. The most prominent issue to arise was the relationship between filmmaker and film participant.

In a self-reflexive way, *The Making of The Colony* documents the resistance made by some of the film's subjects (the director and producers of *The Colony*) to being filmed. For example, a few weeks into production, the series producer called a meeting with the SBSi commissioning editor to discuss *The Making of The Colony,* to which he wanted to call an end. I was permitted to film the meeting, which would determine the future of the documentary. Below is a snippet from that discussion:

> SERIES PRODUCER: We've invested a lot of time and money and energy [in making *The Colony* series], and the concern is that *The Making Of* will destroy all of that, destroy the magic that's been created.
>
> SBSi C.E.: Yeah . . . ?
>
> SP: I mean, we're making magic out there and . . . [the director's] . . . main concern is that it will be destroyed for them, for an audience, to see what went into making it.
>
> SBSi C.E.: So what's the problem specifically?
>
> SP: Well . . . [the director's] not enjoying it basically.
>
> SBSi C.E.: Well that's not her job to make him enjoy that, that's not the job of a documentary filmmaker.
>
> SP: No I know that, but he can always say he doesn't want to be a part of it anymore.
>
> SBSi C.E.: Well to a point. He knows there's a contract to do *The Making Of* as well.

SP: Yeah, well okay. Well, we just want to make sure that SBS will not put something to air that will undermine their investment and commitment to this series. (Scheelings, film)

By including this conflict as part of the narrative, *The Making of The Colony* reflects on the fine line between intimacy and exposure, revelation and exploitation, and allows the viewer to consider these ethical dilemmas, which are inherent in any documentary process, even more so when the film participant does not want to be part of the film anymore. The documentary goes on to explore the participant-filmmaker relationship and the balance of power as it existed within the living-history production. Here the film participants are not competing for a prize, as in most other reality TV shows, and they are also not afforded the capacity to live their own lives as documentary film participants. The coproducer of *The Colony* explained the level of control that the production company had in every detail of the participants' constructed world: "They call us 'the company' and we are the government to them in many ways" (Scheelings, film).

Though these time travelers were expected to uphold the "spirit and intent" of the show by adopting the illusion that they were living in the early 1800s as free settlers on their own land, when they did assume this persona they encountered one of the ironies of their position. As the director of photography stated, "We had to tell people, 'No, this isn't really your farm, it belongs to someone else. This is actually a TV show, and we're here to film you going through this experience, so you can't really tell us to 'fuck off.'" Dissatisfied with the lack of self-determination within this small and inescapable confine, some participants on *The Colony* began to question the living-history process and the role they were expected to play in it. One participant in particular did not like what he perceived to be an aggressive filming approach taken by the director, and this meant ongoing clashes between the two. It was a serious enough problem, in the director's opinion, to warrant having this participant and his family removed from the show, despite their being halfway through the production. The international funding arrangements meant removing one family was not an option. To resolve the issue, the series producer came on location to advise all the participants of the living-history obligation to which they had signed on: "We're here, and you, because this is a TV show ultimately; TV stations are paying all of our bills. And the 'spirit and intent' side of it is that you've agreed to let us film you going through this experience—that's why we're all here. So it is not kosher basically for you to say: 'We don't want you to film'" (Scheelings, film).

The participants agreed that this was "fair enough," and had no objection to this original agreement, but one participant wanted to clarify the extent to which access was a matter of course and when privacy might be afforded in an extenuating circumstance, giving the following example:

> Participant: People were upset here and the cameras started following them, which made them more upset and then followed them even more, so is that part of it? You tell me it is.
>
> Director: We don't instigate [participant's name]. If something is happening, it's happening. We are making a TV program here!

The second unit director on *The Colony* reflected on this issue, of allowing your film participant privacy versus the need to show things as they are, by describing the biggest obstacle experienced in both *The Colony* production and *The Making of The Colony* documentary:

> The great problems we've got on *The Colony* and that [the director] is particularly sensitive about as we all are, and rightly so, is that [one family] are trying to set an agenda of what's on camera and what's off camera and obviously that's completely against the "spirit and intent" of *The Colony* for what they signed up to allow us to film—which is everything and anything that they're doing. And it has been quite clear and obvious to us that *The Making Of* crew are supposed to have been granted total access to the making of *The Colony,* but he [the director] is also trying to, you know, create the agenda of what you can and can't film in terms of the negative and positive aspects. So we had a good laugh at the fact that what's happening to him as a director is also happening to him as talent, and that irony has also been noticed. It's quite amusing. (Scheelings, film)

Though determined to show the moments of triumph and failure of the time-traveling participants in their attempts to relive history, the producers and director of *The Colony* did not have the same conviction with regard to their own journey into living history. In *The Making of The Colony,* Hilton Cordell wanted a one-sided portrayal of themselves, to show all the high points of their production with no challenges along the way. As I mentioned earlier, an EPK for the series was not the film SBSi had commissioned, but rather a more honest, behind-the-scenes account of *The Colony*'s production, a documentary in the traditional understanding of the genre. This distinction ultimately resulted in Hilton Cordell's insisting the film be suppressed.

While SBSi did not agree with the rationale or the need for suppression, believing the documentary to be a "balanced" and "compelling" account, it nevertheless appeased the fears of Hilton Cordell by choosing not to exercise its contractual rights, agreeing not to screen *The Making of The Colony* as the final episode. Not satisfied, Hilton Cordell wanted the documentary suppressed indefinitely.

The SBS Web site forum devoted to the series was inundated with discussions from *The Colony* cast and crew when it was revealed that *The Making of The Colony* would not be aired. Over a few days the exchange became an online event to the extent that it was considered necessary to erase the discussion history and block contributors from logging back onto the public forum. The message was clear: it was not a topic open to public discussion. Hilton Cordell went on to obtain the master tapes from *The Making of The Colony* production, with which it would construct its own behind-the-scenes version for DVD release.

Another matter of note is that some of the participants in *The Colony* who were unhappy with how they were portrayed by Hilton Cordell tried to exert control over the screening of the series. Taking legal action, they requested the series be either reedited or suppressed from broadcast. *The Colony* participants were unsuccessful, and the series screened as scheduled. As is usual in participant-filmmaker balance-of-power relations, once the personal release contract is agreed to by the film participant, he or she signs away all future rights to veto the film's public screening. That Hilton Cordell was able to claim for itself these rights that its own film participants were denied is an exceptional case. The suppression of the in-house, publicly funded documentary, *The Making of The Colony*, also indicates the extraordinary influence that one company can have on a public broadcaster, which raises questions about independence in the public broadcasting sector.

Documentary film remains one of the most effective ways to enhance understanding on a mass level. For this reason, if for no other, it is worth the effort to make sense of the documentary now, to linger on the history that shaped it, and to dwell for a while on its possible future. (Ellis and McLane 326)

Though the documentary tradition remains identifiable, the role of the documentarist is as diverse as the individuals making the films. What is clear, however, is the inherent assumption that a documentarist intends to represent actuality and, moreover, to do so with integrity of purpose. Notwithstanding this, as commercial success plays an increasingly important role in the production of documentary films, the documentarist's original responsibility is in danger of being overshadowed by the perceived need to make "great TV."

In the case of *The Colony*, the series producer's statement "we're making magic out there and *The Making of* will destroy all that" was used to justify his intolerance of public knowledge of—let alone discussion about—the production process of his "documentary" series. For this to be accepted by the broadcaster, SBSi, as a legitimate reason not to screen the behind-the-scenes documentary fuels the contention that a commercial imperative (even in public television) is overriding social values that once defined the documentary form, not to mention public broadcasting. Furthermore, when open debate among the "community of practitioners" is silenced according to the personal wishes of one company, an essential part of the practice that has always characterized the profession is denied. These issues raise the question of where the contemporary documentary film is now situated.

The motivations that began the documentary tradition incorporate a commitment to the truth, not a determined suppression of what is real. The assumption that anything "too real" needs to be hidden from the audience is a troubling notion. The genre was never intended as a magic act, and revealing illusion does not destroy the craft, but rather is what defines it.

Commenting on American and British historical reality TV shows, and referring to the documentary tradition to which some of those program makers assert their format belongs, the film scholars Ellis and McLane say, "Few would claim that this is documentary" (333). Voicing a similar sentiment, a *Sydney Morning Herald* TV reviewer stated that the obvious hurdle for the makers of *The Colony* was knowing "the difference between documentary and reality TV, and being sure which side of the line you sit on" (Idato). The attempt to make an educational history program by using a reality TV concept while proclaiming documentary practice, creates not only a path of ambiguity and confusion but also, in Hilton Cordell's case, a disproportionate fear of exposure for not delivering on original claims. These findings are not isolated to *The Colony* but appear to relate to a broader trend in television production. As the historian Iain McCalman concluded from his involvement in a BBC "extreme history" series, "If we'd been allowed to be openly reflexive about the imperatives of the present or sceptical about our ability to recapture the past, the series might have been enhanced. . . . Instead, it seems to me to have succumbed to an identity crisis, unsure whether it was historical documentary or reality TV" (McCalman 484).

Reflecting on some of the problems that arose in the production of *The Colony* and *The Making of The Colony* I think it necessary that a new distinction be made on top of "serious intent" to differentiate the documentary from the ever-forming reality hybrids. My findings suggest that the employment of integrity in revealing reality and reflexivity in that process would take us a step closer to genuine documentary and historical inquiry. The willingness to be transparent and to make methods public—or at the very least accessible—should be what separates the documentary from other factual forms. Online public forums created to discuss television programs are currently centered on the *content* and not the *process* of production, and this does not come close to answering the necessary questions that need to be asked of documentary outcomes. To understand how "living history" can contribute to documentary tradition and practice as well as history pedagogy, revealing and discussing rather than trying to hide the challenges and perceived failures would better serve audiences and program makers. Such transparency would also align it closer to the disciplines of documentary film and history pedagogy.

Despite the observations I have made here, *The Colony* was categorized and nominated by the Australian film and television industry as a contender for "most outstanding documentary series" at the 2006 TV Week Logie Awards. As the film scholar Bill Nichols has said with regard to defining the documentary: "At one level we might say documentary is what those who regard themselves as documentarists produce. This begs the question of who defines the documentarists, or, perhaps better, acknowledges that this group is largely self-defining" (15).

I do not discount the merit of truth and exploration in historical reenactment, but they need to be balanced and understood within the context and priority of telling the story of history, and, without careful planning of both, we are left with this new documentary genre resembling something more like a poor man's *Survivor*. The intention of "living history" to make a worthwhile contribution to history education and to the craft of the documentary is not in question. How it can ultimately achieve this aim, however, warrants careful consideration.

Notes

1. *Hearts of Darkness: A Filmmaker's Apocalypse* (1991) and *Burden of Dreams* (1982) are the best-known examples.

2. *Network* (1976); *The Truman Show* (1998); *Series 7: The Contenders* (2001) are some examples.

3. Though the information provided does not offer the promised findings, the reader is nevertheless urged to support the production: "Be more adventurous. Help bring programs like COLONIAL HOUSE to your PBS station . . . pledge online!" (*Colonial House*).

4. This phrase, "serious intent," used as a means of separating documentary from reality TV, originates from a paper that the film scholar Brian Winston presented at the Australian International Documentary Conference in 2003.

5. Peter Watkins is the pioneering British filmmaker of the documentary historical reenactment, best known for *Culloden* (1964) and *The War Game* (1966).

Works Cited

Anstey, Edgar, and Arthur Elton, dirs. *Housing Problems*. Documentary film. British Commercial Gas Association, 1935.

Australian Television Archive, www.australiantelevision.net/colony/about .html.

Bowie, Geoff, dir. *The Universal Clock: The Resistance of Peter Watkins*. Documentary video recording. Prod. Yves Bissailon. National Film Board of Canada, 2005.

Colonial House. PBS, www.pbs.org/wnet/colonialhouse/.

The Colony. Six-part TV series. SBS Television, 2005.

Cunningham, Sophie. "Television in 2005." *The Age*, January 1, 2005.

Ellis, C. Jack, and A. Betsy McLane. *A New History of Documentary Film*. New York: Continuum, 2005.

Gaines, Jane M., and Michael Renov, eds. *Collecting Visible Evidence: Volume 6*. Minneapolis: University of Minnesota Press, 1999.

Gibbon, Belinda. *The Colony: The Book from the Popular SBS Living History Series*. Sydney: Random House, 2005.

Grierson, John. *Grierson on Documentary*. London: Faber, 1966 [1946].

Hill, Annette. *Restyling Factual TV: The Reception of News, Documentary, and Reality Genres*. London: Routledge, 2007.

Idato, Michael. "Armed and Dangerous." *Sydney Morning Herald*, January 4, 2005, www.smh.com.au/articles/2005/01/03/1104601280868.html.

Kilborn, Richard, and John Izod. *An Introduction to Television Documentary: Confronting Reality*. Manchester: Manchester University Press, 1997.

McCalman, Iain. "The Little Ship of Horrors: Reenacting Extreme History." *Criticism* 46.3 (2004): 477–487.

Meade, Amanda. "Real Life Gets Respectable." *Australian*, July 1, 2004, www.theaustralian.news.com.au/story/0,20867,10001429–27648,00.html.

Nichols, Bill. *Representing Reality: Issues and Concepts in Documentary*. Bloomington: Indiana University Press, 1991.

Scheelings, Aurora, dir. *The Making of The Colony*. Documentary film. SBS Television, 2005.

———. *The Making of The Colony*. Documentary film. Rushes. SBS Television, 2005.

Contributors

Michelle Arrow is a senior lecturer in the Department of Modern History, Macquarie University, where she teaches Australian history, history and media, and the history of popular culture. Her first book, *Upstaged: Australian Women Dramatists in the Limelight at Last,* was published in 2002 and was short-listed for five national prizes. In 2004 Arrow worked as a television presenter on the ABC-TV history series *Rewind.* She has published widely on the issues of representing history on television and on histories of aspects of Australian popular culture and its audiences. Her latest book, *Friday on Our Minds: Popular Culture in Australia since 1945,* was published in 2009.

Lee Barron is senior lecturer in Media and Communication at Northumbria University. His main research and teaching interests are in the areas of cultural theories and popular culture, including music, film, television, and celebrity. He is the author of journal articles, book chapters, and reports on popular culture, teaching and learning, and sport. His writings have appeared in journals such as the *Journal of Popular Culture, Chapter and Verse, International Review of the Aesthetics and Sociology of Music,* and *Disability & Society.* His recent publications include "The Seven Ages of Kylie Minogue: Postmodernism, Identity, and Performative Mimicry," *Nebula* (2008); "The Habitus of Elizabeth Hurley: Celebrity, Fashion and Identity Branding," in *Fashion Theory: The Journal of Dress, Body & Culture* (2007); and (with Ian Inglis) "Scary Movies, Scary Music: Uses and Unities of Heavy Metal in the Contemporary Horror Film," in *Music, Sound and Horror Cinema,* ed. Philip Hayward and Rebecca Leydon (forthcoming).

Ken Dvorak currently serves as the secretary-treasurer of the Southwest Texas Popular Culture/American Culture Association. His research interests include analysis of educational technologies and their influence on teaching and learning, particularly film and television analysis. His publications have appeared in the *Journal of Popular Culture; Journal of American Culture; Journal of Film & History, Quarterly Review of Film and Video,* and *Film and History: An Interdisciplinary Journal of Film & Television Studies.*

LEIGH H. EDWARDS is associate professor of English at Florida State University. She specializes in nineteenth- and twentieth-century U.S. literature and popular culture, with particular emphasis on interdisciplinary American studies and media studies approaches and on intersections of gender and race. She is the author of *Johnny Cash and the Paradox of American Identity* (2009), which examines how Cash's work and image illuminate key foundational tensions in the history of American thought.

TOBIAS HOCHSCHERF is a lecturer at Northumbria University, where he teaches a wide range of undergraduate and postgraduate modules in film and television studies. His research interests focus on European film and television cultures. He is particularly interested in television aesthetics, transnational film practices, and representations of the cold war in film and television. His research has been published widely in academic journals and edited collections. He is area chair and co-organizer of a number of academic conferences in Britain and the United States, and he has spoken about his research at a range of institutions. Raised in Hamburg, Germany, he was spared firsthand experience of British school dinners.

SU HOLMES is Reader in Television Studies at the University of East Anglia. She is the author of *British TV and Film Culture in the 1950s* (2005), *Entertaining TV: The BBC and Popular Television Culture in the 1950s* (2008), and *The Quiz Show* (2008). She is currently working on a monograph on the seminal 1974 documentary serial *The Family* (*After Reality TV: Revisiting The Family*), and is coeditor of *Understanding Reality TV* (2004), *Framing Celebrity* (2006), and *Stardom and Celebrity: A Reader* (2007). Her key research interests are in British TV history, popular TV genres, and celebrity.

CASSANDRA JONES is a doctoral candidate in American Culture Studies at Bowling Green State University. Her research interests include racial and gendered embodiment in digital spaces.

JAMES LEGGOTT lectures in film and television studies at Northumbria University. He has published on various aspects of British film and television culture, such as traditions of social realism, regional cultures, and contemporary cinema. His research interests also include science fiction in film and television, literary adaptations, and reality television. He is the owner of three Jamie Oliver cookbooks.

SARAH A. MATHESON teaches film and popular culture in the Department of Communication, Popular Culture & Film at Brock University in St. Catharines, Ontario. Her recent work has appeared in the *Canadian Journal of Film Studies* and *Film and History,* and in the anthology *Programming Reality: Perspectives on English-Canadian Television.*

FRED NADIS is the author of *Wonder Shows: Performing Science, Magic, and Religion in America* (2005). He has a PhD in American Studies from the University of Texas and writes about technology and culture.

DEBBIE CLARE OLSON is a doctoral candidate in the Department of English, Oklahoma State University. Her most recent publication is "Lu jot bèt bi? African Visual Rhetoric and the Search for Authenticity," in *Facts, Fictions, and African Creative Imaginations,* edited by Toyin Falola and Fallou Ngom (2009), the first volume in Routledge's new series on African studies.

SAYANTI GANGULY PUCKETT is a doctoral candidate in the Department of English at Oklahoma State University. She specializes in seventeenth- to nineteenth-century British literature and nineteenth-century colonial Indian literature.

LAURIE RUPERT is a doctoral candidate at Oklahoma State University. Her area of focus is nineteenth-century American literature; however, she has published and presented a number of papers in the area of film. She is currently employed as a seventh grade English teacher at Ford Middle School in Allen, Texas.

AURORA SCHEELINGS is an independent filmmaker and doctorial candidate at Griffith University, Brisbane, Australia.

JULIE ANNE TADDEO currently is a Visiting Associate Professor, Department of History, University of Maryland–College Park. She previously taught at Temple University and University of California at Berkeley, where she also was the Assistant Director of the Center for British Studies. Her courses specialize in Victorian and twentieth-century British culture, gender, and class. She is the author of *Lytton Strachey and the Search for Modern Sexual Identity* (2002) and several articles on British modernism, sexuality, and twentieth-century popular culture. Her current projects include edited books on reality TV and the British novelist Catherine Cookson.

Index

Illustrations are indicated by italicized page numbers.

Aborigines
    Australia's history debates and,
        218, 219, 220, 221
    in *The Colony*, 229–230
"access" programming, 100–101
ACTRA, 150
advertising, influence on *Big Brother*,
    33–34
Alam, Faria, 38
Alberta Report, 154
Alexander, Jason, 139
Allcorn, Juli, 224, 226
Allcorn, Paul, 224
All in the Family (television show),
    126
Ally McBeal (television show), 158
Alters, Diane F., 133
Amazing Race, The (television show),
    140
American dream, the
    An American Family and, 85–86,
        91–93
    makeover narrative and, 166
American Family, An (television show)
    the American Dream and, 85–86,
        91–93
    beginnings of, 83, 85
    British counterpoint to, 98
    British television and, 99
    critical reception, 115
    criticisms of, 116
    disillusionment and, 91–93
    feminism and, 109
    Craig Gilbert and, 83–89 *passim*,
        91, 94, 95–96

the heritage of documentary and,
    115
homosexuality and, 87–88
influences and strategic choices in
    the making of, 84–85
intent of, 83
the Loud family, 84–94 *passim*
manipulation of material, 83,
    86–91 *passim*, 93–96 *passim*
narrative climax, 116
opening montage, 90–91
popularity of, 138
presentation of marriage and the
    family in, 85–91
rise of reality TV and, 94–95
significance of, 96
therapeutic culture and, 104
American family, the
    as "family in crisis," 123–124
    family values media debates,
        137–141
    functional vs. dysfunctional,
        129–131
    historic links to TV, 125–126
    "modern" and "postmodern," 124
    narrative stances toward social
        change and, 127
    narrative tropes of, 128–129
    1950s fantasy family, 141n6
    nostalgia for the nuclear family,
        129, 131
    as presented in *An American Fam-
        ily*, 85–91
    reality TV reframes the ideals of,
        123–127

American family, the (*continued*)
  trends in textual representations of, 129–136
"*An American Family*": *A Televised Life* (television show), 99
American Idol (television show), 137
Andrejevic, Mark, 173, 190
Andrews, Maggie, 159
Apprentice, The (television show), 53–54, 173
Are You Anybody? (Laron), 23
"artful surveillance," 19
asexuality, fatness and, 70–71
"As Seen on TV" products, 161
audience, *Big Brother* and, 33
Austen, Jane, 203
Australian Broadcasting Corporation (ABC), 217
Australian historical reality TV
  Australian history in, 225–233
  constructing the past in, 222–224
  first forays into, 217
  See also *Colony, The* (television series); *Outback House* (television show)
Australian history
  in Australian historical reality TV, 225–233
  Australians' sense of, 220–222
  debates over, 217, 218–219, 220–221
  "pioneer legend" discourse, 220–221
  "stolen generations," 229
authority, Allen Funt's concerns with, 18

Bachelor, The (television show), 128
Baker, Jonathan, 140
Barnes, Guy Gorell, 204, 205
Barr, Roseanne, 43n, 168n7
Barris, Chuck, 138
Barrymore, Michael, 37
Battle for Ozzfest (television show), 133
Baudrillard, Jean, 191

Bazalgette, Peter, 38
Beauty and the Geek (television show), 71
beauty ideals, 77–78
Becker, Ron, 134
Beckham, David, 55
Beckham, Victoria "Posh Spice," 43
Behind the Dog Tag (radio show), 13
Bergson, Henri, 17
Big Brother (television show)
  appeal of, 32
  audience, 33
  contestants as social actors, 35–36
  evolution and transformation of, 27–29, 33, 41–43
  French version, 29
  influence of advertising on, 33–34
  on the Internet, 33, 34–35
  narrative and, 40–41
  notions of celebrity and, 27–28, 32–33, 36–37, 39–40, 43
  ontological uncertainty and, 35
  origin and development of, 30
  premise and metanarrative, 30–31
  role of the television audience in, 33
  sibling contestants, 136
  as a social experiment, 49
  social settings and, 36
  as spectacle, 42–43
  surveillance motif in, 31–32
  television format and, 34
  See also *Celebrity Big Brother* (television show)
Big Brother: Celebrity Hijack (television show), 43n
Big Brother House, 30
"Big Food Fight," 61
Biggest Loser, The (television show)
  class and, 79n2
  compared to the Presidential Fitness Challenge, 78–79
  construction of the show, 67–68
  contestants as "ambassadors to our states," 73–74
  depiction of fatness, 65

fat identity and double-consciousness, 71–73
fatness and asexuality, 70–71
fatness as moral failure, 69–70
fatness as spoiled identity, 68–69
frontier mythology and, 69, 72–73, 75–76
naturalization of Eurocentric beauty ideals, 77–78
public ownership of the fat body, 74–77
racialism and, 78
reunion show, 77
theme song, 65
third episode, 66–67
warfare rhetoric and, 72–73
Billy Elliot (film), 54, 57–58
Bingham, Traci, 37
Biressi, Anita, 102
Black.White. (television show), 130
Blair, Tony, 49, 60
Bonanza City, 171
Boorstin, Daniel, 39, 43
Bourdieu, Pierre, 33, 34
Bowie, Geoff, 242
Bowlby, Rachel, 160
Bowler family, *200*
Brady Bunch, The (television show), 90
Bravo, 134
Broadcasting Act of 1991 (Canada), 151
Brown, Gordon, 57
Bunim, Mary-Ellis, 94
Burgess, Michael, 212
Burns, Pete, 37
Bush, Laura, 135
business consulting, Allen Funt and, 23–24
Byron, Lord, 205

Cabezuela, Robby, 212
Caldwell, Rob, 74, 76
cameras
"hidden camera," 164
surveillance and, 19

Campos, Paul, 70
Canada
equity clause in broadcasting, 167n2
reality TV and, 146, 147–148
Canadian Advisory Council on the Status of Women, 150
Canadian Broadcasting Corporation (CBC)
reality TV and, 147–148
report on sex discrimination in broadcasting, 149–150
Canadian Radio-television and Telecommunications Commission (CRTC), 148, 150–151
Candid Camera (television show), 11
appeal of, 18–19
beginning and growth of, 15
criticisms of, 19, 21–22
Funt's defense of, 19–20
Funt's goal for, 20
last incarnations of, 24–25
methods and categories of observation in, 16–18
privacy and, 20–21
social concerns during the time of, 12–13
in the Soviet Union, 21
surveillance "victim" example, 12
Candid Microphone, The (radio show), 11–13, 14, 19
CanWest Global Communications, 151
capitalism, *Kid Nation* and, 182–183
captivity narrative, 212–213
Carmichael, Deborah, 209
Carphone Warehouse, 34
Castells, Manuel, 188
Catherine Tate Show, The (television show), 60
Cathy Come Home (documentary-drama), 106, 107
Cawelti, John G., 92
celebrity
Big Brother and, 27–28, 32–33, 36–37, 39–40, 43

celebrity (*continued*)
  Celebrity Big Brother 2006 and,
    37–39
  cultural intermediaries and, 33
  reality TV and, 173
Celebrity Big Brother (television
    show), 27, 28, 34, 120n15
Celebrity Big Brother 2006 (television
    show), 37–39, 40, 41
Certeau, Michel de, 75
Changing Rooms (television show),
    52
Channel 4 (UK), 49–51
"Chantelle," 39
"chav" culture, 57, 61n4
Chidley, Joe, 154
childhood, *Kid Nation* and, 171–172,
    183–187
Chronicles of Summer (documentary),
    96n1
cinema verité, 96n1
civilized-savage dichotomy, 212–213
Clack, Lynn Schofield, 133
Clarke, Alison, 161
class (economic)
  The Biggest Loser and, 79n2
  The Family and, 105
  Jamie's School Dinners and, 57–59
  Kid Nation and, 175–178
Clift, Montgomery, 209
Close-Up! (television show), 96n2
Clune, Tracy, 198
Colonial House (television show),
    136, 201, 240
Colony, The (television series)
  Aboriginal participation, 229–230
  aim of, 244
  arrival scene and first day, 244–247
  Australia's history debates and,
    217, 219
  background to, 237–238
  claims of documentary practice
    and, 236, 237–238, 240–241
  documentary on the production of
    (see *Making of the Colony, The*)
  flag-making episode, 232

illusion of reality in, 243–248
interpersonal conflict as the focus
    of, 227
legal action against, 252
notions of pioneering on, 227–228
obstacle in the production of, 251
premier date, 239
priority for, 243
production and financing, 233n2,
    237
promotion and marketing, 238
race relations and, 229–230
representation of European-
    Aboriginal conflict, 227–228
success of, 254
volunteers and applicants, 224, 238
volunteers' dissatisfaction,
    250–251, 252
volunteers' expectations for,
    224–225
women's lives on, 232
Come Dine with Me (television show),
    60–61
comedy
  The Family and, 117–118
  See also female comedy
confessional poetry, 25n2
consciousness II, 87
consciousness III, 87
conservatives, family values media
    debates and, 139
consumerism
  Kid Nation and, 176, 182–183,
    190, 191
  The Shopping Bags and, 158–162
"Cookalong Live," 61
Cooke, Bill and Lisa, 209–211, 212,
    213
cookery shows. *See* reality cooking
    shows
Coontz, Stephanie, 125–126, 137,
    141n1, 141n6
Coronation Street (television show),
    115, 117
"corporate multiculturalism,"
    130–131

Corus Entertainment Ltd., 155
Cosby Show, The (television show), 126
cosmetic surgery, *Plastic Makes Perfect*, 163–167
County Durham (England), 57–58
"cowboy vs. Indian" plot, 212–213
Crossroads (television show), 115
Culloden (documentary), 255n5
cultural intermediaries, 33
Cumming, Alan, 43n
Curthoys, Ann, 220–221

D'Acci, Julie, 149
Daily Express, 107
Daily Mirror, 117
Daily Telegraph, 99–100
Dating Game, The (television show), 138, 204
Davis, Curt, 85
Davis, Sammy, Jr., 126
Davison, Graeme, 220, 223
Day, James, 83
Deery, June, 166
democratic realism, 19
Desperate Housewives (television show), 138
"detective" cameras, 19
Diana, Princess, 50, 60
Diana: The Witness in the Tunnel (television show), 50
DiGiovanni, Debra, 165
direct cinema, 96n2, 101
divorce, 129, 142n8
Doane, Mary Ann, 168n7
documentary
    Candid Camera and, 18–19
    The Colony and, 240–241
    commitment to truth and, 253
    current crisis in, 242–243
    debate among practitioners and, 242
    direct cinema and, 96n2
    epistemological debates, 113
    The Family and, 101–102
    gendered nature of, 108

historical reality TV and, 236
    perceptions of in the 1970s, 114
    recommendations for distinguishing from historical reality TV, 254
    social consciousness and, 241–242
    as surveillance, 19
    television's influence on, 113
    See also *Making of the Colony, The* (documentary)
Donovan, Anto, 230
double-consciousness, fat identity and, 71–73
Double Talk (television show), 153
Dowling, Brian, 37, 120n15
Doyle, John, 156, 158–159, 162, 163
Dragon's Den (television show), 53
Dranoff, Linda Silver, 149
Drew, Robert, 96n2
Duggan, Lisa, 139
Duncan, Andy, 50
Dunkley, Christopher, 110, 114
dysfunctional families, 129

Eavesdropper at Large (Funt), 20
Ehrenreich, Barbara, 89–90
electronic press kit, 238
Ellis, Jack, 96n2
Ellison, Ralph, 14
elove (television show), 155
Emmerdale Farm (television show), 115
Endemol Entertainment, 30, 38
Entertainment Weekly, 132
Eriksoon, Sven Göran, 38
Eurocentric beauty ideals, *The Biggest Loser* and, 77–78
exposés, *Candid Camera* and, 16–17
Extreme Makeover: Home Edition (television show), 123–124, 134, 135

Fabrication of Aboriginal History, The (Windschuttle), 219
"fake celebrity," *Celebrity Big Brother* and, 28

"false historicity," 222
family. *See* American family, the; nuclear family
Family, The (television show)
    "access" programming and, 100–101
    analytical treatment and, 99
    An American Family and, 98
    British values, 103–104
    comedy and, 117–118
    contemporary views of, 99–100
    critical perceptions, 116–117
    documentary culture and, 101–102
    as "documentary serial," 115
    domestic routine and, 108
    feminism and, 108–110
    fly-on-the-wall programming and, 101
    gender roles and, 108–109
    generic discourses and evaluation, 113–118
    identity and, 107–108
    individualization and, 104
    issues of privacy and, 102–103
    mediation, 110
    narrative climax, 115–116
    a "New Real-Life Documentary Serial for BBC," 100–104
    notions of reality TV and, 99
    opening sequence, 117
    performance and agency, 110–113
    serial narrative design, 115–116
    social and political context, 104–110
    therapeutic culture and, 103, 104
    typicality and, 111–112
    the Wilkins family, 100, 102–103, 107–116 *passim*
Family Affair, A (M. Wilkins), 103
"family in crisis," 123–124
Family of Man, The, 21
The Family: The After Years (television show), 112
family values media debates, 125, 137–141
"family wage," 124

Fat Club/Celebrity Fit Club (television show), 53
fat identity, double-consciousness and, 71–73
fatness
    American cultural notions of, 65–66
    asexuality and, 70–71
    depicted on *The Biggest Loser*, 65, 68–69
    double-consciousness and, 71–73
    as moral failure, 69–70
    public ownership of the fat body, 74–77
    as spoiled identity, 68–69
Fearnley-Whittingstall, Oliver and Hugh, 61
Federal Communications Commission (FCC), 139
"Feed Me Better" campaign, 47–48
female comedy
    carnivalesque, 168n7
    Plastic Makes Perfect and, 165
feminism
    An American Family and, 109
    Canadian television and, 156–158
    The Family and, 108–110
    The Shopping Bags and, 158–162
    See also second-wave feminism
Festinger, Leon, 17
fetishizing the "ordinary," 184–185
Feuer, Jane, 172
Ficklin, Benjamin, 209
Ficklin, Jared, 209, 212, 213
Film Finance Corporation (FFC), 237
Financial Post, 154
"Finding Data, Reading Patterns, Telling Stories" (Corner), 118
Finkelstein, Maura, 210, 211, 213
Flaherty, Robert, 19, 22
Flynn, Paul, 38
fly-on-the-wall programming, 101
Ford, John, 171
Forman, Tom, 189
Foster, Derek, 147, 167n1
Foucault, Michel, 31

Fox TV, 139
"franchise" series, 146
Frankenstein (Shelley), 207
Freaky Eaters (television show), 53
Frontier House (television show), 136, 198
frontier mythology
    The Biggest Loser and, 69, 72–73, 75–76
    Kid Nation and, 190, 192
    Texas Ranch House, 208–214
Fuller, Victoria, 140
"Full-Figured Phantom," 75
Full Monty, The (film), 54
Funt, Allen
    autobiographies, 15, 20
    life and career of, 13–16, 23–24
    self-perceived roles of, 11–12, 14, 15
    Stern's novel *Golk* and, 14, 22–23
    See also *Candid Camera* (television show)
Funt, Evelyn, 15
Funt, Peter, 24
Furedi, Frank, 102, 104

Galloway, George, 38
game shows. *See* reality TV game shows
gender
    The Family and, 108–109
    Kid Nation and, 179–181
    and Jamie Oliver on *Jamie's School Dinners,* 55–56
    Outback House and, 226
    Texas Ranch House and, 211–212
Giddens, Anthony, 133
Gilbert, Craig, 83–89 *passim,* 91, 94, 95–96
Gill, A. A., 59
Gillan, Jennifer, 135
Girl Talk (television show), 152, 153
Giroux, Henry, 183, 184
Globe and Mail, 156
gluttony, 70
Godfrey, Arthur, 15

Goffman, Erving, 35
Go Girl! (television show), 153
Golding, William, 171
Golk (Stern), 14, 22–23
Good Housekeeping (magazine), 55
Goodman, Ellen, 176
Goodman, W. Charisse, 75
Goody, Jade, 34, 37
Gosford Park (film), 202
Gotti, John, 135
Gotti, Victoria, 135
Graden, Brian, 132–133
Graef, Roger, 101, 111
Gray, Herman, 126
Greene, Richard, 230
Greening of America (Reich), 84, 85, 86–87
Grierson, John, 241
Grierson, Ruby, 241–242
Gripe Booth, The (radio show), 13
Griswold v. Connecticut, 21
Groot, Jerome de, 231
Growing Up Gotti (television show), 135
Guardian, 117

Hamburger, Philip, 21–22
Happy Days with the Naked Chef (Oliver), 56
Hardie, Melissa Jane, 74
Hatch, Dan, 225, 226
Hawks, Howard, 209
Hayes, Chanelle, 43
Healy, Chris, 223
Heath, Edward, 105
Heller, Dana, 165, 166
Hell's Kitchen (television show), 120n15
Herizons, 152
Herman, Wendy, 155
"hidden camera," in *Plastic Makes Perfect,* 164
Hidden Persuaders, The (Packard), 20
Hill, Annette, 134, 135
Hilton Cordell Productions, 237, 238, 239, 244, 249, 251, 252, 254

Hirst, John, 219, 220, 221
"historical experience" programs, 136
historical reality TV
    claims of documentary practice
        and, 236
    constructing the past in, 222–224
    distinguishing documentary from,
        254
    emotional affectivity of, 223
    importance of, 233
    limitations of, 217
    personalization of conflict and,
        222–223
    possibilities of, 217–218
    reliance on social memory,
        223–224
    See also Colony, The (television
        series); House series; Outback
        House (television show)
Hohnke, Tracy, 232
Hohnke family, 224
Holmes, Su, 27
home makeover shows, 134–135
homosexuality, An American Family
    and, 87–88
Hoover, Stewart M., 133
Hoppe, Beth, 197, 199
"'Horror of Corpulence,' A" (Huff),
    65
Houghton, Chantelle, 28, 38, 39, 40,
    41
House series, 136
    early success and growth of, 197
    formula, 199, 201
    Manor House, 202–203
    media critics on, 199
    participants' perceptions of,
        198–199
    Regency House Party, 203–208
    relationship to history, 197–199,
        201–202
    strengths and weaknesses, 214–215
    Texas Ranch House, 208–214
    See also each individual series
Housing Problems (documentary),
    241–242

Howard, John, 219
Huff, Joyce L., 65
Hughes, John, 222
Hunt, Tristram, 198, 208, 214, 223,
    231
Hurley, Declan, 225
Hurley, Trish, 224–225
hybrid television, 51–54

Ian Wright's Unfit Kids (television
    show), 53
identity
    The Family and, 107–108
    fatness and, 71–73
Images of Women (CRTC report),
    150–151, 159, 160–161
individualization, The Family and,
    104
inmate world, 30
Inness, Sherrie A., 124
Insider, The, 140
Internet
    Big Brother on, 33, 34–35
    "Jennicam," 30
    Kid Nation Web site, 171, 188–
        189
Invisible Man (Ellison), 14–15
Isaacs, Jeremy, 50
Iversen, William, 90

Jacobs, Jason, 118–119
Jalees, Sabrina, 165
Jamie at Home (television show), 52
"Jamie's Fowl Dinners," 61
Jamie's Ministry of Food (television
    show), 59
Jamie's School Dinners (television
    show)
    debate generated by, 47–48
    gender roles and, 55–56
    as hybrid television, 51–54
    issues of class and stereotyping,
        57–59
    masculinity and, 55
    Jamie Oliver as a "crossover"
        product, 54–56

origin and intent of, 47–48
as a political makeover show,
  56–57
public service broadcasting and
  tele-intervention, 49
significance of, 49, 60–61
swearing and, 61n3
Jeffersons, The (television show), 126
"Jennicam," 30
Joe Millionaire (television show), 139
Johnson, Luke, 50

Kapur, Jyotsna, 171, 182–183, 192
Keating, Paul, 218–219
Keaton, Buster, 17
Kelly, Clinton, *146*
Kent, Le'a, 68
Kerr, Graham, *48*
Kid Nation (television show)
  adult commentators and, 187–188
  advertisers, 193n
  chicken killing episodes, 174–175
  class-based sociopolitical structure,
    175–178
  competing/conflicting notions of
    childhood and, 171–172
  consumerism, 187, 190, 191
  controversy over child labor laws,
    189–190
  "cult of the child," 190–191
  cyberspace and online participa-
    tion, 187, 188–189
  the death of childhood and,
    183–187
  expectations of adult maturity and,
    185–186
  expectations of masculinity,
    186–187
  fetishizing the "ordinary," 184–
    185
  final episode, 191–192
  frontier mythology and, 190, 192
  gender and, 179–181
  the "Journal," 175–176
  marketing, 187, 189
  play and labor in, 178–181

ratings, 190
  show construction, 171, 174,
    175–176
  showdowns, 176
  socioeconomic conditions in,
    182–183
  Survivor as the model for, 173
  Web site, 171, 188–189
Kid Nation 2, 188, 190
King, Allan, 84
"Kino Pravda," 96n1
Kipnis, Laura, 137
Kirby, Durward, 15
Koori Clan, 248
Kuhn, Manfred, 93

Lamb, Caroline, 205
Lardner, John, 22
Larger Than Life (television series),
  102
Laron, Marilyn Ina, 23
Last Chance for Animals, 174–175
Lattas, Andrew, 220
laughter, Henri Bergson on, 17
Lawler, Kate, 36
Leacock, Richard "Ricky," 96n2
Learning Channel, 134
Leave it to Beaver (television show),
  126
LeBesco, Kathleen, 69
Leese, Peter, 105
Lenska, Rula, 37
Lester, Susan, 85
Liddiment, David, 51
Life Network, 146, 148, 162
  See also Slice Network
Lifestyle, 151–152
  See also Women's Television Net-
    work (WTN)
living-history production. *See* histori-
  cal reality TV
Lloyd, Danielle, 34
Loft Story (television show), 29
London, Stacy, *146*
Lonely Crowd, The (Riesman), 14
Longford (television show), 50

Lord of the Flies (Golding), 171
Loud family, 84–94 *passim*
Lucas, Matt, 43n
Lumby, Catharine, 231
Lygo, Kevin, 50
Lynch, Jessica, 135

Macdonald, Ross, 84, 89
Maclean's, 154
Maggot, 37
Major, John, 57–58
"makeover" programming
    Plastic Makes Perfect, 163–167
    Slice Network and, 162
Making of a Counter Culture, The
    (Roszak), 84
Making of the Colony, The (documen-
    tary)
    background to, 238–239
    censorship of, 248–255
    illusion of reality in *The Colony*
        and, 243–248
    planned airing of, 239
    priority for, 243
    theoretical context for, 239–243
Man Alive (television show), 102, 103
Manor House (television show), 201,
    202–203
marriage
    family values media debates and,
        139
    as presented in *An American Fam-
        ily*, 85–91
Married by America (television show),
    139
Married Couple, A (King), 84
Marsh, Jodie, 37
masculinity
    Kid Nation and, 180, 186–187
    Jamie Oliver on *Jamie's School
        Dinners* and, 55
    Outback House and, 226
    Texas Ranch House and, 210
Matistic, Kristina, 159, 161–162
Maynard, John, 230

McAllister, Orlaith, 37
McCall, Davina, 42
McCalman, Iain, 240, 241, 254
McGraw, Jay, 134–135
McGraw, Phil, 135, 140
McKernan, Michael, 232, 238, 244
McMurria, John, 135
McNutt, Matthew, 74, 76
McRobbie, Angela, 158
Mead, Margaret, 94
MediaWatch, 150
"Meet Joe Schmo" (*Candid Camera*),
    25
Mellencamp, Patricia, 153
Mittell, Jason, 114
"modern family," 124
Modleski, Tania, 124
Moffatt Communications, 151, 155
Money Talks (film), 24
Moore, Michael, 53
morality, fatness and, 69–70
Moseley, Rachel, 56
multiculturalism, "corporate,"
    130–131
Murray, Jonathan, 94
Myerson, Bess, 15

Naked Chef, The (television show),
    52, 53, 55
Naked Society, The (Packard), 20–21
Nanny 911 (television show), 123,
    133
Nanook of the North (Flaherty), 19
narrative, *Big Brother* and, 40–41
Nation, 139
national identity, *The Biggest Loser*
    and, 73–74
Newlywed Game, The (television
    show), 138
Newman, Richard, 37
New Mexico, 189, 190
New Yorker, 21–22
New York Times, 188
Nicholas, Liza, 199
Nichols, Bill, 254

1984 (Orwell), 30
1900 House (television show), 197, 200, 202
Norton, Juliette, 54
nostalgia, for the nuclear family, 129, 131
nuclear family
   historical perspective, 141n1
   nostalgia for, 129, 131
   reality TV shows on threats to, 135–136
Nunn, Heather, 102

Oasis, 55
O'Connor, Carroll, *126*
Ofcom, 50
Off, Shirley Anne, 151–152, 153–154, 155
Oliver, Jamie
   "branding" of, 53
   evolution as a social reformer, 56–57
   Jamie's Ministry of Food, 59
   Jamie's School Dinners and, 48, 52–53, 54–56, 58–59 (see also *Jamie's School Dinners*)
   meeting with Tony Blair, 60
   Return to Jamie's School Dinners and, 60
   swearing and, 61n3
O'Meara, Jo, 34
One, The (television show), 147
One Day at a Time (television show), 126
One Pair of Eyes (television show), 102
On the Buses (television show), 117
Open Door (television show), 101
Open for Discussion (television show), 153
Orwell, George, 30
Osbourne, Jack, 132
Osbourne, Kelly, 43n, 132
Osbourne, Ozzy, 131–132, 133
Osbourne, Sharon, 131, 132, 133

Osbournes, The (television show), 52, 131–133
Ottawa Citizen, 155
Otto, Peter, 220
Outback House (television show)
   applicants, 224
   Australia's history debates and, 217, 219
   indigenous depiction in, 228–220
   notions of pioneering and, 225–227
   opening episode, 224
   representation of European-Aboriginal conflict, 228–229, 232–233
   social memory of the past and, 224
   volunteers' expectations for, 225
   women's historical experiences and, 230–232

Packard, Vance, 20–21
Palmer, Gareth, 135
"panopticon," 31–32
Panorama (documentary), 52
parenting, "self-reflexive," 133
parenting shows, 133–135
Parents Television Council, 139
Parris, Matthew, 51
Parsons, Talcott, 129, 133, 137
PBS, 83, 136
personalization of conflict, historical reality TV and, 222–223
personal myth, the House series and, 199
philanthropy, 53–54
Philip Morris, 15
Philips, Craig, 36
Pictures of People (television show), 20
Piestewa, Lori, 135
"pioneer legend"
   Australian history and, 220–221
   The Colony and, 227–228
   Outback House and, 225–227
Pirie, Caroline Ross, 204

Plastic Makes Perfect (television show), 163–167
Playboy Channel, 24
poetry, confessional, 25n2
political makeover shows, 56–57
postfeminism, 158
postmodern family, 124, 135
postmodernism, quest for the real and, 183–184
POV Women (television show), 152, 153
Powell, Helen, 56
Prasad, Sylvie, 56
Presidential Fitness Challenge, 78–79
Preston, 37
"Principles and Practice in Documentary Programmes" (BBC), 105–106
privacy
    Candid Camera and, 20–21
    The Family and, 102–103
private realm, 231
progress, American myth of, 69
"Proud" (song), 65
pseudo-events, 39
public service broadcasting, 49
public voyeurs, 20

Quayle, Dan, 125

Rabinovitch, Robert, 147–148
race
    The Biggest Loser and, 78
    Celebrity Big Brother controversy, 34, 120n15
    The Colony and, 229–230
radio shows, 13
    See also *Candid Microphone, The*
Radio Telefis Eireann, 237
Radio Times, 103, 105, 114, 115
Radway, Jan, 141n7
Ramchandani, Naresh, 41
Ramsay, Gordon, 55, 61, 61n3
Rappaport, Paul, 166
Reagan, Ronald, 137

Real Housewives of Orange County (television show), 163
"Reality, Identity and Empathy" (Hunt), 198
reality cooking shows, 47
    See also *Jamie's School Dinners* (television show)
reality TV
    critiques of, 98, 172–174
    focus on ratings and money, 95
    gender divisions and, 108
    history of, 30
    manipulation of material and, 95
    narrative stances toward family and social change, 127
    negative comments on, 29–30
    notions of the history of, 98–99
    reframing ideas of the American family, 123–127
    subgenres, 127
reality TV game shows, 30
Real World, The (television show), 94–95, 125
Red River (film), 209, 210, 211, 213
reflexive celebrity, 36–37
Regan, Jonny, 35
Regency House Party (television show), 198, 203–208, 214, 215
Reich, Charles, 84, 85, 86–87, 91–92
Renov, Michael, 236
Renovate My Family (television show), 134–135
Representing Reality (Nichols), 113
Return to Jamie's School Dinners (television show), 53, 60
Riesman, David, 14
Riis, Jacob, 19
Ringley, Jennifer, 30
Ritchie, Guy, 55
River Café, The, 55
Rivers, Joan, 43n
Rivett, Gail, 162
Roberts, Adele, 35
Roberts, Brian, 75
Roberts, Ian, 201

Roberts, Ken, 15
Rodman, Dennis, 38
Rollins, Peter C., 209
Roosevelt, Theodore, 137
Rosenblatt, Rebecca, 166
Rosenstone, Robert, 222
Roszak, Theodore, 84
Rotherham (England), 59
Rouch, Jean, 96n1
Rowe, Kathleen, 168n7
Royal Commission on the Status of
    Women (Canada), 149
Ruoff, Jeffrey, 84, 89, 99, 104, 109,
    115, 138

Sainsbury, Margaret. *See* Wilkins,
    Margaret
Saroyan, William, 20
"scopic technologies," 173
Scottish Women's Liberation Group,
    109
scullery maids, 231
Searchers, The (film), 213
Seaton, Beth, 222–223
second-wave feminism, 108–109,
    149–151
Secret Millionaire, The (television
    show), 54
self, *Big Brother* contestants and,
    35–36
"self-reflexive" parenting, 133
serial narrative, *The Family* and,
    115–116
sex, 24
Sex and the City (television show),
    158
sex discrimination in broadcasting,
    Canadian report on, 149–150
Sharing the Wisdom (television show),
    152, 153
Shaw Communications, 155
Sheff, Jody, 210, 213, 214
Shelley, Mary, 207
Sheluchin, Glen, 224
Shetty, Shilpa, 34, 120n15

Ship, The (television show), 240, 241
Shopping Bags, The (television show),
    158–162
Shorter, Edward, 124
Showbiz Moms and Dads (television
    show), 135
Sight and Sound, 101, 115
Simpsons, The (television show), 60
single-mom series, 135
Slice Network
    arrival of, 162
    Plastic Makes Perfect, 163–167
    programming, 162–163
    rebranding, 146
sloth, 70
Slotkin, Richard, 69, 72
Smile When You Say I Do (film), 24
Smith, Matthew J., 173–174
soap operas, 115
social actors, 35–36
social class, *Jamie's School Dinners*
    and, 57–59
Social Contract agreement, 106
social memory, historical reality TV
    and, 223–24
social settings, 36
soundtracks, *Jamie's School Dinners*
    and, 52
Soviet Union, *Candid Camera* in, 21
Space between Words, The (Graef),
    101
Spall, Timothy, 52
Spears, Britney, 139
Special Broadcasting Service (Austra-
    lia), 217
Special Broadcasting Service Inde-
    pendent (SBSi) Television, 237,
    238, 239, 252
Spigel, Lynn, 125, 137
spouse-swapping programs, 129–130
Spurlock, Morgan, 53
Steichen, Edward, 21
Stelter, Brian, 187–188
stereotyping, *Jamie's School Dinners*
    and, 57–59

Stern, Richard, 14, 22–23
Stevens, Sharon, 182
"stolen generations," 229
Supernanny (television show), 50, 133
Supersize Me (film), 53
surveillance
    in *Big Brother,* 31–32
    Candid Camera and (see *Candid Camera*)
    "detective cameras," 19
    documentary studies and, 19
Survivor (television show), 68, 173
swap formats, 52

Tait, Sue, 158
Talbot, Mary M., 159
Tarrying with the Negative (Žižek), 184–185
Taylor, Elizabeth, 74
Taylor, Ella, 126, 138
tele-intervention, 49
Television and Genre (Mittell), 114
"Television Archive, The" (Jacobs), 118–119
T'elle'vision, 151
Texas Ranch House (television show), 201, 208–214
therapeutic culture, *The Family* and, 103, 104
Things I Hate about You (television show), 128
This Week (television show), 102
Thompson, Jack, 244
Thornham, Sue, 149, 160
Tichi, Cecelia, 137
'Til Death Do Us Part (television show), 117
Tinniswood, Adrian, 203
Toronto Star, 155–156
totalitarianism, 18
"Towards Equality for Women," 150
Trading Spouses: Meet Your New Mommy (television show), 129–130
True Life (television show), 173

Trump, Donald, 173
Tuchman, Gaye, 149
Turner, Frederick Jackson, 208

Underground Man, The (Macdonald), 84
United Kingdom History Channel, 237
Upstairs, Downstairs (television series), 202
Urlocker, Michael, 154

Wallner, Anna, 159, 161–162
Ward, Lindsey, 180
warfare rhetoric, 72–73
War Game, The (documentary), 255n5
Watching Race (Gray), 126
Watkins, Peter, 242, 255n5
Watson, Paul
    critique of reality TV, 98
    The Family and, 98, 100, 101, 104, 105, 107–108, 115–116, 117
Wayne, John, 209, 210
wealth, 93
What Do You Say to a Naked Lady? (film), 24
What Not to Wear (television show), 52, *145*
White, Mimi, 134
White Gates, 15
Who's Your Daddy? (television show), 136
Wife Swap (television show), 129–130
Wilkins, Margaret, 102, 103, 106–107, 108–110, 112
Wilkins, Marion, 112–113, 115–116
Wilkins, Tom, 115–116
Wilkins family, 100, 102–103, 107–116 *passim*
Will, The (television show), 136
Williams, Raymond, 127
Windschuttle, Keith, 219
Winfrey, Oprah, 74

Winston, Brian, 255n4
Wiseman, Frederick, 25
WNET, 83, 93–94
W Network (W)
    arrival of, 155
    criticisms of, 155–156
    historical narrative of, 155–156
    postfeminism and, 158
    reality and lifestyle programming,
        156
    rebranding, 146
    The Shopping Bags, 158–162
Wolfe, Patrick, 233
Women's Network, The (television
    show), 152
women's programming (Canada)
    emergence, 149–151
    feminism and, 156–158
    Plastic Makes Perfect, 163–167
    reality TV and, 148
    The Shopping Bags, 158–162
    See also Slice Network; W Net-
        work (W); Women's Television
        Network (WTN)

Women's Television Network (WTN),
    146, 148
    audience and, 156–157
    early reactions to, 154
    feminism and, 156–158
    history of, 151–155
    original mandates, 153–154
    programming, 153, 154–155,
        157–158
    rebranding, 155
    See also W Network (W)
Wood, Andrew F., 173–174
working class, The Family and, 105
World in Action (television show), 51
Wrigley, Ruth, 40–41

X Factor, The (television show), 41

You Are What You Eat (television
    show), 53

Zerbisias, Antonia, 155–156
Žižek, Slavoj, 184–185
Zoonen, Liesbet van, 108, 231

LaVergne, TN USA
08 March 2011

219179LV00001B/21/P